Literary Lives

Founding Editor: **Richard Dutton**, Professor of English, Lancaster University
This series offers stimulating accounts of the literary careers of the most admired
and influential English-language authors. Volumes follow the outline of the
writers' working lives, not in the spirit of traditional biography, but aiming to
trace the professional, publishing and social contexts which shaped their writing.

Published titles include:

Literary Lives
Series Standing Order ISBN 978–0–333–71486–7 hardcover
Series Standing Order ISBN 978 0–333–80334–9 paperback
(*outside North America only*)

You can receive future titles in this series as they are published by placing a standing order. Please contact your bookseller or, in case of difficulty, write to us at the address below with your name and address, the title of the series and one of the ISBNs quoted above.

Customer Services Department, Macmillan Distribution Ltd, Houndmills, Basingstoke, Hampshire RG21 6XS, England

Emily Dickinson

A Literary Life

Linda Wagner-Martin
*Frank Borden Hanes Professor of English and Comparative Literature,
University of North Carolina at Chapel Hill, USA*

First published 2013 by
PALGRAVE MACMILLAN

Palgrave Macmillan in the UK is an imprint of Macmillan Publishers Limited, registered in England, company number 785998, of Houndmills, Basingstoke, Hampshire RG21 6XS.

Palgrave Macmillan in the US is a division of St Martin's Press LLC, 175 Fifth Avenue, New York, NY 10010.

Palgrave Macmillan is the global academic imprint of the above companies and has companies and representatives throughout the world.

Palgrave® and Macmillan® are registered trademarks in the United States, the United Kingdom, Europe and other countries.

ISBN 978–1–137–03305–5

This book is printed on paper suitable for recycling and made from fully managed and sustained forest sources. Logging, pulping and manufacturing processes are expected to conform to the environmental regulations of the country of origin.

A catalogue record for this book is available from the British Library.

A catalog record for this book is available from the Library of Congress.

Typeset by MPS Limited, Chennai, India.

*For Andrea Wagner Duff
and in the Memory of
Evelyn Welshimer Reiser*

Contents

List of Illustrations

Preface and Acknowledgments

Poetry in the twentieth and the twenty-first centuries owes an incalculable debt to Emily Dickinson and her immensely original and revealing poems. As the flood of critical reaction that began midway through the twentieth century showed, Dickinson's work set a nearly unreachable standard for poets in both the United States and the world—the English speaking world and the world of other languages as well. Few constructions of language, either before Dickinson's poems or after, had such power to reach readers, or such enigmatic and evocative force to make readers create significant and individualized meaning.

Categorized as the poet of nature, Dickinson spoke for the simplicity of existence in the untouched, unspoiled natural world. Hailed as the poet of family, she, ironically, wrote seldom about relationships among parents, aunts and uncles, siblings, and cousins. Instead, she gave her reader the poet as *isolato*, as separable intent consciousness, able to perceive—and record—the best or most moving of human interactions. Described as a philosophical poet, Dickinson wrote a great deal about death but very seldom about either organized religion or happiness. Limned as the poet of simple verities, Dickinson yet employed a great amount of allusion and metaphor: a learned woman, she fought consistently for her human right to live in the family home and to benefit from the caretaking available to her there. As an unmarried woman, one who was never gainfully employed, Dickinson also became the prototype for the self-protective woman writer, a person whose love of language and ambition to create great art dominated much of her adult life. It is of Dickinson's mature life, and her daily dedication to her writing, that this study speaks.

Grateful acknowledgment is made to the following for permission to reprint previously published material:

Excerpts from *The Poems of Emily Dickinson: Variorum Edition*, edited by Ralph W. Franklin, The Belknap Press of Harvard University Press, copyright Harvard University Press and the Trustees of Amherst College, 1998; and from *The Letters of Emily Dickinson*, edited by Thomas H. Johnson, The Belknap Press of Harvard University Press, copyright Harvard University Press and the Trustees of Amherst College, 1958.

I would to thank Palgrave's Ben Doyle and the Palgrave Macmillan team, and the copy editors Linda Auld and Mervyn Thomas.

Note on Conventions

Because Emily Dickinson's poems were nearly all unpublished in her lifetime, and because she did not authorize the forms in which the printed poems appeared, there is no secure typography and punctuation. I use Ralph W. Franklin's three-volume variorum edition for all poem numbers, dates, notes, and formats.

I have maintained Dickinson's non-traditional use of the apostrophe, and her unique spellings ("opon" for "upon," for example).

1
Reaching 1850

In the spring of 1850, Amherst, Massachusetts was a thriving if comparatively isolated town of 4000. When the three Dickinson children (Figure 1.1) were growing up there, the village was still reached from nearby communities only by stage which traveled the roads and under the covered bridges from Hadley. A resident of Springfield could have come the 18 miles by train to Northampton; then the stage would take over. Finally, in 1853, the Amherst-Belchertown Railway was completed (Ward *Emily Dickinson's Letters* 31). For all the difficulties of travel, however, the Edward Dickinsons were considered a family that did travel. It was the mark of their prestigious position in the traditional—and traditionally classed—town. Their journeys took them to the eastern coast, to Boston and Philadelphia and, occasionally, to Washington, DC. If they went abroad, which was unlikely, they traveled to England, France, and perhaps Italy: these were the countries they read about in the elite books of the English-speaking world. In effect, such patterns of travel reflected their intellectual interest: the white and educated New Englanders kept themselves surrounded by other white people. While some Amherst families employed African American household help, most residents who hired cooks, laundresses, and yard workers drew from the newly-arrived Irish population (Murray 3, 10).

In the spring of 1850, Emily Dickinson was approaching 20. William (usually called Austin) was already 22, a student at Amherst College; and Lavinia (Vinnie) was 17. Emily had already completed her studies at Amherst Academy, and had gone for most of a year to the Mount Holyoke Female Seminary. Sometimes her attendance was sporadic because Emily was considered fragile. In a century when deaths from tuberculosis decimated the population (deaths occurred among teenagers as readily as among parents), people who appeared to be frail, or who

1

Figure 1.1   O.A. Bullard's painting of the three Dickinson children (*Dickinson Room. By permission of the Houghton Library, Harvard University*)

developed serious coughs with colds, were sheltered (Mamunes 3–4). It is thought that 22 percent of deaths in Massachusetts during the mid-nineteenth century came from tuberculosis (Habegger 640–1).

In 1850 Emily was a proud, talented, and (at times) self-satisfied young woman on the edge of adulthood, a woman trained into the dimity convictions of the so-called separate spheres of the nineteenth century. Upper-class women were protected from the hard work that many lower-class women were forced to undertake. Living in the comfort of their fathers' homes (at least until their marriages to equally well placed suitors), these middle- and upper-class women helped with household tasks, had social lives with other similarly educated young people, and saw the way religious beliefs persuaded good young adults to behave (Kelley Ch 1). While not luxurious, this life of social propriety was coercive. Once Emily had finished her formal education, she realized how codified women's social roles were. As she wrote to Abiah Root, her former classmate from Amherst Academy, "I expect you have a great many prim, starched up young ladies there, who, I doubt not, are perfect models of propriety and good behavior. If they are, don't let your free spirit be chained by them" (LI 13).

Emily Elizabeth Dickinson from early on in her childhood considered herself a free spirit. She also seemed to grasp the role of observer, the role of Other. In the words of Charlotte Nekola, one of the issues in high relief during the mid-nineteenth century was "how to claim self within an ideology of self-denial . . . womanhood was defined as absence of self" (Nekola 148). Emily Dickinson recognized this inherent conflict: being female "hindered rather than fostered the development of ego, voice, and imagination" or, in other words, within the cult of true womanhood, the female imagination was, at times, equated with selfishness (Nekola 149). As a result, Emily looked on at accepted social behaviors—and she often participated in them during her late teens—but she also came to see herself as her father's daughter and Austin's sister: one of a family triumvirate of witty intellectuals. In that role, Emily became almost genderless.

Whether because of her own talents—among them her across-the-board academic competence—or because her parents had already tried to erase the parameters of gender difference for her, Emily felt as if she were Austin's equal. As her letters to him show, once he is away in college and then teaching school, she cajoles, jokes, and exaggerates with the perfect understanding that Austin loves her, as does her father, without making judgments. In the hierarchy of family power, Emily had early on become Edward's second son; it might well be said that she was his favorite son.

To identify as Emily did with men, and with the privileges of a man's education, was often a means of emphasizing the life of the mind rather than that of housekeeping. Judging from the periodicals and newspapers to which the Dickinsons subscribed, homelife was itself an intellectual pursuit. Amherst residents received two mail deliveries a day. The Dickinsons took three Northern newspapers as well as *Harper's New Monthly Magazine*, *Scribner's Monthly*, and—from its founding in 1857—*Atlantic Monthly* (Stewart 322). In the words of one historian, "the *Atlantic* was not a channel for American literature—it *was* American literature" (Pollitt 167). Staying abreast of national and state news, as well as literary, scientific, and humanistic interests, was easy; it was also expected. But while the "men" of the family were reading the latest journals and papers, the routine housekeeping tasks were also ongoing. Much as she tried to avoid them, Emily still felt the conflict: should she be reading or should she be washing dishes? With what seems to be near derision, Emily jokes about her mother's obsession with those perpetual household duties. She writes about the reason she could not send along her mother's good wishes: "Mother would send her love—but she is in the 'eave spout,' sweeping up a leaf, that blew in, last November" (Habegger 63). As Dickinson's recent biographer Alfred Habegger describes this extended joke, pointing out that the letter was probably written in August, long after the leaf got lodged in the roof gutter's spout, he terms Emily's drawing "an unforgettable picture of an obsessed New England housekeeper driven from the comforts of home and much too busy to send her love, let alone to write" (Habegger 64).

Critics often commented on the fact that the "quiet and self-effacing" Emily Norcross, the woman Edward Dickinson had chosen to be his bride, was "excellent at managing her household" (Longsworth Amherst 22). She was responsibly educated and from a relatively affluent family in Munson. Yet as their correspondence from the several years of their engagement suggests, Emily was not a reader. She also seemed unwilling to write, or wrote with a practicality that expressed little romance: she was not a reader/writer as her daughter Emily Elizabeth would come to be, or was instinctively. Even as Barbara Mossberg contends that Dickinson's relationship with her mother was much less distant than some critics have suggested (Mossberg 38), there are few references in Dickinson's early letters that show any pride in either her mother or her role within the family. It does seem clear that the Norcross family, and perhaps eventually the Dickinson family in Amherst, professed the doctrines of the Popular Health Movement of the 1820s and the 1830s. Women understood that doing their own chores and cleaning—as well as gardening—could satisfy their physical need for exercise, and there are mentions—sometimes urgent—of the need for both Emily and Vinnie to get outdoors (Ehrenreich and English 69–70).

Longsworth also speculates that Emily Norcross may have inherited her "fearful, anxious temperament" from her own mother, Betsey Fay Norcross (Longsworth Amherst 22). Emily Norcross seemed to take immense pride in doing the housework and running the Dickinson house impeccably. As Habegger (62) points out, however, her life was marked by "her drivenness, her extreme thrift." To illustrate these characteristics, he tells the story of Emily's accepting boarders (boys who were attending Amherst College and preferred staying with a reputable family), just a few months before her first child was due. The boys, a son and a nephew of a leading Springfield attorney, may have been seen as giving Edward Dickinson some sort of political advantage. But acknowledging the fact that throughout the Dickinsons' early years of marriage, the Norcross family worried about Emily—urging her to return home for rests, sending her girls from their family to help out—her decision to invite the boys to board seems foolhardy.

The truth about the Dickinson family was that poverty haunted their lives. Whereas critics have emphasized the fact that Emily Norcross insisted on being, literally, the maid of all work, seeing the family's financial situation whole excuses at least some of her obsessiveness. After Edward Dickinson had proposed to her and she had eventually accepted, he deferred their marriage for several years while he tried to pay off debts his father, Samuel Fowler Dickinson, had accumulated. Samuel was one of the founders of Amherst Academy; he was continuously in financial difficulties, although he wanted to be seen as one of Amherst's leading citizens. As he poured what resources he had into Amherst Academy and Amherst College, his children knew they would need to help with this task—and with his other projects. Finally a bankrupt, Samuel "left Amherst in disgrace" (Murray 65) and moved to northern Ohio for a position; he died there, miles from his family, and left a legacy of possible chicanery as well as bankruptcy. Eventually in 1825 the family had to sell the Homestead, which Samuel had built in 1813, and which they then rented a part of during their early married years (Longsworth Amherst 15, Murray 65).

It also seems clear, because the Dickinsons never had a full-time maid (according to the 1850 federal census 7 records), that all the children helped with the housework, the laundry, the tailoring, the cooking, and the yard. Aife Murray (66) tells the story that Emily was to be apprenticed to a baker when she was 14; such a plan seems at odds with the fact that all three of the Dickinson children had the best possible educations, Emily and Vinnie as well as Austin. As Murray notes, Emily was "already accomplished in knitting . . . needlework and mending." She went to school and had piano lessons, had many indoor plants, and "privately arranged German lessons" (Murray 66). It was not until March 7, 1850 that Edward Dickinson ran an ad for "a girl or woman to do the entire work of a small family" (Murray 73). Meanwhile, in the 1850 census, Emily Dickinson had listed her occupation as "keeping house," and then in a later letter complains when Vinnie is away, "my two hands but *two*—not four or five as they ought to be, and so *many* wants—and me so *very* handy—and my time of so *little* account—and my writing so *very* needless" (LI 82).

Alfred Habegger also traces the anxiety stemming from financial losses from early in the family's history: putting off their wedding for several years, trying to maintain a house (or at least part of a house) with so little help, and infecting their children with their own financial worries. He believes that Emily especially felt "her parents' anxiety about financial insolvency" (Habegger 57). It is probable that this financial worry helped to shape Emily's choice of studies at both Amherst Academy and Mount Holyoke. She turned again and again to scientific curricula. In college, she took "ancient history and rhetoric" as well as "all science courses: algebra, Euclid [geometry], physiology, chemistry and astronomy" (Gordon 42). The authority on the way Emily Dickinson both studied science and drew from it for her poetry is Robin Peel, whose 2010 book thoroughly discusses both the courses (and their texts and emphases) and relevant Dickinson poems. Peel's aim is to present Emily as a "scientific investigator," drawing on what she sees as the exciting new, scientific culture (Peel 13–14). He asks that readers see Emily Dickinson "as a concealed natural philosopher/scientist" working in ways that mimic scientists contemporary with her (14). (One thinks of Emily's trip home from college in 1848 for the dedication of the telescope in the Amherst Observatory, installed as part of the Octagon Building, an excitement the whole town shared. The various segments of The Smithsonian Institute and Museum in Washington, DC, were not in place until a decade later, 1859, Peel 21).

The connection between Emily's consistent interest in science and her family's often precarious finances may be that she saw some opportunities for employment in the newly categorized field: Peel notes that some of her structures in her early poems were geared to making "scientific claims" and emphasizing scientific details; in fact, it could be that her creation of the fascicles (the small tied-together booklets of her poems) was a way of preserving field notes (Peel 17). To undergird this interest was the obvious fact that many of the journals carried essays about matters that were more scientific than philosophical: family discussion would have privileged "science" almost unconsciously.

Peel points out that the fascination with the new that marked the 1830s and 1840s changed during the later years of Emily's education. Rather than just describing and observing, people interested in science were now applying the principles, especially in medical fields. Creating hypotheses became the standard for proving material learned, rather than memorizing the long blocks of information that had previously marked science class methodology (Peel 78, 17). He notes how seriously Emily took her herbarium, and how often in her poetry she closely observed "flowers, insects, and birds . . . as if she were making a scientific record" (91, 172). Throughout her poems, Dickinson uses the metaphor of sight, as in "I see New Englandly" (Peel 81). There are also more volcanoes, winds, and storms in her poems than might be expected.

All the courses of study at Amherst Academy were more scientific than most curricula because the third president of the school was Edward Hitchcock, a well-known geologist with strong interests in paleontology. While Emily often followed the classes that Austin had chosen, Vinnie seemed to prefer a more humanities-based course of study. Again, Emily was no doubt aligning herself with Austin as a way of interesting her father in her intellectual prowess.

With the sometimes strange juxtapositions that occur in any culture, the impetus to study science came at a time when Massachusetts was overtaken with protestant revivalism. The coercion to accept Christ, to become a Christian and an active church member, was almost frenetic at mid-century. Cynthia Griffin Wolff acknowledges that despite Emily Dickinson's comparatively wide knowledge of science and philosophy, all her educable life she struggled with the question of conversion (Wolff 87): "Even by the middle of the nineteenth century, Amherst— both college and town—still looked upon conversion as one of the crucial events that marked the division between carefree youth and responsible adulthood . . . . [conversion] was a recognized public rite of passage" (Wolff 93).

Emily Norcross had converted in 1831, but no other family members had done so. It was, however, the revival meetings in the winter and spring of 1850 that succeeded in proselytizing much of Amherst. On August 11, 1850, Emily's father converted; in November, Vinnie professed her faith (Wolff 104). Emily maintained the position that had grown during her months attending Mount Holyoke: she was a non-believer.

The Mount Holyoke experience was unexpectedly coercive. Mary Lyon, the head of the college and a protégé of Edward Hitchcock, created an atmosphere at the school that was "unremitting and inescapable." Women were recognized at assemblies on their standing as converts or non-converts; Emily Dickinson was grouped in the "No hope" category and saw many of her peers in that classification weeping because they were not saved (Wolff 100–1). (Habegger speaks about the non-believers having to attend what he calls the "painful collective inquiry sessions," 199). In one instance, at the deathbed of a beautiful classmate [Emma Washburn], the unconverted students were asked to come so that Emma might urge their conversions. Her death in itself (occurring from "galloping" consumption) was a scarifying event, but to have her implore her friends to follow her to God was unforgettable (Mamunes 45–6). Emily Dickinson felt even more of an outsider during this revival turmoil, especially when several of her best friends converted later in 1850.

It is also true that much of Emily Dickinson's education came from the people she knew and loved—either in person or through her many letters. It is impossible, then, to replicate what she had learned at the close of her formal education by simply studying the textbooks from her classes, at either Amherst Academy or Mount Holyoke. For more than two years, Ben Newton, one of her father's law clerks/students, had been Emily's tutor. She called him that a decade later—after his death—as she wrote about him and his tutelage to friends, and it seems clear that from the time she left Mount Holyoke at her father's insistence, worried as he often was about her timorous health, until Newton moved from Amherst back to Worcester, the two spent great amounts of time together. Newton was an open-minded man, not yet committed to Christ, interested in new writers like the Brontës and Elizabeth Barrett Browning, and encouraging about Emily's poetry. He told her she would one day *be* a poet. From a poor farm family, Newton had not attended college but he was apt, smart, and dedicated to becoming a lawyer. He was also ill with consumption, the primary malady of the mid-nineteenth century in Amherst and its surroundings. At 26, Newton had already spent years earning the money for his law study—probably working as a teacher—but he remained terrifically poor: biographers have long wondered how he paid for his two years in Amherst, and the following year in Worcester, after which he finally earned his degree (Mamunes 14–15). Emily was only 17 but she was well-educated, intent on becoming what she could be even though resistant to conversion, appreciative of the beauties of nature—as was Newton—and deeply worried about her own illnesses (which seem at this time to be connected with consumption although somewhat later, Lyndall Gordon suggests, she may have developed fainting and seizure disorders as well). (Gordon 78–135).

Rife with novels, stories and poems about the sad lives of consumptives, mid-nineteenth century American culture provided examples aplenty of both the gruesome hemorrhage scenes—often death scenes—and the impossibility of any couple's marrying when one or the other was consumptive. Death waited around corners; the still-living partner and whatever children had been born were marked for lives of only sorrow. Not only was Emily reading *Jane Eyre*; another of the popular novels that Emily admired was this story of consumption, Ik Marvel's *Reveries of a Bachelor* (1850). The huge following that Marvel's (Donald Grant Mitchell's) writing enjoyed made his books sound more senti-mental than they were. They worked with commonplace themes and situations, but they were pertinent to Emily's interests in her nineteenth year. It was difficult to avoid the consumptive-love theme during this period: Philip Goodwin's *Lily White*; T. S. Arthur's *Seed-time and Harvest*; Samuel Elliot's *Dreams and Realities*; Harriet Beecher Stowe's *Uncle Tom's Cabin* with the death of Eva and the illness of her mother; Josephine Franklin's *Rachel*—a novel of "unutterable anguish" as well as the incessant loss of blood in the mother's last hemorrhage: each work posits the dismal life after the great loss of the consumptive, as well as the possibility that the tendency for the disease will be inherited by the children of any such union (Mamunes 100–47). There are also the poems written by Emerson, Irving, and Lowell on the deaths of their wives from consumption.

It was the 1847 collection of Ralph Waldo Emerson's poems that Ben Newton gave Emily after he left Amherst, a collection that included Emerson's poem upon the death of his young, beloved wife Ellen. When Emily wrote to her friend Jane Humphrey, she commented about the gift, which she called "a beautiful copy" and about the letter, saying that she would write to Newton "in about three weeks" (Habegger 219). Saving her reply to coincide with Valentine's Day and its extensive cele-bration, Emily wrote one of her most impressive early poems. "Awake ye muses nine, sing me a strain divine" calls on all the spirits of the arts and of lovers, announcing in its first lines "Oh the Earth was *made* for lovers, for damsel, and hopeless swain,/ for sighing, and gentle whisper-ing, and *unity* made of *twain*,/ all things do go a courting, in earth, or sea, or air,/ God hath made nothing single but *thee* in his world so fair!" (Franklin 49). Unlike Emily Dickinson's poems in the decades to come, this apostrophe to the conventional spirits—expressing conventional love sentiments—shows the poet's apt handling of poetic traditions. Her irregular rhyme scheme, like her irregular capitalization of the first word in each line, shows her defiance of the rote even here: the long lines and the inherent ambition of this Valentine's Day poem, com-pared with the poem she wrote in 1852, shows how strong her early talent was. But there are very few poems extant from this early period in Emily's writing. (The 1852 Valentine's Day poem is written in quatrains; it expresses an even more conventional sentiment.)

Not only did Emily realize what a gap the absence of Ben Newton would create, and attempt to fill that gap through serious attention to what was to become her art; her father, Edward Dickinson, bought for her Carlo, the half-St. Bernard, half-Newfoundland who was to be her companion for the next 15 years. Josephine Pollitt spoke decisively early on in her 1930 biography about the bond between father and daughter: Emily "was from the first his companion spirit in that household. He liked to sit in the dim parlor and listen to her playing the piano; he preferred her bread and prune whips . . . he guarded her health jealously. It was he who took her driving with him that she might be out in the fresh air . . . ; he who mixed the doses of medicine" (Pollitt 239).

Another use in Emily's mind for her comparatively deep training in science was to ferret out information about the various illnesses that marred her young life, illnesses that also carried off good friends and acquaintances. When Emily was only 13, her good friend Sophia Holland died of consumption. As she wrote to Abiah Root, "I gave way to a fixed melancholy" (in Wolff 77). In the spring of 1848 she lost her friend Jacob Holt; previously she was aware of the deaths from consumption of Susan Gilbert's mother Harriet (in 1837) and Sophia Holland's mother, Fanny (in 1844). Her own family saw the death of their minister's wife Elizabeth Parsons that same year and of, most closely, in 1860, Emily Lavinia Norcross, their aunt, whose children Lou and Fanny were like sisters to the Dickinson children (Habegger 640). In 1850, Susan Gilbert's older sister Mary died soon after giving birth Emily refers to her as "dear Mary, sainted Mary" (Hart and Smith 7); as did Leonard Humphrey, a preceptor at Amherst Academy. In 1851, four of Emily's earlier classmates died and in 1852, her cousin and former roommate at Mount Holyoke—Emily Norcross—was dead of consumption (Longsworth Amherst 30). Given the web of mourning that was already surrounding Emily Dickinson, her phrase in an 1852 letter to Susan Gilbert might seem less of an exaggeration: "when you come, *if we all live till then*, it will be precious, Susie" (Hart and Smith 26; my italics).

Science however could never replace her love for literature. With her girlfriends, which more and more often included Susan and Mattie Gilbert, and Vinnie (and sometimes even Austin), Emily read works from both England and the United States. Among her regular correspondents by this time were Abby Wood, Abiah Root, Harriet Merrill, Sarah Tracy (the group, including Emily, known as "the five"), according to Cynthia Griffin Wolff (75). To those young women one might add Emily Fowler, who was Noah Webster's granddaughter, and Jane Humphrey. These

readers were perusing not only Ik Marvel and Charles Dickens (*Bleak House* at the time) but *Only* and *A House Upon a* Rock by Matilda Anne Mackarness, *Alton Lock* by Charles Kingsley, *Head of a Family* and *Olive* by Dinah Maria Craik, and Mary Elizabeth Stirling's memorial *The Light in the Valley* (Hart and Smith 20). Most significant in 1850, setting her work apart from the merely "popular," was Elizabeth Barrett Browning's *Sonnets from the Portuguese.*
It should be said that 1850 was a crucial year for United States culture. Preceded by Harriet Tubman's escape from slavery on the Underground Railroad in December of 1849, and privy to the publication of *Narrative of Sojourner Truth* in 1850, in September of 1850 the Fugitive Slave Law was enacted, forcing abolitionists in northern states like Massachusetts to decide what their convictions were about freeing the African American slaves. More frequently in the media than the 1848 Seneca Falls Convention had been, the Fugitive Slave Law took more than equal billing with the scientific and literary events that peppered print "news." Elizabeth Barrett Browning's *Sonnets* were frequently commented upon since she was herself something of a hero: ill from childhood, protected by her father from any taste of real life until he lost his fortune and moved the family from their palatial home into a Wimpole Street apartment, Elizabeth Barrett was rescued from her secluded life by the passionate love of Robert Browning, another British poet, though one not so acclaimed as she. After the couple married and moved to Italy, Elizabeth Barrett Browning—against medical advice—bore a son. It might be said that the Brownings were one of the first glamorous couples of the time, celebrated for their great love more frequently than for their poems.
For readers who knew poetry and poetic conventions, *Sonnets from the Portuguese* was an unconventional book. Sonnet cycles were usually written by male lovers, praising the beauties of women, who were the intended recipients of the poems. In this case, the poet's voice is female and the great love expressed goes clearly to a male lover. Probing the roles that her society assumed were always gendered, Emily Dickinson felt a kind of ownership with Elizabeth Barrett Browning's accomplishment, and when the latter's long, almost epic poem, *Aurora Leigh*, was published in 1856, Emily read and re-read it until she knew whole sections from memory. Years after Elizabeth Barrett Browning's death from consumption in 1861, Emily still wore her hair "looped over her ears and knotted in back," reminiscent of the way Barrett Browning had styled her hair (Benfey Amherst 204). She also had a framed picture of this admired author on her bedroom wall, and also "sent pictures of Barrett Browning to several of her friends" (Benfey Amherst 205).

One might suggest that the reason Emily and her friends so admired the British writers is that *class* is the foremost issue in their writing: Charles Dickens, for example, presents the poor of London but there is no danger that he will become a part of that group. Each of the Brontës, as well as George Eliot, writes to make poverty ennobling, but none of their characters goes hungry. During mid-century United States writing, in contrast, if one chooses to use Harriet Beecher Stowe's *Uncle Tom's Cabin* as a focal point, *race* is the thematic overlay. For the women and girls of Amherst, living comfortably in their years at Amherst Academy and surrounded by the best-educated populace of any northern town, class, gender issues, illness, religious beliefs, and heterosexual romance are much more interesting themes than the amorphously distant matter of race.

It seems clear that at the mid-nineteenth century Dickinson and readers like her and her friends were the products of their conventional study of 300 years of accepted British literature. It is a bit before this time that Emily asks Emily Fowler if the way people talk (or write) "taking all the clothes off their souls" does not make her "shiver" (in Habegger 234). The confessional had no place in either good literature or decent living. To the British canon had been added the Americans Ralph Waldo Emerson, James Russell Lowell, John Greenleaf Whittier, Nathaniel Hawthorne, Washington Irving, and a few others but when Walt Whitman's first *Leaves of Grass* appeared in 1855, even though it was recommended by friends, Emily did not read it, commenting that she had heard it was "disgraceful." Look as we might for an explanation of the new and unexpectedly modern elements in the poetry Dickinson was to write beginning in the mid and later 1850s, there is nothing apparently helpful to be found in her classwork. Neither is there anything helpful in her reading, especially since she reads much more prose than poetry.

Over the next four or five years, from 1850 to the appearance of her interesting poem "I have a bird in spring," perhaps the poet may have been studying not the writing of poetry so much as the living of a surprisingly unpleasant life. To borrow one of Dickinson's metaphors from geology: the accumulating layers of that life, studded as it was with pain and loss, may have created a seismographic synthesis. Her 1854 poem, "I have a bird in spring," might itself have been, simply, a kind of eruption.

2

Dickinson's Search, to Find the Poem of Her Being

Emily Dickinson had no access to classes in writing (except the writing of argumentative essays or the working out of exercises of intricate stanzas, rhyme, and meters in a set poetic form). When she reached the surety of a set of lines like

> I have a Bird in spring
> Which for myself doth sing—
> The spring decoys . . . .
>
> In a serener Bright,
> In a more golden light
> I see
> Each little doubt and fear,
> Each little discord here
> Removed. . . . (Poem #4 Fr 59)

her own satisfaction was her reward. Where did she learn to anchor the tercet with that short third line? How did she discover that breaking a stanza pattern could be even more effective than simply repeating that pattern? Perhaps more to the point, where are all the poems Dickinson wrote between her Valentine's Day poetry in 1850 and this 1854 poem for Susan Gilbert?

Experimenting as she obviously was, Dickinson had by 1854 created a template in her mind and ear that governed the writing of her distinctive poems. Again, there will be a large gap between this 1854 poem, enclosed in a letter to Susan, and the quantity of poems that she wrote (and kept) which are now in the authoritative three-volume Franklin edition, all dated 1858.

The characteristic qualities apparent already in this 1854 poem are the use of nouns as more than single parts of speech: "Bird" which is described once as "Robin" but more often as "that Bird of mine" stands in for the poet's valued possession. Evanescent in the writer's life, the Bird changes hands, and for a time is Susan's. Depending on whether or not Susan as image stays or goes, the Bird finally returns to the poet-speaker, despite her "doubting heart." The warmth of the "golden light . . . In a serener Bright" parallels the warmth of the melody conveyed by the Bird, and the stasis of the short lines underscores the peacefulness of the closing word, which comprises the entire last line, "Return."

Dickinson's use of a far-reaching noun that takes on the qualities of metaphor pairs with her scattered yet purposeful rhythms. Although the stanzas look like sexains, each is comprised of two careful tercets; the tercets themselves, however, differ according to the pace of the poem. The third line of each tercet, as we have seen above, is shorter, creating the pause that divides the halves of each stanza. Replicating a spoken sentence, each tercet winds down to a shorter and shorter rhythm: for example, the third line in the first stanza is a complete sentence; the third line in the fifth stanza is only a modifier ("The spring decoys" in stanza one shortened to "Though flown" in stanza five). Accordingly, the whole poem slows.

Any visible rhyme pattern is also interrupted, again purposefully. Whereas the last lines of the stanza's tercet might well rhyme, in that the first two lines are rhymed, they do not: "spring/sing" and "nears/appears" are rhymed but "decoys" does not rhyme with "gone." Finally, in the third stanza, the last word of line three does rhyme with the last word of line six, "mine" and "thine." This rhyme of the middle stanza (of the five stanzas that constitute the poem) is the only perfect pattern. Stanzas four and five parallel stanzas one and two in that the pattern of rhyming lines is interrupted by the non-rhyming of lines three and six. Whereas critics have for decades seen Dickinson's use of hymnal traditions in her poems, this poem shows her breaking with even those voice-replicated forms.

Poet Hayden Carruth commented at length on what he called Dickinson's "idiosyncratic usages": "She chose to let her aural imagination range freely, and one result is that her off-rhymes, which vary from close to distant, together with her reliance on well-known rhyming patterns (hymns, ballads, etc.) force the reader to hear rhymes where none exists" (Carruth 151).

Her employment of poetic conventions—and her breaks from the expected choices—also reinforces her literal meaning. The valuable object (which the Bird images) belongs at first to only the poet. Then it becomes a shared possession, making a journey "beyond the sea" where it learns "Melody new for me" and takes its place in "a safer hand." Assuming the Bird now lives "in a truer Land," as the property of "thine," the poet feels confident that the object will return, enhanced. "Though flown," the Bird will eventually come back. But this is hardly the emphasis the poet wants, so she writes a final tercet that creates the stable pace, representative of the secure calm which she intends:

> Shall in a distant tree
> Bright melody for me
> Return.

Dickinson's choice of language also came into the purview of Richard Wilbur in his seminal essay of 1959. He points out that the poet gave up the eloquent and formal language of her time that would have changed her voice: "She inherited a great and overbearing vocabulary which, had she used it submissively, would have forced her to express an established theology and psychology. But she would not let that vocabulary write her poems for her." Instead, "the poems of Emily Dickinson are a continual appeal to experience" (Wilbur 11).

It may be too that the effectiveness of this poem illustrates one of the principles of Dickinson's writing here in the early 1850s. Often, increasingly often, Emily's poems were included in letters to friends. (The second stanza of this poem, though it seems to have been originally written for Susan Gilbert, was later included in a letter to Elizabeth and Josiah Gilbert Holland (Franklin 60).) Part of Dickinson's habit of enclosing poems in her letters, or appending a part of a poem in the prose of a letter, seems to have begun with her letters to Susan Gilbert. No doubt this practice intensified in the year Susan was away teaching. It seems clear, from the perspective of poetic practice, that there is a seamless movement from prose to poetry and back: the language of both modes itself becomes stressed into similarity, and a fusion of reason and feeling comes to mark the poet's choice of both diction and pace.

In the case of "I have a bird in spring," the situation of creating the poem is signaled both by the way the letter opens, "Sue—you can go or stay," and the prefatory material before the poem proper begins. "We have walked very pleasantly-Perhaps this is the point at which our paths diverge-then pass on singing Sue, and up the distant hill I journey on" (Franklin 59). It is rare that a prose context would provide so much information. In this case, because Emily had decided that her friendship with Susan Gilbert was of paramount importance in her life, to have her brother Austin propose to her friend was an unexpected complication. Her best friend was about to become her sister-in-law; and more to the point, in some respects, Austin and Susan as Mr. and Mrs. Austin Dickinson were to live directly beside the Dickinson homestead in a house that Edward Dickinson had built for them. The emotional impact of this situation was clear.

Another complication for Emily's friendship with Susan Gilbert was that Susan's older sister, Mattie, had earlier been in love with Austin. His choosing Susan, despite what some saw as Susan's reluctance, was therefore another difficult emotional situation, especially because both Emily and Vinnie were close friends of Mattie's as well as of Susan's.

To illustrate the divisiveness of Susan's engagement to Austin, there is one segment of a letter from Emily to Susan, written in 1852, in which she shows her somewhat desperate need to be close to her beloved friend:

> I have heard all about the journal, Oh Susie, that you should come to this! I want you to get it bound—at my expense—Susie—so when he takes you from me, to live in his new home, I may have *some* of you. I am sincere (Hart and Smith 26).

This paragraph is written in the margin of the first page; the letter itself primarily laments that Susie was not in Amherst for a sugaring, though Mattie was. Emily writes, "Only think of it, Susie; I hadn't any appetite, nor any lover, either . . ." (Ibid.) In a letter to Austin soon after his engagement, Dickinson had written, "I guess we are very good friends tho', and I guess we both love Sue as well as we can" (LI 236).

Several years have passed by the time of this "Bird" poem: Emily seems reconciled to the necessity of existing with Susan as a married woman. In a way, the poem is a kind of negligent dismissal: Emily, the speaker, has her art, her poetry, her life of the imagination, an existence she has long thought she and Susan shared. She will also take solace in the natural world. The bird will become her talisman.

By the time Dickinson writes what is generally considered her first mature poem, the 1858 "One sister have I in our house—," she has no doubt written many now-lost works. It seems clear that much of her writing during the richest period of her production—between 1858 and 1865—bears more resemblance to "I have a bird in spring" than it does to "One sister have I in our house." In order to investigate both the emotional state of the poet's psyche as well as her technical prowess, the following summary of Dickinson's life from 1850 to 1854 may be useful. In speaking of the pressure that helped to shape her art, it also seems evident that several areas of stress marked her existence during that time.

Perhaps the most important stressor for Emily was the pressure to find her role within the Dickinson family—to, in effect, *belong* within the family. Her formal education was finished. Her life, as the older daughter of one of Amherst's leading families, was prescribed: if she did not marry, suitably, she would live in her father's house and participate regularly in the town life.

It seems pertinent as well to begin with the fact that Emily was taken to live with her Aunt Lavinia when she was 2 years old, since her mother could barely cope with having her third child and, as we have seen, the Dickinsons did not employ household help. Whereas the child Austin stayed home, awaiting Vinnie's birth, Emily was taken to the Munson household for at least a month. Such separation would surely have created some kind of anxiety. The fact that Emily and her mother were never as close as Vinnie was with Emily Norcross may have had other causes, but Emily at least felt that a distance existed. In her letters she often comments about Vinnie's role in keeping house, as here in an 1851 letter: "The dishes may wait dear Susie—and the uncleared table stand, *them* I have always with me . . . . Vinnie is sewing away like a fictitious seamstress" (Hart and Smith 11). Often Dickinson comments on Vinnie in relation to their mother:

> Vinnie sweeps—sweeps, upon the chamber stairs; and Mother is hurrying around with her hair in a silk pocket handkerchief, on account of the dust. Oh, Susie, it is dismal, sad and drear eno'—and the sun don't shine . . . and here's nobody to smile! (Hart and Smith 19).

Emily's baking and cooking is a means of both pleasing her father and of taking on one of the household roles that needed to be filled. For housecleaning, however, Emily was content to leave the management— as well as the work—to her younger sister. As Emily Norcross became less and less able to do housework, even with the addition of a maid, Vinnie became the head of housekeeping tasks.

Both Emily and Vinnie loved to garden, as did their mother. Emily's carefully made and preserved herbarium, 66 pages of pressed flowers which she had collected with great zeal, attests to her interest. Habegger describes the oversized book, with its 400–500 flower specimens, as a treasure that grew out of both her study of botany in school and a fashionable urge to make such a collection (Habegger 154–9). In his words, "Since many wild plants are highly localized and have a brief flowering season, serious collecting requires close observation and persistent wandering." Many of Emily's days, especially the days when she was forced to miss school because of health concerns, were spent in this wandering.

In the scheme of her whole life, Emily's loss of the friendship—and perhaps the romantic interest of—Ben Newton was a definite blow. In the midst of losses of other friends, her separation from her tutor was cause enough for her father to give her Carlo; he knew that replacing her previous walking partner would be difficult, and he could not be at home often enough to provide that service himself. Just as Edward took Emily out driving, her walking was a prescribed part of protecting her from developing more serious illnesses.

Even though Ben corresponded with her, it is hard to avoid seeing the pain in her letter to Austin once she has read in the newspaper that Ben has been married on June 4, 1851, to Sarah Rugg. (She writes as a postscript, "B F N is *married*," Mamunes 64, LI 116.) Biographers comment that in their correspondence, Ben had not mentioned Sarah, nor had he told Emily he was to marry. Knowing that a consumptive friend was in many ways prohibited from thinking of marriage did not erase the sting of Ben's having found a partner for himself. That Sarah was considerably older than he, and that his will did not mention her, suggested to early biographers that he was marrying a nurse rather than a wife (Whicher 86).

The letter writing between Newton and Dickinson continued. But before two more years had passed, Emily was reading the death notice for Ben—again, she writes to Austin: "Oh Austin, Newton is dead. The first of my own friends. Pace" (Whicher LI 236). Often quoted is the sentence from the apparently last letter Newton had written to Emily: "If I live, I will go to Amherst—if I die, I certainly will" (in Mamunes 70).

Depressed, quite naturally, about Newton's death, Dickinson commented to Austin that even the birds could not cheer her as they sang their morning songs (see LI 249). That "I have a bird in spring" dates from the year following Newton's death, repeating the bird image in a positive light, suggests some reconciliation between Emily's deep grief and her art.

Along with the loss of Ben Newton, Dickinson had lost other friends to either disinterest—as when Abiah Root stopped writing to her (Martin 87)—or to death. Such experiences marked her development; years earlier, after she had gone to the funeral of Sophia Holland in the spring of 1844, she is sent on trips to visit both Aunt Lavinia in Boston and Uncle William in Worcester (Kirk xv). As the deaths of friends and acquaintances continue, the fact that Dickinson has not converted makes her acceptance of these losses unusually difficult. Where can she turn for solace in her non-religious life?

Moving house from the Homestead to the North Pleasant Street house and back to the Homestead again seemed to oppress Emily (as it clearly oppressed her mother, who was hardly able to function after each move). Part of the physical shifting between homes reminded the Dickinson family of the precariousness of their finances. Dating from 1833 when Samuel Dickinson had sold his half of the Homestead to General David Mack, followed by Edward Dickinson's selling his half to Mack in April of 1840 so that his family could move into an entire house on North Pleasant Street, Emily was aware that her "home" could be evanescent. As she noted in a letter, "They say that 'home is where the heart is.' I think it is where the *house* is, and the adjacent buildings" (LI 324).

Emily's room in the house on North Pleasant Street overlooked a cemetery and the mandate that she walk outside may have put her in closer proximity with that location than most people would have liked. Lyndall Gordon states that there was a funeral almost every day that the Dickinsons lived in the Pleasant Street house (Gordon 33). In contrast, in 1855 when Edward purchased the Homestead (Figure 2.1) back from

Figure 2.1 Photograph of the Homestead in winter (*MS Am 1118.99b(83)* *By permission of the Houghton Library, Harvard University*)

the Macks, he saw acquiring the homeplace as a mark of prosperity. Aife Murray calls it "the triumph of the family's class change." Moving from North Pleasant Street, the family went "from the 'haves' to the 'have-mores' . . . . Edward made his wealth a public fact by his ostentatious clothing, livery, and home" (Murray 152).

Edward Dickinson invested over $5000 in remodeling the house, and his family moved back in mid-November of 1855. That Emily is sur-prised at how difficult such a move is—barely a three blocks walk from one house to the other—comes through in her letter to the Hollands: "I cannot tell you how we moved. I had rather not remember." She calls the occasion a "melee" and "a catastrophe . . . I supposed we were going to make a 'transit,' as heavenly bodies did—but we came budget by budget, as our fellows do, till we fulfilled the pantomime contained in the word 'moved.' It is a kind of *gone-to-Kansas* feeling, and if I sat in a long wagon, with my family tied behind, I should suppose without a doubt I was a party of emigrants!" (LII 324).

Edward Dickinson simultaneously designed and built the Italianate house he called "The Evergreens" for Austin and Susan; it was built next door to the Homestead and was finished in time for their return from their honeymoon to Niagara Falls in 1856. Surrounded by the sudden grandeur of the refurbished Homestead and the appearance next door of the new, fashionable house, the Dickinson family saw that they had to have permanent household help. In 1856 they hired Margaret O'Brien Lawler as maid. (There is to be another Margaret—Maggie Maher—later in the Dickinsons' life, and it is this Margaret who preserved many of Dickinson's poems.) During the near-decade that Margaret O'Brien served, supporting her widowed mother before her own marriage, Emily reclaimed the luxury of writing time (Murray 245). As Murray points out, Dickinson wrote between 100 and nearly 300 poems a year until Margaret left: the year the household was first without Margaret, Emily wrote only ten poems, and her writing seemed to be stalled for the next three years—until Maggie Maher was talked into leaving another employer and coming to the Dickinsons' household (Murray 10).

The reader remembers Dickinson's description of her mother's mala-dies in that early letter to the Hollands (January 20, 1856): "Mother has been an invalid since we came *home*, and Vinnie and I 'regulated,' and Vinnie and I 'got settled,' and still we keep our father's house, and mother lies upon the lounge, or sits in her easy chair. I don't know what her sickness is . . ." (LII 324).

Unsympathetic with what may well have been depression (as it seems to have been post-partum depression after Vinnie was born), Emily may have unconsciously seen her mother's inability to do housework as one source of her own lack of writing time—and of her beginning the practice of writing very late at night, and then sleeping late in the morning. From a slightly more comprehensive perspective, critic Wendy Martin suggested in her 1984 study that whereas Austin was the favored child, and his education and his time for study given priority, Emily may have learned to use her own ill health to buy herself mental and emotional privileges: "Clearly, it did not occur to Dickinson that her mother's perpetual invalidism was a physical enactment of the insignificant . . . position she held in her husband's world, a world that literally rendered her invalid" (Martin 3).

More than 40 years ago, historian Carroll Smith-Rosenberg studied correspondence between women friends during the nineteenth century; she concluded that the protestations of love between women then were as erotic as letters between heterosexual lovers. (Smith-Rosenberg Signs). It has been a presumption of some Dickinson biographers that Emily felt great passion for Susan Gilbert—and in some respects, such passion was what Emily expressed in her letters to her friend. For instance, this paragraph from Emily's June 1852 letter:

Stay, Susie; yet *not* stay! I cannot spare your sweet face another hour more and yet I want to have you gather more sheaves of joy—for bleak, and waste, and barren, are most of the fields found here, and I want you to *fill* the *garner. Then* you may come, dear Susie, and from our silent home, Vinnie and I shall meet you . . . Susie, I do bring you a Sister's fondest love—and gentlest tenderness (Hart and Smith 46).

Repeatedly, Dickinson links herself with Susan Gilbert, seeing the other as a kind of mirror image—as when she uses the descriptors of "prose and poetry" that later mark one of her best-known poems. Here she notes that she and Susan "please ourselves with the fancy that we are the only poets—and every one else is prose" (Hart and Smith 9). Difficult as it is to judge the intensity of Dickinson's friendship, it seems clear that there is a sense of possessiveness that could be read in multiple ways. Paula Bennett sees Dickinson as a "nostalgic" poet, writing in the vein of many women nineteenth century poets (Bennett Woman 5); Betsy Erkkila thinks Dickinson's emotional life stemmed from her friendships with a number of women—not only Vinnie and Susan but "Abiah Root, Abby Wood, Emily Fowler Ford, and Jane Humphrey and later her friend Elizabeth Holland and her cousins Louise and Frances Norcross." She too places much of Emily's poetry in the convention of "affection and dissidence," which has as one element "a joyous irreverence toward male law" (Erkkila 161–2). Critic Jan Montefiore points to Dickinson's use of the riddle form, a means of underscoring her reliance on ambivalence and disguising her direct meanings. Her book acknowledges, too, the degree of speculation about Dickinson's sex-life (which she calls a "mystery") and insists that readers must separate the work from the woman, in some cases reading it "as fantasy" (Montefiore 167–8).

Calling Susan "sister" often during the 1850s, Dickinson also mentions the losses of their friends, women who have died as well as Ben Newton's 1853 death. Survivors as they are, Dickinson and Susan Gilbert bear a connection that also isolates them in some respects; they become dependent on each other in ways that Vinnie, for example, who is younger, cannot share. Yet Dickinson's 1858 poem couples Vinnie, her biological sister, with Susan Gilbert, her sister in spirit. And judging from the imagery in her extant letters, the poem comes as no surprise. Dickinson, who in this period signs herself "Emilie," uses a matter-of-fact tone to commemorate her love for Susan (perhaps on the latter's December 19, 1858, birthday): "One Sister have I in our house–/And one, a hedge away./ There's only one recorded,/ But both belong to me."

As the poem describes Vinnie's role—wearing "my last year's gown"— Dickinson reverts to her bird image to describe the fact that her spirit sister came into their family by building "our hearts among." Stanza three makes clear the difference:

> She did not sing as we did—
> It was a different tune—
> Herself to her a music
> As Bumble bee of June (Franklin 61).

As Dickinson places this sister in her undeniable love ("Today is far from Childhood"), she also creates a crescendo that leads to this remarkable ending: "From out the wide night's numbers—/Sue—forevermore!"

Here the consistent hymn-like stanzas, complete with a-b-c-b rhymes, suggest how practiced Dickinson has become in honing a poem to maintain compelling meaning. Still reliant on the nature imagery that she used throughout her lifetime, she here chooses to use the bird and bee imagery selectively: this poem is more plain spoken than most of her emphatic, metaphor-centered poems. "One Sister have I in the house" illustrates carefully the commentary Mutlu Konuk Blasing wrote years ago. Insisting that friendship between women can be the crucial subject for a poem, Emily brings a newly serious treatment to that sometimes frivolous subject. Blasing sees this as a significant move; she sees Dickinson as relentlessly "ironic," evoking "new positions for poets to speak from. She is the first to exploit the opportunity marginality offers—to women and to others—to examine the rules by which not only poems but central social discourses are constructed" (Blasing 670). Even as "One Sister have I in the house" is not in itself ironic, it is dated by Dickinson to be considered in the midst of a number of ironically structured poems from 1858. The first year of Dickinson's prolific writing, 1858 shows her mining the great losses she has known during the 1850s—and in the poems that result, establishing many of the principles for what will become her characteristic work.

3
Losses into Art

Critic Elizabeth Petrino makes the case that while Emily Dickinson seemed to be following various conventions of nineteenth century women's poetry, especially in the lyrics of loss, death, and love, she frequently "transformed" those conventions (Petrino 210). Four of Dickinson's 1858 poems about death, for example, illustrate the ways she often chose to reach such a sense of transformation.

"Nobody knows this little rose" is more familiar today than most of Dickinson's poems because it is one of the rare poems to have been published. Appearing anonymously August 2, 1858, in the *Springfield Daily Republican*, the poem has no title but is headed "To Mrs. _____, with a Rose/ [Surreptitiously communicated to The Republican]" (Poem #11 Fr 66–7). It is generally assumed that Susan Gilbert Dickinson gave the poem to her close friend Samuel Bowles, editor and publisher of the newspaper.

The gift poem genre—this poem evidently accompanied by a rose—was familiar to women readers of the nineteenth century. Written in the hymn-like quatrains, until Dickinson later transcribed the poem as a single stanza in the first of her fascicles, the poem draws once again on the natural imagery she found so comfortable. Yet, rather than being a direct announcement, the first lines suggest the transcience of the flower/gift/rose, which the last line emphasizes. "Nobody knows this little rose" makes the poem both metaphysical and, in some ways, autobiographical: in both poems and letters Dickinson often describes either herself or a beloved as a rose—and sometimes as a daisy, her father's favorite flower.

The internal rhyme ("No .../knows . . . rose) gives a sonority to the enigmatic rose. The fact that a flower might be understood, apprehended—i.e., *known*—personifies it and gives it more than its factual identity as

24

a flower. The same personification animates the other natural objects the poet chooses so that the act of dying turns the poem into a lament. The poem closes

> Only a bird will wonder;
> Only a breeze will sigh;
> Ah! little rose, how easy
> For such as thee to die!

In a literal sense, "to die" may be the fate of a rose but it must not be the fate of a personalized rose such as the poet herself or any of her beloved friends. The poet's use of the animate "such as thee" also aids in the humanizing of the rose. Death may be "easy" but as the two exclamation marks suggest—it must not even be imagined.

In a later version, one dated 1861, Dickinson modifies the closing two lines so that the personification is even more emphatic:

> Ah, little Rose!
> How Easy, for such as thee, to die! (Fr 66–8)

The spacing of the lines and the capitalization of "Rose" makes clearer the personification, while the faster pace of the now longer last line makes the poem's commentary on death less ambiguous.

Dickinson's shorter "So has a daisy vanished" makes succinct use of the question of an afterlife. In only eight lines the poet introduces the metaphor of the daisy personified, and follows its loss with parallel losses of both the slipper and the day itself. How easily—i.e., naturally—death appears. In the closing couplet the poet chooses gerunds to stress the motion of life: "Blooming—tripping—flowing"—before she asks her direct question, her means of illuminating the mystery of life which has here been overtaken by death. The question is, simply, "Are ye then with God?" (Poem #19 Fr 78).

In another poem dated "late summer 1858," Dickinson writes more somberly about death; this poem incorporates the presence of a "sister" figure within the natural images. "A brief, but patient illness" is also given a religious context: the mourners "knelt in prayer" as they awaited angels. Describing both the dying friend and her mourners, this poem uses its web of information to create a meaningful leave-taking.

> A brief, but patient illness—
> An hour to prepare—

> And one below, this morning
> Is where the angels are . . .

The sense of natural, direct speech cuts through the often flowery rhetoric that conventionally expresses death: "An hour to prepare" tells the reader how sudden the loss has been.

The poem's single stanza of twelve lines has a prayerful effect, achieved through both the repetition of lines 9 and 10 and the brokenness of direct address in line 11:

> We trust that she was willing—
> We ask that she may be—
> Summer—Sister—Seraph!
> Let us go with thee! (Poem #22 Fr 80–1).

Dickinson's 1858 poems that cluster around the theme of death are frequently about the death of a woman. Perhaps the poet is expressing real life situations: her teenaged friends, their mothers, the wives of Amherst's clergy have died. Some of her poems, such as "A brief, but patient illness," create the mood of acceptance; the dying person, even when rushed out of life, remains patient, willing. Dickinson here modulates, without a pause, from *Sister* to *Seraph*. It is those bereaved who are lost, mournful, needing to follow the dead into whatever awaits.

In another poem from this group, however, a poem written just a few months later, Dickinson used her images from nature to emphasize the dangerous independence required for the poem's speaker ("I") to face the act of dying. "I hav'nt told my garden yet" uses the three-stress line in quatrain form to hint at the sheer personal power the act of leaving life may require.

> I hav'nt told my garden yet—
> Lest that should conquer me—
> I hav'nt quite the strength now
> To break it to the Bee—
>
> I will not name it in the street
> For shops w'd stare at me—
> That one so shy—so ignorant
> Should have the face to die.

Whereas "So has a daisy vanished" observes the losses that death occasions, "I hav'nt told my garden yet" makes the knowledge of death an active process. There is little passivity here, even though the dying person is described as being both "shy" and "ignorant," the former a quality long associated with femininity. The apparently traditional quatrain structure is not at all traditional: it is instead filled with slant rhymes—or as the poem comes to its jarring conclusion—with no rhymes at all. A poem that is written not in third person but in first (a rarity for Dickinson) seems to have also broken with other poetic conventions. This poem ends with an apparently unexpected suggestion, a departure which Dickinson names a "Riddle":

> Hint that within the Riddle
> One will walk today— (Poem #40 Fr 92).

Structurally, this poem is similar to three other strong "death" poems from the same period: "I never told the buried gold," "I never lost as much but twice," and "I often passed the village." These, along with the dozen or so other poems that deal with death, all written in the summer of 1858, suggest that Dickinson has begun using a thematic core so as to work through poetic strategies that create varying effects. About half these poems mention religion or a religious outcome. It seems significant that her focus in the summer and fall of 1858 was on death and, perhaps even more importantly, on whatever embroidery her poetry could give it.

This date is important for Dickinson's view of herself as writer because it is during this same time period that she writes the first of her three "Master" letters, letters which remain in her handwriting and, some critics speculate, were never sent to the mysterious "Master" of the salutation. The general consensus is that Dickinson may have been modeling these letters on Charlotte Brontë's letter to Constantine Heger, headmaster of the Brussels school she attended (Martin 101)—because Dickinson was immersed in the writings of both Emily and Charlotte Brontë (who first published as Currer and Ellis Bell). After a decade of writing seriously but in near secrecy, Dickinson was ready to expose her ambition to become a writer. She writes, in the first of the three letters, of wishing for good health for her friend and for herself, as well as wishing "that I were great, like Mr. Michael Angelo, and could paint for you" (LII 333). What such a comment in prose suggests—regardless of the identity of Dickinson's "Master"—is that the serious poet has realized that she needs both an audience and a response. Having lost the man she referred to as her "tutor" in 1853 (and, in reality, earlier than that when Ben Newton left Amherst), she had since that time been working alone in her writing.

Dickinson's fascination with writing about death may be even more important at this time because of what she may have seen as her *returning* health. So long as her life was surfeit with dying, so long as she had fears herself that her life would be short, she was less drawn to the topic. Instead, she feared the topic. In fact, she spent much of her everyday life deflecting other people's worries about her health.

Dickinson's childhood and adolescence were marred by "illness," states of health that were never described. Some biographers have written off these concerns of, largely, Edward Dickinson because all genteel young women were over-protected. Placing Dickinson's possibly frail health in the context of what occurs in the lives of upper-class or at least middle-class young women during the early 1800s robs any investigation of pertinence. Two recent books—Lyndall Gordon's 2010 *Lives Like Loaded Guns, Emily Dickinson and Her Family's Feuds* and George Mamunes' 2008 *"So Has a Daisy Vanished"—Emily Dickinson and Tuberculosis*—provide both new information about and new perspectives on the matter of Dickinson's various illnesses. Gordon contends that what many have read as possible consumption, or the threat of consumption, may have been a clear seizure disorder, if not epilepsy itself, something similar to it, marked by long periods of syncope (fainting). The loss of consciousness that became increasingly pronounced as she aged may have given rise to the many Dickinson poems that refer to earthquakes (Vesuvius, Etna, Pompeii), human minds that cleave, fits, and throes, expressed in opening lines that startle such as "I felt a Funeral in my Brain." Images are frequently read as metaphors but Gordon suggests there is much more literal description in Dickinson's poems than readers have recognized.

He also provides helpful information about the way epilepsy was viewed in the mid-nineteenth century—as the classic "falling sickness," with many epileptics incarcerated in asylums (Gordon 122). The recognition that there is no treatment for the malady lends a kind of hopelessness to the diagnosis: epileptics could not marry, for fear that offspring would carry the illness. It was also feared that sexual intercourse—along with such unrelated incidences as bright lights, sudden changes in positioning, and other less controlled situations—would bring on seizures. Gordon too points to the fact that the genetic tendency for this illness sometimes occurs in families. Not only did Ned Dickinson (Susan and Austin's older son) develop epilepsy when he was 15, (Gordon 133) but so too did the son of Edward's cousin Irene Dickinson Montague—Zebina Montague, who had graduated from Amherst College and, working in Georgia, planned to marry. Then epilepsy struck. He returned to Amherst and lived with his mother for the next 40 years: he led a dependent life, and never married (Gordon 132).

Readers have long accepted the premise that Dickinson was tubercular, or at least that she needed to be protected from the possibility of her developing consumption. She has coughs, she is made to stay home from school, she is urged to take walks and to garden in the outdoors, she is given Carlo to accompany her (Figure 3.1). She is thin, thinner than she has usually been once she stays home from Mount Holyoke at the close of spring vacation (weighing perhaps 107 pounds). Mamunes provides sobering statistics about the death count among Massachusetts

Figure 3.1 Daguerreotype of Emily Dickinson (*Amherst College Archives and Special Collections, by permission of the Trustees of Amherst College*)

residents, both from "galloping consumption" and a more common, long-suffering form of the illness. He points out that Dickinson's mother, Emily Norcross, gave the appearance of a consumptive: *her* mother and two of her siblings had died of tuberculosis, and when she is photographed at age 42, she appears to be "emaciated" (Mamunes 23). He also tells the story of Emily's good friend Emily Fowler, who was engaged to a man who developed consumption. He freed her from their bonds before he set sail for Cuba to regain his health. She married someone else; he lived another 60 years (Mamunes 78–9).

As Gordon makes clear, there is a secrecy about Emily Dickinson's health conditions that would probably not have existed if her family feared consumption—there were so many cases of that illness that it was, sadly, a familiar story. He suggests that some of the trips Emily, often with Vinnie, takes to Boston, to visit their Aunt Lavinia (and her children Fanny and Lou, the Dickinsons' favorite cousins) for what might be seen as a vacation, are really trips to consult doctors. He points particularly to Dickinson's visit to Boston in 1851, originally scheduled for the summer of that year but then delayed because Lavinia's husband Loring had to undergo a trial for bankruptcy—the family's financial worries were on-going. So from September 4 through September 22, 1851, Dickinson (at age 20) consulted with Dr. James Jackson, a more eminent physician than any available in Amherst. (Gordon points out that Jackson's best-known book, *Letters to a Young Physician,* includes a chapter on epilepsy, 119).

What may be most interesting about Dickinson's meetings with Jackson is the fact that the prescription he gave her—glycerine diluted in water—was filled at a Boston pharmacy, as it continued to be filled. The secrecy of this prescription's being procured (even though it was sometimes prescribed for tuberculosis as well as epilepsy) adds to Gordon's sense that Emily's illness was considered more serious than consumption. For instance, embedded in a long paragraph about other news is Dickinson's request to Austin, then teaching in the Boston area, that he "have the vial filled, and send it by Mr. Watson." She continues that she will be "very glad" to have him do so, but "don't, unless it's convenient" (LI 200).

The heart of Dr. Jackson's treatment for epilepsy, as described in his writings, was based on the stability of the patient's brain. He believed that the patient must "avoid whatever might aggravate or prolong attacks: agitation, fright, fatigue and excitement" (Gordon 120). There is also the possibility that during Emily's early years with epilepsy, the illness might have shown itself as "petit mal" and been much less obvious to other people than "grand mal," with its full blown seizure activity, would have been. Dickinson herself would have known discomfort, symptoms such as disorientation, rapid heart, vision troubles, but she might have avoided the debility of seizures. She might also have been plagued with epilepsy of "absence." Here the patient's consciousness shuts down but there are few symptoms of illness. Gordon refers to the stories Emily Fowler Ford told about Dickinson's dropping dishes and other kitchen objects, and then hiding the pieces of the broken object "in the fireplace behind a fireboard." Obviously, when autumn came, the remnants would be discovered. But as Gordon says, the behavior "suggests absences, either accompanying the condition or the condition itself" (Gordon 136).

There is also the essential mystery of Dickinson's physical development during her adolescence—how did her body mature? how early did her menses begin? Such considerations likely contributed hormonally to her illness, whether that illness was tuberculosis or a seizure disorder, and must also remain unknown today.

Following Gordon's speculation, the fact that Emily often slept with Vinnie—and was lonesome enough to comment on her absence when she was away—may have been another nod to the debility of epileptic seizures. Longsworth states that the sisters shared both a bed and a bedroom (Longsworth *Amherst* 37). The onset of a seizure often occurs as the mind drifts into its deepest sleep: if Dickinson feared going to sleep, to bed, alone (which might be another reason she often chose to write into the night), then to have her younger sister gone from the house would trouble her. Her dependence on Vinnie, who was clearly both strong and discrete, would have provided a comforting security net. There is a remarkably tender passage about Vinnie in one of Emily's letters to the Hollands, "Vinnie is sick to-night, which gives the world a russet tinge, usually so red. It is only a headache, but when the head aches next to you, it becomes important. When she is well, time leaps. When she is ill, he lags, or stops entirely" (Ward 57).

If Dickinson were herself ill with an ailment that came suddenly, with little or no warning, her practice of staying within her house would also be more than an affectation. (She later writes, "A something overtakes the mind—we do not hear it coming" (LIII 919).) That Emily's father built her a conservatory in the corner of the Homestead, which could be reached from both inside the house and outside, also seems informative: she can continue to get fresh air without having to walk far on their grounds. Critic Judith Farr, who considers gardening to be Emily's "second vocation," noted that Edward built the conservatory to show he understood his daughter's great love of flowers. Farr continued that the Dickinson property "during the poet's lifetime was in effect a small farm with a barn, a fruit orchard [Mrs. Dickinson cared for the plum trees], a vegetable garden, and a meadow across the road" (Farr 4, 6).

Her father's strangest behavior, walking with his lantern to Austin and Susan's house to retrieve Dickinson when she had stayed at a party there till midnight, also becomes reasonable in light of his fear of Emily's having a seizure. Even with her dog as companion, had she seized and fallen in the wide yard, she would have been alone (Longsworth Amherst 40). As Gordon concludes, "sickness is a more sensible reason for seclusion than disappointed love . . . What seemed eccentric was merely dread" (Gordon 117).

In 1851, then, Emily's three-week stay in Boston so that she can consult with Dr. Jackson becomes an important part of her medical history. It also parallels Austin's being in Boston teaching at the Endicott Grammar School, very near the Norcross' home. In fact, according to biographers, Austin stayed with Aunt Louisa for a time before moving to Mrs. Reid's boarding house. His teaching job, secured for him by his uncle, was instructing the children of the immigrant Irish; and both he and Emily lamented the ignorance of that population (Bingham 127). That Austin could continue to get her prescription filled in a Boston pharmacy comforted her, even though her letters to him state repeatedly that she misses him.

Between what seems to have been a physician's seminal opinion in 1851 and Dickinson's steady development into a sure poet by the summer of 1858, there is a two-year gap in her preserved correspondence. There are the deaths in 1852 of Edward's sister Mary Dickinson Newman and her spouse Mark—both from pulmonary tuberculosis (the four daughters orphaned by their deaths became Edward's wards, and he moved them from New York to Amherst and housed them near his family). There is the 1853 completion of the railroad link from Amherst to Belchertown, studded with celebrations—and the formation of Dickinson's deep friendship with the Hollands who often traveled that line. There is Ben Newton's death, followed ten months later by Dickinson's letter to Newton's minister, Edward Everett Hale, asking him for information about Newton's last weeks (Mamunes 76). There is Austin's engagement to Susan Gilbert and her various absences from Amherst, first to teach, then to visit her brothers in Grand Haven, Michigan, a town they had helped to settle. There are Emily and Vinnie's trips to Philadelphia (where Emily may have heard Charles Wadsworth preach), to Washington, DC to visit Edward, and to Springfield—several times—to visit the Hollands. In 1854 there is what Longsworth calls "at least one panic attack" for Emily's medical history (Longsworth *Amherst* 36). There is Austin's graduation from Harvard Law School, and his joining his father in a law partnership—and by doing so, relinquishing the dream he shared with Susan that they would move west—perhaps to Chicago—for their new life together (Habegger 339). There is the Dickinson family's move from the North Pleasant Street house back into the refurbished Homestead. There is the marriage between Austin and Susan Gilbert in 1856, with their move into The Evergreens—and subsequently the move of both Clara and Anna Newman (to be cared for) into The Evergreens, until 1869 when Clara married (Mamunes 81). Literarily, there are the deaths of both Emily Brontë and her older sister Charlotte Brontë; and the publication of *Aurora Leigh*, the feminist epic poem written by Elizabeth Barrett Browning. But as we have seen, there remain only fragments of the poems Dickinson has been writing: until 1856, when Margaret O'Brien joins the household as maid at the Homestead, Emily's life, like Vinnie's, has been usurped by housework. Critic Sharon Leder quotes Dickinson's 1850 letter to Jane Humphrey: "The path of duty looks very ugly indeed" (Leder 23). And Gordon notes, "At home, an unending tide of cleaning closed over and seemed to obliterate her." She mocked herself in letters as "'the Queen of the court, if regalia be dust, and dirt'" (Gordon 50).

To date her strong poems from 1858 as markers of the fact that Dickinson had begun to be less fearful of her debilitating illness—even considering that the prescription she thought was helpful may have been only palliative—is coupled with the fact that it is during the summer of 1858 that she begins constructing her tied-together poem booklets, usually referred to now as *fascicles*. Rather than hiding her poetry from all except Susan Gilbert Dickinson and a few other friends, Dickinson may be adopting a practice that Jonathan Edwards had originated. In the words of contemporary poet Susan Howe, Edwards had "carefully sewed his work into handsome notebooks . . . Among his manuscripts are several containing 212 numbered entries he made with different inks and pens over the span of his life. Miscellanies—fragments; like her poems they were never meant for publication" (Howe *My Emily* 53). Dickinson also may have been following the suggestion of Ralph Waldo Emerson, who advocated creating "Poetry of the Portfolio," a form of self-publication so that a writer's poems might be shared with friends (Longsworth *Amherst* 41).

What remains of Dickinson's work, beginning in 1858 with her collecting separate poems into booklets, occurs for the next 15 years in these fascicles. Accomplished now in her art, Dickinson found value in creating a more permanent record—both in sewing the booklets into shape and in choosing more elegant paper for her transcriptions—so that her art would, perhaps, find readers years in the future. One change from the many poems dated summer and fall, 1858, to the even larger group of poems dated summer and fall, 1859, is the more apparently direct commentary on illness. The first four poems discussed in this chapter appeared in what Dickinson labeled Fascicle I; the two poems which close this chapter both appear—along with one of her best-known poems "Success is counted sweetest"—in Fascicle V, dated summer 1859. During the year's work of poems, Dickinson compiled fascicles II, III, and IV; and she has come to write with a steadier, almost recognizable voice. The two poems that seem to be paired in the fifth fascicle—"A throe opon the features," Poem #105, and "A something in a summer's day," Poem #104—illustrate the poet's command of what she will later describe as "telling it slant."

"A throe opon the features" is a clear reference to a physical debility, and as the poem continues, "A hurry in the breath--/An extasy of parting," leads in line four directly to "Death." As if crystallizing symptoms into the fear she had long expressed, Dickinson describes that fear as a specter that shadows her life.

> An Anguish at the mention
> Which when to patience grown—
> I've known permission given
> To rejoin it's own (Fr 141).

Her life, her family's life, has been dominated by the surroundings of illness, an illness that might well lead to her death. Through the patience the poet speaks of in line six, the poem calms; the closing line, speaking of rejoining "it's own," has a hint of unexpected peacefulness.

The reader may remember, however, the anxiety of many of Dickinson's poems about death just months earlier. In fact, to read such a number of Dickinson's poems, all dated either 1858 or 1859, is to recognize the power of the metaphor of death. Difficult to separate in terms of their themes, Dickinson's poems from 1858 and 1859 are all governed (to a greater or a lesser extent) by the notion of Death. The use of the concept of death metaphorically, of course, can be an indicator of sleep or any other loss of consciousness, as well as the resting state after sexual intercourse—and, more literally, of actual death.

What has changed in these poems from Dickinson's fifth fascicle—when read alongside those included in Fascicle I—is a tone: patience, perhaps, but more significantly, the joy to be found in the act of rejoining the living.

Writing "A throe upon the features" in quatrains, Dickinson seems moved by the same set of impulses in "A something in a summer's day," where she speaks in tercets about the weather's solemnizing effect. Stanzas two through four take the reader through possible stages of the loss of both consciousness and *self* consciousness:

> A something in a summer's noon—
> A depth—an Azure—a perfume—
> Transcending extasy.
>
> And still within a summer's night
> A something so transporting bright
> I clap my hands to see—
>
> Then vail my too inspecting face
> Lest such a subtle—shimmering grace
> Flutter too far for me . . . (Fr 140).

The enigmatic "something" that anchors the first two stanzas—where *is* the source of the tranquility expressed? Is it more than Dickinson's usual reverence for the natural world?—lends an air of more than reality to this poem. A calmness that is rare in her poems of 1858 and 1859 marks this poem, and others from the fifth fascicle, and seems to imply that the poet has come into her own, non-derivative power. The six tercets that comprise the poem lead to a concluding quatrain which reifies that tone.

> So looking on—the night—the morn
> Conclude the wonder gay—
> And I meet, coming thro' the dews
> Another summer's Day!

Poised to reach out to a wider group of readers, Dickinson has found several new friends to whom she will send her newest works. Even though she denies the role of "success" in another of her 1859 poems, she clearly is reaching out for it in her most private undertakings.

4
Dickinson's Expanding Readership

1858 and 1859 were crucial years for the development of Dickinson's poetics. Poet Susan Howe says firmly, "Between 1858 and 1860 Emily Dickinson became the poet we know" (Howe My Emily 17). Critic Vivian Pollak affirms that "The poetry of Dickinson's maturity is conventionally dated from 1858" (Pollak Historical 8). In sampling her poems from these years briefly, as we have, it seems that the great quantity of what remains calls for further discussion.

Among the Dickinson poems from 1858 and 1859 are a number of strong poems—seldom repetitious—about the natural world. "My friend must be a Bird-/Because it flies!" she chants; "Flowers—well, if anybody" extends the poet's appreciation of the flower face into a kind of metaphysics ("Can the extasy define,/ Half a transport, half a trouble,/ With which flowers humble men"). In "The Bee is not afraid of me," the reader is returned again to the role the natural object plays in the poet's existence.

Even as Dickinson was writing her memorable poems about nature, she was also carving out a special niche of *small* beauties—sometimes a diminutive flower and sometimes a tiny human speaker (perhaps disguised as a wren). (Although Dickinson was comparatively tall at five feet, five inches, she was slender and often described herself as *small*.) As the poet remarked in Poem #86:

> For every Bird a nest—
> Wherefore in timid quest
> Some little Wren goes seeking round— (Fr 124).

Similarly in "On such a night, or such a night," she emphasizes "such a little figure/slipped quiet from it's chair,//So quiet—Oh how quiet,/ That nobody might know . . . ." (Poem #84 Fr 122).

36

The fusion between the natural world and the human occurs often. It is as if Dickinson has already learned to expand the terms of her metaphors. No longer does one image equate with another, stretching the second term. It is as if both terms expand simultaneously. For instance, in poem #68, natural objects link with life's largest abstractions:

> Some things that fly there be—
> Birds—Hours—the Bumblebee—
> Of these no Elegy.
>
> Some things that stay there be—
> Grief—Hills—Eternity—
> Nor this behooveth me.
>
> There are that resting, rise.
> Can I expound the skies?
> How still the Riddle lies! (Fr 112).

The objects of nature (birds, the bumblebee) pivot on "Hours," the non-natural signifier. In stanza two, only one noun—"Hills"—represents the world of nature. Both "grief" and "eternity" tie the reader to the abstractions of the mind, for which—as in stanza one—there can be no elegy.

With the third tercet, the poet's voice laments her fragile powers. The Riddle remains but her ambition fights against its dominance as she asks "Can I expound the skies?" Through her understanding, and love, of the natural world, she has become wise. And as the first line in stanza 3 says so powerfully, "There are that resting, rise." Perhaps Dickinson's use of language here is what Emily Budick calls non-symbolic, "fluid," even elusive (33). In a larger sense, critic Jed Deppman points to Dickinson's use of "conversationally experimental" techniques—here, asking a question, extending what might be seen as philosophical observations (Deppman 17).

Somewhat later in 1859, two of Dickinson's poems went to Mary and Samuel Bowles (probably by way of her sister-in-law Susan; see Franklin 154–6). As a way of understanding that the poet was amenable to people other than family members reading her work, discussion of these important poems—"Her breast is fit for pearls" (Poem #121) and "These are the days when Birds come back" (Poem #122)—shows a synthesis of elements that drew poems that seemed to be nature poems into the wider philosophical bent of Dickinson's oeuvre.

In "Her breast is fit for pearls" the poet-speaker describes herself as "I—a sparrow." She does not ornament either the breast or the brow of her beloved. Rather, she builds for herself a "*home,*" a "perennial nest," "Sweet of twigs and twine" (Fr 134).

Using an eight-line stanza for this poem, Dickinson creates the sense of enigma through abrupt concision. In the rhythmic tercets of "These are the days when Birds come back," the poet chooses that conversational emphasis Deppman speaks about:

> These are the days when Birds come back—
> A very few—a Bird or two—
> To take a backward look—
>
> These are the days when skies resume
> The old—old sophistries of June—
> A blue and gold mistake . . . (Fr 155–7).

The later stanzas of this poem may refer to Dickinson's gift of wine (she writes about this in a letter to Mary and Samuel Bowles). Less autobiographically, in stanza five, it seems to present the poet's child persona, a conventional "self" in keeping with Dickinson's interest in smallness. About this persona, Paul Crumbley early on defined the poet's various personae in this way: "The poems introduce polyvocality as a direct challenge to the primacy of a single unified voice. Familiar child, bride and Queen or poet speakers, for example, speak for a spectrum of positions that stretch from the conventional to the wild . . . The child communicates shock at the discovery that discourse limits personal power" (Crumbley Pen 2–3). That the child understands firm religious belief is an ironic appendage to the poem, a poem that remains a praise of summer's bounty, no matter what else is included in the work.

Paired in Fascicle Six with "Going to Heaven!" "These are the days when Birds come back" introduces several emphatic "belief" poems.

> Going to Heaven!
> I don't know when—
> Pray do not ask me how!
> Indeed I'm too astonished
> To think of answering you! . . . (Poem #128 Fr 167–9).

Replete in stanza two with the smallness imagery Dickinson chose to use elsewhere—"a little place," the "smallest 'Robe' . . ./ And just a bit of 'Crown'"—the poem strikes the reader as more typical than its apparent theme suggests.

Another poem from this religious grouping is less typical. In Fascicle Five, Dickinson included "Ambition cannot find him!" a poem less about what society thinks of as "ambition" than about "immortality." Another of her eight-line poems, this work makes the point that the persona—evidently a male speaker—was "*Yesterday*, undistinguished!/ Eminent *Today*." Perhaps linked with "Success is counted sweetest," "Ambition cannot find him!" draws on conventional definitions of acclaim to underscore the significance of religious belief (Poem #115 Fr 148–9).

Among Dickinson's poems from 1859 is also the mysterious "Heart! We will forget him!" (Poem #64) which later appeared in Fascicle 2. ("You may forget the warmth he gave—/I will forget the light!)" Along with a poem Dickinson transcribed for Fascicle 4, "This heart that broke so long—" (Poem #83), and the curiosity about the draft of the first "Master" letter in 1858, readers in the twentieth century were piqued to try to ferret out Dickinson's love interest. It seemed not to matter that neither Vinnie nor Austin believed that there had been a great love in their sister's life (Eberwein 28), critics, biographers and readers persisted in their investigations.

The search for that all-important masculine love in Dickinson's life led to several possible candidates (excluding Ben Newton, whose disappearance from Amherst came during the winter of 1849–50, followed by his death less than three years later). Eberwein suggests that Dickinson had fallen in love with Austin's classmate, George Gould, editor of the Amherst College magazine where her first Valentine was published (Eberwein 22). Most critics think her devotion was directed to either Samuel Bowles (with whom—and his wife Mary—she exchanged upwards of 50 letters) or Charles Wadsworth, the Philadelphia minister who moved to San Francisco in 1862. Dickinson may have met him in 1855; he visited her in Amherst in 1860 and again in 1880, after he had returned from California to preach in Philadelphia until his death in 1882. Married in 1846 and the father of three children, Wadsworth was known as a brilliant pulpit orator throughout his career. No correspondence remains (Bingham 508).

Critic Benjamin Lease sees Wadsworth as Dickinson's "Master" because of his "way with words, his manner of delivery." He also emphasizes Wadsworth's "inscrutable roguery," a trait he thinks Dickinson "possessed in good measure herself" (Lease 5, 8). There is also the story about Wadsworth's son William, born late in the marriage; Wadsworth told Dickinson that this child reminded him of her (Lease 10).

Other observers choose either Wadsworth or Bowles (Benfey Amherst 126, Martin 100); for Martin, Samuel Bowles seems the better choice, at least partly because so many letters exist. Between Mary and Samuel Bowles and Dickinson, the letters are intimate and intense, and the Bowleses seem to have preserved the poet's letters carefully. As owner-editor of the *Springfield Republican*, Bowles was a key literary figure in Massachusetts life. Dickinson's own poems, beginning in 1861, are often sent first to Bowles—often by her sister-in-law, Susan Gilbert Dickinson.

Martin also borrows from Adrienne Rich's commentary on Dickinson, to suggest that the poet might have referred to her own creative persona as "Master," as Mary Ann Evans became George Eliot, and Charlotte and Emily Brontë became Currer and Ellis Bell. With these models, Martin concludes, "It is possible that Dickinson also referred to her creative self as male" (Martin 103). Habegger, however, states that Dickinson never used this term to refer to *any* woman (Habegger 350). His attention fell on Wadsworth, and he resists bringing Bowles into the scene—despite his appreciation for Bowles' consistent sympathy for Dickinson—because the family did not meet Bowles until later in 1858 (Habegger 376).

Mentioned first in 1971 and then expanded to become the insistent topic of his 2012 book, *Emily Dickinson in Love: the Case for Otis Lord*, John Evangelist Walsh finds that Dickinson's friendship/relationship with her father's friend may provide the answer to this conundrum. Whereas Lord was married until the time of his wife's death from cancer in December, 1877, he had known Emily from the time of her infancy—being a close friend of the Dickinsons' cousin Zebina Montague at Amherst College—and later, her father's friend and associate. Walsh points to a number of references in Dickinson's early poems to "Lord," ambiguously placed to suggest a deity but doubling as a noun of direct address (see Chapter 18). He suggests that Judge Lord moved his court cases to Boston rather than hear them in Northampton during the months Dickinson was under the oculist's care there (Walsh 71). He also tells the story of Austin's paying off a blackmailer to retrieve a number of Dickinson's letters to Lord after both of the parties have died (Walsh 4–10).

George Whicher, along with prize-winning biographer Richard Sewall, uses Dickinson's correspondence with all these well-placed people to illustrate how much she wanted recognition. He lists "Samuel Bowles, Josiah Gilbert Holland [not realizing that Emily's real pact was with Elizabeth, his wife], T. W. Higginson, Helen Hunt Jackson, Thomas Niles of Roberts Brothers . . . [concluding that] She went to 'professional' literary people because the common reader of poems could not have

read her work—they could not have understood 'her own level'"
(Whicher 116).

As chronology blurs, and the critical battle over Dickinson's allegiance to Bowles or Wadsworth or—a few years later—Higginson,
and very recently, Lord shifts and settles, the imbroglio over that
allegiance seems immaterial. What continues to be important is the way
Dickinson found her way, in poetry, out of the personal seclusion that
surrounded her. In a spring 1859 poem, for example, she wrote "New
feet within my garden go." Through her extensive correspondence with
both the Hollands and the Bowleses, and through what she feels is their
appreciation for her art, Dickinson is ready to *betray* what has become
her customary "solitude" (Fr 118).

One of the reasons for Dickinson's expanding circle of friends and
poem readers is the social activity at the Evergreens. With the recurring
illnesses of Emily Norcross Dickinson, the entertaining which Edward
enjoyed became more and more difficult: even hosting the Amherst
College graduation reception was in danger of being cancelled. But
because Susan Gilbert Dickinson was eager to become Amherst's foremost
hostess, she and Austin began volunteering to take on the family's social
role. Susan was also houseproud at this time: her successful brothers had
contributed $5000 both for finishing the house and for furnishing it.
Successful as Susan's brothers were in Michigan—and that success had
led Austin and Susan to think of moving west—their gift was princely.

Among other events, in 1857 Austin and Susan hosted Ralph Waldo
Emerson when he came to Amherst to lecture. This is the event that
biographers mention—recounting that Emily was already so reclusive
that she did not go to meet the important man. (Habegger suggests
that she might not have been invited.) Emerson returned in 1865.
The Bowleses were other intimates of Susan and Austin, and Habegger
quotes from the reminiscence of Susan's school friend Kate Scott Turner:
"Those celestial evenings in the Library—the blazing *wood* fire—*Emily—
Austin,*—the music—the rampant fun—the inextinguishable laugh-
ter" 373.) Even as Susan loved to be the center of this social activity,
Longsworth reports that Austin was sometimes heard to grumble about
"my wife's tavern" (Longsworth Amherst 53).

Because Austin and Susan's first child was not born until five years
after their marriage, the couple had ample time to work on perfecting
their salon-like existence. Susan Gilbert had lived an unmoored life as
an orphan: her need for this kind of stability was understandable. As
one of the younger Gilbert siblings, Susan had long been dependent.
Trying to live with an older married sister, she found that adoptive

household very unwelcoming so she took a post teaching mathematics at Mrs. Archer's Boarding and Day School in Baltimore during 1851–52. The next year she became an informal family companion to Mary Learned Bartlett, the sister-in-law of her older beloved sister Mary, who had died soon after giving birth. While Susan was useful in the Bartletts' Manchester, New Hampshire, household, helping to care for a new baby, she seemed to be looking for a permanent, family-linked placement (Gordon 64–72).

It was March 23, 1853, that Susan traveled alone to meet Austin in his room at the Revere House Hotel in Boston and they became engaged. Gordon makes the point that Susan was extremely resourceful as she traveled alone around New England, from Baltimore to New Hampshire and Boston (Gordon 74).

In 1858, Edward Dickinson decided that more use of the Evergreens would benefit his extended family's life: he asked Austin and Susan to provide a home for two of his wards, the younger Newman sisters. Clara was 14; Anna, 12. Such an arrangement gave Edward as guardian more access to the Newman sisters' inheritance, and when Clara was married in 1869, more than a decade after moving to the Evergreens, her inheritance was smaller than she had expected. That Edward had first considered moving the two girls into the Homestead seems clear from Aife Murray's comment that moving them next door instead was a "triumph" for Emily (Murray 84). Critic Polly Longsworth adds that Susan Gilbert Dickinson was "far from delighted" to have the wards living with them (Longsworth Amherst 40). There is also some evidence in Emily's letters to Austin that she would not welcome Clara and Anna, because she does not think the teenagers are "like" them.

To sort through the kinds of festivities—the visits, suppers, evenings around the piano, and more formal entertaining—that linked the two Dickinson houses—the Homestead with the Evergreens—is to chart the sometimes difficult partnership between Edward and his household and Austin and his. For instance, in early 1860 the impressive minister that Emily so admired—Charles Wadsworth of Philadelphia—paid a call on Emily at the Homestead. It was mid-March; Vinnie was still staying with Aunt Lavinia Norcross as she drifted into death. In June of that year, June 9, 1860, Edward's good friend Judge Lord and his wife visited the Dickinsons at the Homestead: in August the Governor of Massachusetts and his wife (the Bankses) stayed at the Homestead, and Emily's school friend Helen Hunt came with her husband, Major Hunt, to visit Emily and to urge her to publish her poetry. Of all these memorable events, the most important—for Emily and for her family—was the death of

Aunt Lavinia Norcross, another woman lost to consumption. Aunt Vinnie's death may have been an even deeper loss for Emily who had frequently, imaginatively, replaced her own biological mother with her comforting, and always loving, aunt (Cody 51).

Lavinia Norcross died April 17, 1860. Soon after, Dickinson wrote a rare personal poem to her cousins, Louise (who is 18) and Fanny (who is 12), her aunt's beloved daughters. In "'Mama' never forgets the birds," the poet includes a definite reference to "either of her 'sparrows,'" (Poem #130 Fr 171). More of Dickinson's 1860 poems describe Lavinia's death with the poet's straightly simple language:

> She died—*this* was the way she died.
> And when her breath was done . . . (Poem #154 Fr 193).

This poem is similar in tone to poems #158, #159, #161, and #163.

A few of Dickinson's poems from spring 1860 move away from the beloved's death, so peacefully distilled in these careful words as to suggest a depth of grief bordering on the catatonic. "I have never seen 'Volcanoes'" lists the rage of bereavement—"Fire, and smoke, and gun"—and refers to "pain Titanic" (Poem #165 Fr 202). Dickinson's pair poem for this shows her biting irony:

> Dust is the only secret—
> Death—the only one (Poem #166 Fr 202-03).

And "Ah, necromancy sweet" and "Wait till the Majesty of Death" complete the imagery of grieving loss (Poems #168 and #169 Fr 204–5).

Working her way through her grief over her aunt's death, Dickinson creates a montage of the simple language she equates with this loving woman. She also writes a handful of poems about the small persona who is often equated with the poet herself: "I cautious, scanned my little life" and "As if some little Arctic flower" (Poems #175 and #177 Fr 209–11) here balance with a description of her aunt in "Except to Heaven—she is nought" where, in stanza 3: "The smallest Housewife in the grass,/ Yet take her from the lawn/ And somebody has lost the face/ That made *Existence—Home—*" (Poem #173 Fr 208).

A poignantly related poem "I'm the little 'Heart's Ease'!" links the poet with her aunt, especially in stanza 3 which opens

> Dear—Old fashioned, little flower!
> Eden is old fashioned, too . . . (Poem #167 Fr 203–4).

Dickinson's later April letter to Vinnie, who is still caring for the Norcross family in its bereavement, repeats the sorrow these poems express: Aunt Lavinia had told Vinnie that she loved Emily, and Emily marvels at her thinking of others as she dies. "Poor little Loo! Poor Fanny! You must comfort them./ If you were with me, Vinnie, we could talk about her together./ And I thought she would live I wanted her to live so, I thought she could not die! . . . Dear little aunt! Will she look down? Did she carry my little bouquet? So many broken-hearted people have got to hear the birds sing, and see all the little flowers grow . . . . Well, she is safer now than 'we know or even think.' Tired little aunt, sleeping ne-er so peaceful! Tuneful little aunt, singing, as we trust, hymns than which the robins have no sweeter ones" (LII 362).

There is no comparable lament in any other of Dickinson's letters.

5
Dickinson and War

The Civil War had been brewing for decades. In 1820 the Missouri Compromise brought federal law into the mix of slave versus non-slave settlements. It was followed in 1836 by the Gag Rule and then in 1850 by the Compromise that included the Fugitive Slave law. As the principle of states' rights fought to dominate a philosophical argument, made by many religious groups as well as churches—that slavery was not evil because these dark-skinned people were not human beings, the potential for bloodshed grew. Nat Turner's 1831 rebellion prompted increased militarism throughout the United States, as well as increased prohibitions against slaves being taught to read and write. The mysterious death in 1830 of David Walker, a North Carolina free black, exacerbated tensions in what was not a slave holding state in the way that Virginia and South Carolina were. *Walker's Appeal: in four articles together with a preamble to the coloured citizens of the world* had been published in 1829, while Walker lived in Boston. The Southern states resented this publication; the state of Georgia, for example, offered a high price for Walker's death.

There was no question that the South's "peculiar institution" was going to lead to immense moral and physical conflict. In 1857 the Dred Scott decision held that Negroes were not citizens of the United States, a statement that removed all legal protection from their lives. It also decreed that slaveholding could not be excluded from any of the states or territories. As the invention of the cotton gin and other elements helpful to the production and manufacturing of cotton— a crop long dependent on slave labor—increased profits from this staple of Southern farming (as well as hemp and rice), the Southern states grew more adamant in their legal positions. Nineteenth century culture was dominated by the essay form: the magazines and journals that many Northern subscribers read were filled with arguments that either supported states' rights or lamented the existence of slavery.

In 1858 during the Lincoln-Douglas Debates as the men struggled for a seat in the Illinois state legislature, the differences between Stephen Douglas and Lincoln were already clear; in 1859, October 16, the John Brown Revolt occurred at Harper's Ferry, Virginia. Horrified by the bloodshed, and by Brown's later execution, abolitionists knew their stance was likely to lead to war. When Abraham Lincoln was elected President of the United States on November 6, 1860, it was only a month until the state of South Carolina seceded from the union. In January and February of 1861, many other Southern states—Mississippi, Florida, Alabama, Georgia, Louisiana, and Texas—followed suit. These first seven states met in Montgomery, Alabama, wrote their Articles of Confederation, and elected Jefferson Davis their president; he was inaugurated several weeks before Lincoln's inauguration.

March 4, Lincoln was inaugurated as President. On April 12, 1861, the first shots were fired at Fort Sumter, South Carolina and the next week Virginia seceded. Lincoln proclaimed a naval blockage of these states and North Carolina; in June, the territory of West Virginia was named a state because that population would not leave the union. Tennessee, Arkansas, and—eventually—North Carolina secede. The next month on July 18 Confederate forces won the First Battle of Bull Run. And Dickinson wrote "A slash of Blue—/A sweep of Gray—/Some scarlet patches on the way" (Poem #233 Fr 256-7). In an August, 1861, letter to Mary Bowles, Dickinson writes cryptically, "I shall have no winter this year—on account of the soldiers—Since I cannot weave Blankets, or Boots—I thought it best to omit the season—Shall present a 'Memorial' to God—when the Maples turn" (LII 377). By 1863, after hundreds of battles and thousands of deaths, Dickinson has realized more clearly what the losses of wartime mean, and she tries expressing that grief in several poems—among them "It feels a shame to be Alive/When Men so brave—are dead." With references to a great price "Sublimely paid," the poet moves in stanza four to the crux of the men's sacrifice:

> Are we that wait—sufficient worth—
> That Such Enormous Pearl
> As life—dissolved be—for Us—
> In Battle's—horrid Bowl?

In the conclusion, the poet returns to call "the Men who die" "Saviors—/Present Divinity" (Poem #524 Fr 532-3). (For other "lost" war poems, including a number that Dickinson published in *Drum Beat,* see Dandurand.) With the *Daily Springfield Republican* running news about all battles, no literate Northerner could escape the horrifying realizations. As Sewall had pointed out early, "the Civil War was a living fact for her. . . . how close she lived to the stirring events of her times. Amherst was no backwater" (Sewall 714, 647).

Although critics have recognized that Dickinson's most productive writing period fell between 1861 and 1865, many of them have followed Elaine Showalter's assessment, that Dickinson "did not write about" the Civil War; later this critic notes that Dickinson alluded to the war "in one or two occasional poems" (Showalter 146, 151). Incorporating Douglas Duncan's commentary that the Dickinsons were "segregated . . . from the outer world" provides a view both insular and erroneous (Duncan 104). What well-educated resident of the North could remain oblivious to the war, especially since thousands of young northern men—and some Southern men as well—were fighting for the Union? Particularly in the Dickinson households—both the Homestead and the Evergreens—where the flood of journals, magazines, and newspapers carried news of hardly anything else, the world's fascination with war was being played out intimately as Edward's brother, Samuel Fowler Dickinson, became a "fierce secessionist" (Stewart 322).

One of the difficulties with assessing Dickinson's concern with the Civil War lies in the fact that by 1861, Dickinson had evolved her own cryptic language of metaphor. Whereas Shira Wolosky in her 1984 book had pointed out convincingly that "metaphysical conflict is accompanied by historical trauma" (Wolosky xviii), her commentary is itself somewhat metaphorical: to comment on Dickinson's multiple uses of gunfire, guns, and gunshots—along with the incidences of the suddenness of death—does not peg the poet's responses to specific battles. Wolosky shows how ambivalent other authors contemporary with Dickinson were about the war—Melville, Hawthorne, Emerson, Whitman—and she suggests, correctly, that "it was not merely random death, but insignificant death that seemed inacceptable" for Dickinson (Wolosky 48, 42). Even though she points out that *Harper's,* like the *Springfield Republican,* was filled with the rhetoric of militarism, this critic does not give information about the specific events of the war that might correlate with Dickinson's life or her poems.

Wolosky's emphasis on the way Dickinson used disjunction and discontinuity parallels some of Cristianne Miller's analysis of the way the poet makes use of "densely compacted" metaphors. Miller points out that in mailing her poems to recipients of her letters, Dickinson insures a kind of helpful context for the poetry itself (Miller 1, 13). And poet Susan Howe described Dickinson's process of writing: "Forcing, abbreviating, pushing, padding, subtracting, riddling, interrogating, re-writing" in order to pull "text from text" (Howe My Emily 29).

It is credible that Dickinson was so moved by her personal circumstances during the war years that she wrote differently in the early 1860s. Her work has already moved from "occasional" poems— i.e., those written for Valentine's Day—to the noun-dominated quatrains and tercets that spoke distinctively of both nature and of the human emotions most important to her. But with the encouragement of Samuel Bowles and his wife Mary, as well as with the immense surge of new impressions she was receiving from the surroundings of conflict and war, Dickinson may have felt uniquely poised to write significant poems, poems unlike any so far copied out and into her careful fascicles. Christopher Benfey explains this synergy in terms of "the traumatic experience, direct and indirect, of the Civil War . . . a new sense of precariousness in the lives of artists and writers, and the ways in which art served as temporary anchorage amid uncertainly. This was a period in which art and activism were closely allied" (Benfey Hummingbirds 8). There is also the fact that Dickinson's family is in reasonably good health (with Ned, Susan and Austin's first child, born in the summer of 1861) and that Margaret O'Brien, the family maid, manages much of the work in the Homestead without the help of either Vinnie or Emily.

Isolated, in that normal existence was usurped by the war, the Dickinsons in Amherst were living the war years vicariously. Critics still saw Samuel Bowles as influential in Dickinson's art, but his influence remains unclear. Whereas the Bowleses saved many of the poet's letters to them, the other side of the correspondence is missing, probably due to Vinnie's destroying Emily's correspondence after her death, as she had promised her sister she would. Indirectly, because Bowles published the *Springfield Republican*, materials that appeared in the newspaper carried his seal of approval—or so today's readers assume. Given the hortatory nature of nineteenth century essays, and the factual demands of journalism, there would have been little poetry published (and some of that would also have been hortatory). Judging from the highly personal tenor of Dickinson's letters to both Mary Bowles and Samuel, it seems clear that the poet felt an immediate bond with the couple. For instance, in late August, 1858, Dickinson wrote in a letter to Samuel, "In such a porcelain life, one likes to be sure that all is well, lest one stumble upon one's hopes in a pile of broken crockery." She also tells him, "My friends are my only estate" (LII 338). Several years later she repeats the sentiment: "My friends are very few. I can count them on my fingers—and besides, have fingers to spare" (LII 366). (See Habegger 446–51 for possible explanations for the cooling of the friendship, and Martin (109) for comments about the later role of Maria Whitney in Bowles' life.)

The correspondingly personal elements that began appearing in Dickinson's poems during 1860 may have had little connection with these sentiments. But again, for the poet to feel free to write with unusual intimacy may have opened the way to new subjects for her art. Included in letters to Samuel Bowles, for example, are two powerful poems, "Title divine—is mine!/ The Wife—without the Sign" which is a gendered commentary on God's favors, and "Victory comes late," which includes the poignant "*Crumbs* fit such little mouths—/*Cherries*— suit *Robins*—/The Eagle's golden breakfast—*dazzles them!*" This poem characterizes the poet as a small natural identity: "God keep his vow to *"Sparrows"*/ Who of little love–/ Know how to starve!" (Poems 194 and 195 Fr 228–30). Sent originally, Franklin believes, to Bowles, the poems, which combine religious motifs with natural and human, were also sent to Susan Gilbert Dickinson.

Dickinson closed the letter to Bowles in which "Title divine—is mine!" was included, "Here's—what I had to 'tell you'—You will tell no other? Honor—is it's own pawn" (Fr 228). There are many other poems from the early 1860s directed to Bowles, and because Austin's and Susan's first child was born in July of 1861, one natural conclusion is that Dickinson realized she could no longer prevail on the decades-long friendship with Susan Gilbert Dickinson. Hurt as she was by Susan's absorption with the baby (and the several baby nurses she was teaching to care for Ned), Dickinson turned to an equally sympathetic, and knowledgeable, reader.

Dickinson's uses of metaphor also flourished during these years. "Bring me the sunset in a cup—" combines the imagery of the smallest bird with the Biblical strategy of finding a place in the Father's "house" (and pairs with the shorter and more direct "'Houses'—so the Wise men tell me—/'Mansions'! Mansions must be warm!") (Poems #140 and #139 Fr 180–1). Filled with unexpected comparisons, a surprising number of Dickinson's poems from the early 1860s treat religious themes, perhaps in recognition of the national conflict—both already expressed and to come. As Habegger notes, connecting Dickinson's fear about the war and its damages to the family losses—Aunt Lavinia who died in 1860 and two years later, Uncle Joel Norcross's young wife Lamira who also died of consumption and left two children, as did Lavinia—"The war multiplied and generalized her sense of mortal risk and large issues and a nearness to ultimates." He then quotes from Dickinson's letter to Joel Norcross, "So many brave—have died, this year—it dont seem lonely—as it did—before Battle begun" (Habegger 400). Using Dickinson's increasingly frequent letters to her cousins Lou and Fanny Norcross to illustrate how often she mentions the damages of war, Habegger also reminds the reader that their father, Loring Norcross, had died in 1863. In her biographer's assessment, Dickinson "saw that her new powers had something to do with the national ordeal. It was as if her own fundamentals had been endorsed" (Habegger 400).

Critic Aife Murray notes that Dickinson wrote literally hundreds of poems during these Civil War years. Murray lists 88 of Dickinson's poems written in 1861, 227 in 1862, and 295 in 1863 (Murray 79). Attributed in part to the efficient services of the full-time maid Margaret O'Brien, Dickinson's incredible quantities of poems must reflect the fusion of the emotional force—of war, of its losses, and of her own carefully-balanced writing life—with the techniques she had been practicing, and experimenting with, for at least a decade. There had been much experimenting with both language and structure during that decade.

Helen Vendler has pointed out that it is with Dickinson's poems of 1861 that she begins her practice of sequential description: Vendler calls it "seriality" and uses the poem "I'll tell you how the Sun rose" as an example. The layers of description here create the perfect balance: Dickinson fills each segment in the same order. (Vendler calls this "chromatic seriality," Vendler 65–6.) The critic points out that within several more years, and the writing of several hundred more poems, Dickinson has already taken liberties with the perfection of this form.

To note Dickinson's evolving this structure in the early 1860s, years which mark the start of her most prolific and most intense writing period, provides a way of seeing her growing control of "meaning." Vendler places Dickinson as a recipient of the writers of the European lyric, faced as she is with her own style of thinking, which is marked by 'its cryptic ellipses, its compassion, its enigmatic subjects, its absent centers, and its abstractions" (Vendler 64). So in order to control this flood of meaning, Dickinson invents "poetic temporal structures that mimic the structure of life," life marked by Vendler's perception of what she sees as the poet's primary themes: "nature's appearances, death's certainty, and an uncertain immortality" (Vendler 65).

To show the differences in effect as the poet's system breaks apart (as her subjects grow to be more and more complex), Vendler discusses "The Heart asks Pleasure first" (1863). Perhaps more importantly the critic's discussion of two of Dickinson's 1862 poems shows the disruption of the linear forms from the impact of the poet's content: "I felt a Funeral, in my Brain" and "After great pain, a formal feeling comes" as well as the later "I felt a cleaving in my Mind" (1864) (Vendler 67–74). Considered to be among Dickinson's finest poems, these works also illustrate what poet Adrienne Rich called the real force of Dickinson's art, the poet's ability to "retranslate her own unorthodox, subversive, sometimes volcanic propensities into a dialect called metaphor: her native language . . . It is always what is under pressure in us, especially under pressure of concealment, that explodes in poetry" (Rich 161).

Vendler's attempts to create a systematic order in the flood of Dickinson's writing—during 1862 and 1863 particularly—does not come close to explaining the power the poet had achieved in poem after poem. These several hundred poems are the bedrock of Dickinson's reputation and as Hayden Carruth noted, many of these hundreds of poems are unrevised—despite their sense of having come "tumbling out of the poet's imagination in a kind of careless exuberance." He points out, however, that there is nothing "careless" about these poems: "They have great power, and part of their power is their strangeness" (Carruth 152).

Witnesses to the pain Dickinson was both experiencing and accommodating during the Civil War years, these poems—many of them—crystallize the emotional trajectory of Dickinson's life experience. When she concludes "After great pain, a formal feeling comes" with the memorable

This is the Hour of Lead—
Remembered, if outlived,
As Freezing persons, recollect the Snow—
First—Chill—then Stupor—then the letting go— (Poem #372 Fr 396).

the poem, and its placement in her fascicles (this, fascicle 18), serves as a culmination of many poems expressing grief. Whether there are any specific battles, or names, or dates, Dickinson reflects the news of war during 1861 and 1862 whenever she sits down to write.

Perhaps more to the point, if Dickinson is writing autobiographically, is the opening of the poem's second stanza: "The Feet, mechanical, go round—/ A wooden way/ Of Ground, or Air, or Ought . . ." Life, for most people, even during war, continues. Such a life may seem normal. For critic Morag Harris, however, the poet's use of the word "Ought" as a place noun is a coded reference to the women's roles Dickinson finds herself expected to fill. It is a reference she uses often to show the power of the patriarchal family and its community (Harris 129). In these poems, however, what seems to be more crucial than gender is the recognition of pain and its sorrow, as in "The Soul has Bandaged moments—/When too appalled to stir," a poem that parallels "I felt my life with both my hands/ To see if it was there" and "'Twas just this time, last year, I died" (Poems #360, #357, #344 Fr 385, 381, 369–70). The most direct expression of this mood comes in the poem which closes with "The Quick of Wo." The poem is "If Anybody's friend be dead/ It's sharpest of the theme/ The thinking how they walked alive—" (Poem #354 Fr 378–9).

Many of these poems parallel Dickinson's letters to Lou and Fanny Norcross about the deaths of Amherst men in battle, and particularly about Austin's friend, Frazer Stearns (LII 397–98), who was "killed at Newbern . . . His big heart shot away by a 'minie ball.'" More significant to Dickinson, judging from the details in her second letter, was the young man's burial in Amherst, "enclosed in a large casket shut entirely, and covered from head to foot with the sweetest flowers. He went to sleep from the village church. Crowds came to tell him goodnight, choirs sang to him, pastors told how brave he was." Carefully observing a person's leave-taking, Dickinson may have already been developing the idiosyncratic but effective measures for her own funeral in years to come. Perhaps the most important line of her long descriptive letter is the last, "Austin is stunned completely." As she wrote to Samuel Bowles at that time, "Austin is chilled—by Frazer's murder—He says—his Brain keeps saying over 'Frazer is killed'—'Frazer is killed,' just as Father told it—to Him. Two or three words of lead—that dropped so deep, they keep weighing . . ." (LII 399).

This sense of Austin's numbed living through the war, remotely, quietly, protected from serving by his rheumatic heart (and perhaps by his new fatherhood and his family's class and position) shows another significant dimension to Dickinson's empathy. As with many of her letters—especially when she writes to Mary Bowles and other women about difficult or unsuccessful pregnancies—the poet's reticence does not mask her feelings. Dickinson, the woman, cares. Dickinson, the poet, cares. She cares enough to try to give language to her feelings and, more importantly, to the feelings of the person to whom she writes. Oftentimes, silence would be more easily accomplished.

The mobilization of Amherst resources to aid the Union was partly achieved by Edward and Austin Dickinson. It may not have been true, although some critics have stated that Austin bought his replacement for service in the Union army; it was rather that the town took steps to offer funds for that purpose. At first Austin was not drafted, but on May 13, 1864, he found his name in a group of five men who were drafted (described by Murray as "four other Dickinsons and George Cutler in the Ninth District," 165). The rate for volunteer service, or replacement service, was from $300 to $500 a person. Since January 1, 1863, a sentence in Lincoln's *Emancipation Proclamation* decreed that slaves freed under the President's edict would "be received into the armed service of the United States to garrison forts, positions, stations, and other places, and to man vessels of all sorts in said service." Accordingly, these five Amherst men were replaced by "Chauncey 'Julius' Pierce of Sunderland . . . and four African American men: Maryland-born fugitive slave Howard Paxton, who was thirty-six (receiving $443); Hills factory hand Henry Thompson ($338); eighteen-year-old Joseph Solomon ($365), who returned after the war to Mill Valley as a farmer; and Lorenzo Sugland, who as a child became a state pauper but received no bounty for his enlistment at age eighteen" (Murray 166). Murray comments that Amherst was known for being rather "backward" in filling its military quotas. That May, 1864, the vote in town meeting was to pay back "monies spent in filling war quotas and to procure substitutes for those drafted." The records do not show whether Austin paid his own fee to a substitute or allowed the town to pay "$500 for his war substitute" (Murray 166). Critic Susan Stewart, however, claims that Austin himself paid the $500 to the Irish immigrant who replaced him (Stewart 323).

The more localized events of the Civil War—whether men leaving to serve and their subsequent returns and funerals, or the closing of Amherst College—were visible to everyone in the area. By April 1862, the 235 students at the college were enlisting: 78 joined the Union army, four returned to their Southern homes to enlist with the Confederacy. By May of 1862, all classes at Amherst College were cancelled (Stewart 322). In terms of the war's most horrific battles, the carnage was well underway.

6

Colonel Higginson as Mentor

Dickinson's poems as well as some of her letters help to graph the patterns of her health, her poetics, and her awareness of the horrors of war. For instance, in March 1860 she writes to her cousin Lou, "I've had a curious winter, very swift, sometimes sober, for I haven't felt well, much, and March amazes me!" (LII 360). Her later letters show that, despite Vinnie's being in Boston to care for Aunt Lavinia (Lou's and Fanny's mother), the poet did not expect her beloved aunt to die. As we have seen, Dickinson wrote a number of poems about that loss. But intermingled with those poems are others that seem to illustrate concerns about her own health. Some are based on "recovery"—of health? Of consciousness? Of goodness?—as in "Just lost, when I was saved!" and "'Tis so much joy! 'Tis so much joy!" works which seem simpler than a poem from the same period like "To learn the transport thro' the pain" (Poems #132, #170, and #178 Fr173, 205–6, and 212). Other poems seem to describe a person's wounded physical body, as in "A *wounded* deer—leaps highest" with its imagery of both bleeding and a "hectic" cheek, a clear tubercular symptom, and particularly the lament "Dying! Dying in the night!" a poem in which "Dollie" (Dickinson's name for Susan Gilbert) is able to give the speaker comfort that no heavenly messenger can bring (Poems #181 and #222 Fr 215 and 249).

During the early years of the 1860s, for all her prolific writing, the poet seems to be depressed: several critics speak about Dickinson's "break down" (Pollock 3, Longsworth Amherst 46, Benfey Hummingbirds 124). It might well be that her health is trying, and as she struggles to accept the deaths of loved ones—including that of Elizabeth Barrett Browning on June 29, 1861, as well as Lucy Dwight, wife of pastor Edward Dwight, her aunt Lavinia, and her aunt Lamira—she finds acceptance hard to come by. As she writes in "I never hear the word *'Escape'*/Without a quicker blood!," the poet might have welcomed the chance to leave her sorrowing home—replete with community anxieties as well as familial (Poem #144 Fr 184–5). As she had years before written to the Hollands, "I can't stay any longer in a world of death!" (LII 341). Compared with the deluge of grief that she was experiencing during the 1860s, her earlier sorrow might have, in retrospect, seemed slight.

Habegger extends his earlier remarks about the way the Civil War affected Dickinson: "To detach her from the war is to miss seeing how her poetry of the early 1860s, a great and classic descent into a personal inferno, was made possible by the staggering disaster in the distance" (Habegger 400). Both Sharon Leder and Andrea Abbott would agree, seeing Dickinson as a public poet who pretended to be private so as to escape criticism over her sometimes controversial views (Leder and Abbott 2). Zofia Burr has recently pointed out that what she terms "the canonization" of Dickinson has made her into a private poet—and that what poems of hers have been admitted to that canon give readers a "skewed and limiting" sense of her art (Burr 12). Emily Stipes Watts had made a similar point decades earlier, by noting that critics tried to place Dickinson's work into a male-defined set of rules (Watts 125). Paula Bennett, too, comments on the fact that most women poets in the nineteenth century wrote "a poetry of interiority but an interiority shaped and informed by public concerns" (Bennett Public Sphere 39).

It is Bennett who sees the fact that Dickinson reached out so peremptorily to Thomas Wentworth Higginson was a way of breaching her "private" standing. Bennett states that when Dickinson wrote to the well-known literary figure she "deeply compromised" the nature of her poetry—and it seems clear that when Dickinson wrote *two* letters to Higginson in less than a month after the April, 1862, appearance of his *Atlantic* essay, "A Letter to a Young Contributor," she was making herself and her views a subject of note in his consideration of those young writers (Bennett Public Sphere 38). Given the fact that we now have Susan Goodman's study of *The Atlantic Monthly*, today's readers can begin to absorb the power of that journal. It has been clear for decades that the Dickinsons subscribed to *The Atlantic*; in spring of 1861, Dickinson writes to Susan Gilbert at the Evergreens that she needs to borrow the April issue because it contains "Life in the Iron Mills," the novella by Rebecca Harding Davis, one of the first United States stories to focus on contemporary poverty (Hart and Smith 98). A few months later, early in 1862, Susan herself writes to Higginson praising his essays on nature that have appeared in *The Atlantic* (Habegger 451–2). When the April, 1862, issue appeared, with an invitation seemingly directed to

Emily, both Susan and Emily herself would have felt that a response was appropriate—or at least legitimate. As Goodman notes, Higginson was particularly interested in women writers—and saw that there was very little market for work by women. That gendered emphasis would have added to the appeal of his essay/letter (Goodman 30).

For any reader of *The Atlantic*, as Pollitt had suggested, the monthly journal WAS American literature—as well as American history, politics, philosophy, religion, science, and various of the arts. For instance, when Darwin's *Origin of the Species* appeared in 1859, the next year *The Atlantic* ran a twenty page essay about various reviews of the monumental treatise ("Darwin and His Reviewers," 406–25), saying protectively, "We are not disposed nor prepared to take sides for or against the new hypothesis" (408). In October 1860, another seminal essay, "The Election in November," said emphatically "We believe that this election is a turning point in our history," stating further that the issues most important to the election hinge on the definition of the entity "Constitution" (492–502, this quote 494). In January 1861, in the essay "Charleston Under Arms," the unnamed essayist treated the controversial subject of secession, closing his formal essay with this sentence: "In South Carolina, they see but one side of the shield,—which is quite different, as we know, from the custom of the rest of mankind" (488—505). In these early years of publication, *The Atlantic* did not give names of authors (though Habegger points out that the *Springfield Republican* could supply those missing names if anyone inquired); within another few years, names were appended. That practice of anonymity may have made Dickinson more interested in submitting her poems to Higginson for his use in *The Atlantic*.

The letter Dickinson wrote to Higginson dated April 15, 1862—a year after the war had begun—was a series of short paragraphs, sent without any signature. Her signature, however, was enclosed on a card in a separate envelope within the letter. In the letter proper, she asked if her "Verse is alive" (enclosing four poems—as Goodman says, "unlike any he had read," Goodman 30; see Wineapple, entire). The poems included were "Safe in their Alabaster Chambers," "The nearest Dream recedes unrealized," "We play at Paste," and "I'll tell you how the Sun rose," at least the first of which had been reworked after suggestions from Susan Gilbert Dickinson.

Dickinson then asks for his commentary, because she thinks that "The Mind is so near itself—it cannot see, distinctly." Toward the end of the short letter, she repeats almost to its exact phrasing, what she had earlier asked of Samuel Bowles: "That you will not betray me—it is needless to ask—since Honor is it's own pawn" (LII 403). The importance of her asking for advice on examples of her painstaking art is underscored by this single sentence.

Dickinson's choice of poems also provides a wide range of her work: she is showing herself to be an adept critic. Two of the four poems are early: one dates from 1859; a second, from 1861. "Safe in their Alabaster Chambers" (Poem #124 Fr 159) had already been published by Samuel Bowles in *The Springfield Daily Republican* on March 1, 1862, titled "The Sleeping" with a dateline of "Pelham Hill, June, 1861." "I'll tell you how the Sun rose" (Poem #204 Fr 235) illustrates Dickinson's near-perfect set of quatrains, complete with slant rhymes as well as exact rhymes. Taken from Fascicle 10, this poem is an example of the young poet persona observing the natural life that surrounds her.

The other two poems appear to be very recent. "We play at Paste" (Poem #282 Fr 299) may have been written expressly for this submission to Higginson because Dickinson's metaphor is about her aesthetics. First, the poet works in "paste" until he/she improves to compose in "pearl." It is through this practice that the poet earns "new Hands" and achieves what the speaker seems to see as "*Gem*-tactics." (Habegger notes that in Higginson's essay on "*Gym*nastics," the three beginning letters provided the same kind of punning emphasis, 454.)

Dated similarly, "The nearest Dream recedes unrealized" (Poem #304 Fr 324–5) does not use any kind of pun or word play. The poem has become a two-stanza verse after its original division into quatrains. For submitting to Higginson, Dickinson has also softened the poem's tone. The original first line read "The maddest dream-recedes-unrealized" and line eleven used "defrauded" instead of "bewildered" to express the observing boy's disappointment. Much darker in effect than a poem such as "I'll tell you how the Sun rose," this poem draws from the same nature-based landscape but its metaphoric resonance is one of relinquishment, not tranquility.

After Higginson's prompt reply, in which he suggests some conventionalizing of her poetic form (in Leyda 357), Dickinson wrote him another letter, somewhat longer though not more informative; this time she includes three poems. Dickinson's second letter is a good illustration of what critic Sharon Cameron terms her capacity to pose; it is also Cameron's point that although Dickinson asked for comments from both Bowles and Higginson, she never used their advice (Cameron 54).

Dickinson's second letter to Higginson tells him nothing. More than coy, it is intentionally misleading. For instance, when Higginson asks how old she is, no doubt in relation to her art, Dickinson replies

"I made no verse—but one or two—until this winter" (LII 261). Given the many fascicles of carefully preserved poems already hidden in her room, Dickinson must have thought that assuming to be a novice would benefit her poems, in his judgment. Further on in the letter, she delivers the statement that has bothered so many of her critics: "I have a Brother and Sister—My Mother does not care for thought—and Father, too busy with his Briefs—to notice what we do" (LII 261). Another dodge used in the letter comes in answer to Higginson's question about her size; her two sentences together play on the "little girl" narrative voice that Crumbley and others have identified: "I could not weigh myself—Myself" is combined with "My size felt small—to me ...." (LII 262).

The intent of Dickinson's second letter is that Higginson see her as his supplicant, and to that end she writes, "I would like to learn—Could you tell me how to grow—or is it unconveyed—like Melody—or Witchcraft?" (LII 261). Metaphoric in its very coupling (is writing like the aptitude for music that Dickinson so joyfully evinced, or—to darken the quality—is writing like some enormous, unconventional belief in witchcraft?), this central section of the letter attaches to the three enclosed poems—"Then came a Day at Summer's Full" and "Of all the Sounds Despatched abroad," poems in memoriam for lost friends (Poems #325 and #334 Fr 343–9 and 356–60), held within the third poem, which serves as an earlier "nosegay," "South Winds jostle them" (Poem #98 Fr 135–7). Generally more difficult than the first four poems Higginson had seen, these three tie in with Dickinson's query that he be her preceptor.

The most significant section of Dickinson's second letter to Higginson is her unusually personal remark about the "terror" she has lived with since the September before—"I could tell to none—and so I sing, as the Boy does by the Burying Ground—because I am afraid" (LII 261). In a letter replete with subterfuge, her confession about this personal mental state jars. Whereas the death of Mrs. Dwight or the illness of Samuel Bowles might be her reference—or the urgency of her recognition of the real import of war, it seems more likely that Dickinson has had a serious frightening episode, a break in her own health patterns, perhaps physical, perhaps spiritual. For her to admit to a fear that she describes as *terror* seems most uncharacteristic. It may, indeed, be a reason for Dickinson to be looking outside her intimate family circle for information as well as comfort.

Given critic George Mamunes's belief that Dickinson was more seriously ill with consumption than her later history would show, his equation of the September episode is with her hemorrhaging a quantity of blood, usually one of the more serious markers of the illness (Mamunes 128–32). Similarly, Lyndall Gordon might tie this date to Dickinson's experiencing a convulsive seizure (116–18). From a somewhat different perspective, critics Roger Lundin (135) and Maryanne Garbowsky suggest that 1861 would be an appropriate interval for the poet's panic attacks—first recorded in 1854—to resume (67).

To jump ahead several generations, Virginia Woolf's often mysterious illnesses, described in 2012 by her biographer Hermione Lee, share many symptoms of Dickinson's carefully hidden maladies. Lee describes the "severe physical symptoms—fevers, faints, headaches, jumping pulse, insomnia,—signaled and accompanied by phases of agitation or depression . . . it seems possible, though unprovable, that she [Woolf] might have had some chronic febrile or tubercular illness" (Lee xv).

Although Woolf's illness occurs more than half a century later than Dickinson's, notice the emphasis here on avoiding drugs. Woolf's doctors emphasized "a regime of restraint: avoidance of 'over-excitement,' rest cures, milk and meat diets, no working allowed" (Lee xvi). Another similarity in Lee's descriptions of Woolf's illness (and by implication Dickinson's) is the predominance of the unconscious period during a faint. Dickinson fainted and was unconscious for hours: she then declines slowly for two years after that event until her death. For Woolf, a fainting spell in August, 1925, "led to months and months of illness" (Lee xvii).

Whether the silences that surrounded so many of the particularities of Dickinson's health can be attributed to social mores, to the sheer embarrassment of investigating women's illnesses, or to the self-censorship of the Dickinsons as a family as they wrote letters to friends and family members (and to the usual reticence of Dickinson herself—except in this letter to Higginson), today's reader must borrow Hermione Lee's word "unprovable." What existed for Dickinson was the terror and the fear of which she writes to Higginson, giving him compelling details that no reader can forget.

In her third letter, June 7, 1862, when Dickinson asks again if Higginson will be her mentor, surely she considers that September episode a part of her being. She changes tactics in this letter: she includes no poems. The letter itself, however, is written in a set of poem-like constructions. Perhaps a bit overwritten, this letter thanks Higginson for both his praise and his corrective comments (if her own ironically truth-dealing commentary can be overlooked when she says that his second set of comments seemed more just "because you bled me, first") (LII 408). Effusive in her thanks ("if I tried to thank you, my tears would block my tongue—") she continues her emphasis, after a reference to her beloved first teacher, her "dying Tutor" Ben Newton. She then stages her commentary so that it includes Higginson's previous critique:

> You think my gait "spasmodic"—I am in danger—Sir—
> You think me "uncontrolled"—I have no Tribunal.
> Would you have time to be the "friend" you should think I need?
> I have a little shape—it would not crowd your Desk . . . (LII 409).

Closing the letter with a direct question—"But, will you be my Preceptor, Mr. Higginson?"—Dickinson seems amenable to his caution that she does not want to publish yet (he uses the word "delay"). But she does suggest, in some detail, the kind of relationship she would like: "If I might bring you what I do—not so frequent to trouble you—and ask you if I told it clear—'twould be control, to me" (LII 409).

Considering that Dickinson was writing over two hundred poems during this year, Higginson might well have demurred at her suggestion. We do not have his side of their correspondence, of course, but in Dickinson's July, 1862, letter she rehearses the same information. She emphasizes again her modesty—she is female, the thought of publication is "foreign" to her. And because in a recent letter he has asked her for a photograph, she again refuses to supply any such portrait, saying, "You will think no caprice of me" (LII 411). She does, however, describe herself "I had no portrait, now, but am small, like the wren, and my Hair is bold, like the Chestnut Bur—and my eyes, like the Sherry in the Glass, that the Guest leaves" (LII 411). The four poems she encloses this time are "Of Tribulation these are they," "Your Riches taught me poverty," "Some Keep the Sabbath going to Church," and "Success is counted sweetest"—the first two recent, the "Sabbath" poem dating from 1861 and the "Success" poem from 1859 (Poems #328, #418, #236 and #112 Fr 351–2, 440–3, 258–60 and 145–7). As if selecting different kinds of work for his judgment, Dickinson does not date or explain any of the poems. She clearly has made her choices on the basis of work *she* finds effective.

In Dickinson's August, 1862, letter, she encloses two poems, "Before I got my Eye put out" and "I cannot dance upon my Toes," (Poems #336 and #381 Fr 361–3 and 406–8). More apparently autobiographical than most of the work Higginson has seen, these poems should have prompted a somewhat different commentary. Instead, Higginson did not answer this letter. On October 6, 1862, Dickinson sent him a two-sentence note, which read "Did I displease you, Mr. Higginson? But won't you tell me how?" and was signed as were the previous three letters, "Your friend, E. Dickinson" (LII 417).

In the essay that Higginson wrote nearly thirty years later, publishing texts from both his letters to her and hers to him, he commented about this brief note: "Sometimes there would be a long pause, on my part, after which would come a plaintive letter, always terse, like this" (in LII 418). Following Dickinson's letter of October 6, 1862, Higginson was completely involved in his Civil War tasks: he assumed duties as commander of the First South Carolina Volunteers, the first black regiment that fought for the Union (see Higginson's book, *Army Life in a Black Regiment*): he became *Colonel* Higginson.

One of the surprising layers of Higginson's involvement with Dickinson was that he had already assumed a role as public intellectual—supporting women's rights, temperance, abolition—a role that made him clearly visible to all readers of *The Atlantic,* as well as to all abolitionists, even before the Civil War began. He had entered Harvard at age 13; he had begun his professional life as a member of the Protestant clergy; in 1854 he had led a vigilante assault to free a fugitive slave from a federal court house, in the course of which a marshall was shot to death. He was one of the "Secret 6," men who supported John Brown's raid on the arsenal at Harper's Ferry. Taking over the responsibility for the regiment of 900 ex-slaves, housed on Sea Island off the coast of South Carolina, Higginson found his past life—including his correspondence with Dickinson—growing pale. Although she never wrote to him about his radical views, or his role during the Civil War (she did hope he would, "with honor, avoid Death"), Dickinson sent only current poems, hoping they would seem "more orderly" to Higginson (Habegger 458–9).

Dickinson's seventh letter to Higginson, assuming we have the complete record, was dated February of 1863, and it includes her recent poem "The Soul unto herself" (Poem #579 Fr 578–9). Because the *Springfield Republican* had printed long items about Higginson and his African American troops in the issues of both January 1, 1863, and February 6, 1863, her letter speaks with familiarity of his wartime struggles, and she laments not having seen him before his departure for the South. She writes that Carlo, "My Shaggy Ally," keeps her company, though months later she laments to the Norcross cousins, "Nothing has happened but loneliness, perhaps too daily to relate" (LII 423–4, 427). By September 1863, Dickinson is in great pain because of her eye ailment, and she is in even greater pain because of the progress—or lack of progress—of the Civil War.

It is this kind of critical emphasis—on the Dickinson-Higginson early letters—that made somewhat plausible the contention that Dickinson was remote from the war. To concentrate on a single thread of her activity produces a narrowing vision: for Dickinson, like her family and especially for Susan and Austin—who are much more socially involved with Massachusetts intellectual life—every conversation began with news of a recent battle. Despite the fact that the North had most of the manufacturing industry and nearly all the United States steel production, the South seemed to be winning the war. The Southerners' passionate belief—in both states' rights and the necessity of protecting the institution of slavery—fueled the Confederacy.

The tone of the conflict was probably set in the first major battle—the First Battle of Bull Run (July 18–21, 1861) when the expectation was that the Union would win. So sure was the North of victory that carriages and wagons from Washington, DC, set out to observe the battle. But when Stonewall Jackson's augmented forces regrouped and the Confederate forces won, those carriages with their civilian observers became a part of the confused retreat along with the thousands of Union soldiers.

Admittedly, major battles were fought far from Amherst, Massachusetts, but drawings and photographs created the context for readers who cared what was happening—and most everyone did care. Serious battles raged throughout 1861 and 1862. People had heard the names: the Allegheny Mountain battle, the Battle of Belmont (Missouri), the Second Battle of Bull Run (Manassas), the Battle of Ivy Mountain/Ivy Creek (Kentucky); in North Carolina, the Battle of Hatteras Inlet; in West Virginia, the Battle of Kessler's Cross Lanes; in Tennessee, the Battle of Fort Henry; the Battle of Williamsburg, which was part of the Peninsular campaign against Richmond, Virginia, now serving as the Confederate capital; and numerous skirmishes and battles on rivers, over railroads and their access, and naval battles on many rivers as well as the Atlantic coast.

By the time of the battle of Shiloh/Pittsburg Landing in Tennessee (April 1862), the Union forces of 30,000 men under the commands of General William T. Sherman and General Ulysses S. Grant meet 45,000 Confederate men, led by General Albert S. Johnson, a commander who was killed there from blood loss of an untended wound and then replaced by General Pierre Beauregard. Winning narrowly, the Union had more than 13,000 dead; the Confederates, retreating to Corinth, Mississippi, had nearly 11,000 casualties. By June, 1862, the Confederate army—under siege—was driven out of Corinth.

More visibly, however, especially once the Confederate troops were commanded by General Robert E. Lee, those troops won. As in the Seven

Days Campaign (June 1862) Lee attacked the larger Union Army of the Potomac, under George McClelland, near Richmond. During the week of battles, over 30,000 men died, and the visibility of this conflict—along with other such battles—was starting to persuade British and European observers that they should support the Southern forces.

Momentum continued through the Confederate victory at Fredericksburg, Virginia, in December of 1862 when the Union armies lost over twelve thousand men, compared with only five thousand Confederate deaths. "Battle" had been redefined: lost lives and mangled survivors' bodies were the rule, not the exception. The war that Lincoln had thought might last 90 days, and that the Confederacy had not expected to be fought at all, was leading to more and more death and destruction.

The fortunes of victory and defeat began turning on January 1, 1863, when President Lincoln issued the *Emancipation Proclamation*. His emphasis on the human issues of slavery made the war into a moral conflict—so that the participation of outsiders could no longer be justified. It was clear that slavery should be considered a sin. No matter how profitable crops raised with slave labor might be, the issues of human freedom outweighed that profit. Lincoln had circulated a preliminary version of the document in September of 1862, soon after the Union victory at Antietam, but even though the document called for the Confederate surrender—lest all slaves in those states and territories become free—people paid less attention to the document than expected: the Confederate states did not surrender. Former slaves began fighting for the Union, though they received lower pay than did white soldiers. By March, 1863, the Confederacy had turned to impressment (as the Union forces were using conscription), inflation was astronomical, and Southern women were waging "bread protests." The South had lost over 175,000 men.

There are more devastating losses to come: in May, 1863, the battle of Chancellorsville costs 30,000 lives from both armies; in July, the battle of Gettysburg—stretching over several days to include Pickett's Charge, Cemetery Ridge, and Little Round Top—gave the North a victory, but nearly 45,000 men died in those three days. Much of the combat was hand-to-hand.

While the armies on both sides were more and more depleted, key battles such as the mid-September Battle of Chickamauga in Tennessee became shocking markers. 18,000 men died at Chickamauga.

On July 27, 1863, Tom Kelley (who regularly works for the Dickinsons) tries to enlist in the Union army (to receive a bounty for his family) but he is not "accepted as a soldier" because he is "feeble, too feeble to go to war" (Murray 246).

On November 19, 1863, the commemoration of the Gettysburg cemetery was held: Lincoln's short "Gettysburg Address" was a preliminary statement to the main oratory by Edward Everett, the invited speaker from Massachusetts. In Lincoln's remarks, however, he changed the accepted definition of national purpose, calling for a "new birth of freedom" so that "government of the people, by the people, for the people, shall not perish from the earth." Lincoln's address was most significant in that it stated, "all men are created equal."

During the last years of the Civil War, Lincoln may have won the conflict by appointing Ulysses S. Grant commander of the remaining 550,000 Union soldiers. May 3–4, 1864, the Union Army of the Potomac began its scourge of Virginia—the Wilderness, Spotsylvania Court House, Mechanicsville, Cold Harbor and eventually—a year later—Fort Stedman. (In the latter battle, the Confederates lost nearly 5,000 men.) When William T. Sherman marched his 60,000 Union troops from Chattanooga to Atlanta, capturing that city at the end of his hundred-mile conquest, and then continuing to the Sea, he insured Lincoln's re-election on November 8, 1864. In March, 1865, Lincoln took his second oath of office; on April 9, 1865, General Robert E. Lee surrendered at Appomattox Court House—with only 15,000 men remaining in arms; on April 14, Lincoln was assassinated at Ford Theater by John Wilkes Booth, a Maryland actor. With the advent of Andrew Johnson as President of the United States, the Civil War ended and the turmoil of Reconstruction began.

Given Dickinson's highly personal reactions to the war's carnage, and understanding that for much of the last two years of conflict she was forbidden to use her eyes, one does not look for battle-by-battle commentary in her remaining letters. In a letter to Higginson from June, 1864, she acknowledges his having been wounded in July, 1863, and his leaving the Army in May 1864 (LII 431). She also complains—bitterly, for her—about having to live in Boston, without Carlo, for the eye treatments that are to save her sight. Dickinson's necessary retreat into the darkness of her eye illness provides an unintentional parallel to the grim continuation of the final years of warfare. Brave as she had tried to be, writing to the Hollands that "in a world where bells toll . . . *My* business is to love," Dickinson had no recourse but to live the events of the Civil War as if they were surrounding her Amherst, Massachusetts, environs (LII 413).

7
Life Without Home, For the Last Time

In Dickinson's 1864 letter to Higginson, her grief at living away from the Homestead suffuses her prose: "I was ill since September, and since April, in Boston, for a Physician's Care—He does not let me go, yet I work in my Prison, and make Guests for myself." It is this letter that speaks with sympathy of her dog, "Carlo did not come, because that he would die, in Jail, and the Mountains, I could not hold now . . ." (LII 431). Her word choice is vivid—"Prison," "Jail," being away from her "Mountains"—and then toward the end of page one, Dickinson asks "Can you render my Pencil? The Physician has taken away my Pen." The word for a synthesis of these emotions must be either *bereavement* or, in Dickinson's spelling, *wo*.

In 1864, Dickinson is approaching the age of 34. She has an ordered life; she has accomplished an immense amount of work and writing (so much that her family members, even Susan Gilbert Dickinson, have very little idea of the quality and the quantity of her poetry). Since the family has hired Margaret O'Brien as their full-time maid, Dickinson's life has grown easier in that it is less often interrupted. She can dodge Vinnie's requests that they go to Northampton to shop; she has been absolved from the tasks of being an active church member; she has trained her family so that they understand that she leads her own sometimes self-absorbed life. Yet into this world of pleasant and satisfying work has come the unexpected illness—iritis, or rheumatic iritis (anterior uveitis), the inflammation of the middle layer of the eye, which includes the iris. The condition makes light painful, makes reading difficult, makes writing arduous, and—because of the eyes' deep-seated aching—turns the patient into a remote and fearful being (Longsworth Amherst 46, Guthrie 9–12, Habegger 485).

Tucked into the world Dickinson had made of the Homestead and the Evergreens, with occasional private meetings with Susan in the "Northwest Passage," the back hall of the former, Dickinson let her fear of going blind take her away from her place of safety (Hart and Smith 101). In 1864 and 1865, on two separate occasions of many months duration each, she moved to Boston and boarded with Mrs. Barnabas Bangs at 86 Austin Street in Cambridgeport. She lived in this house from late April to November 21, 1864 and from April to October, 1865 so that she could work frequently with Dr. Henry W. Williams, MD, the outstanding oculist-ophthalmologist on Arlington Street in Boston. Living there with her (and probably the reason she found lodgings with Mrs. Bangs) were her beloved young Norcross cousins, Lou and Fanny; after their father's death in early 1863, they could not afford to remain in the family house, and so they became boarders (Bingham 432–3). Dickinson had consulted with Dr. Williams in Boston on February 4, 1864; at his suggestion, she then moved to the area (LII 429).

When Dickinson first arrived, Dr. Williams came to her; she could not see to travel through the streets. "Emily was very ill. Her eyes were causing her serious trouble and she seemed to be suffering from nervousness and depression" (Pollitt 196). She learned to knit. She could write only sparingly; by August, however, she could go to Dr. Williams' office for her treatments, which were said to be painful. Even with Lou and Fanny as companions, Dickinson missed her voracious reading; listening to the boardinghouse conversations—especially at mealtimes—did not replace her usual methods of learning. As she wrote in Poem #512, "Unto my Books—so good to turn—/For ends of tired Days" (Fr 522).

The break into what had become Dickinson's profitable life—most activities scheduled around her writing and reading time—was much more debilitating than biographers and critics have seemed to recognize. In the assessment of Benjamin Lease, drawing from Whicher's early biography, Dickinson's "quest was not as lonely or idiosyncratic as we have been led to believe. She shared with family and friends (Wadsworth and Higginson foremost among them) her life and thought and poems—and her lifelong search for answers to unanswerable questions. She experienced with them (and through them) a terrible war. She shared with these kindred spirits her passion for sacred books and her passionate dedication to a sacred vocation. The uncompromising honesty of her quest has spoken eloquently to our time" (Lease 130). James R. Guthrie, in speaking of her unhappiness, speculates on the "reserves of patience, optimism, and . . . imaginative resilience" she needed to summon (Guthrie 13).

"Home" to Emily Dickinson spelled out the worth of her very existence. She was, therefore, ecstatic to leave Mrs. Bangs' house in November—President Lincoln had won his second term but unbelievable war news still dominated the press—and return to the Homestead, to Carlo, Vinnie, Susan and Austin, little Ned, her parents, and her garden. Judith Farr has long contended that for Dickinson her garden "was a refuge, a sanctuary, and a studio of sorts" (Farr 23). Light still bothered her eyes, so she frequently did her gardening in the evenings (Farr 33).

Correspondence with Elizabeth Holland would have been a relief (Elizabeth feared, with good reason, for her own eyesight) but the Hollands were occupied with their own family, and Josiah was writing a life of Abraham Lincoln. According to Theodora Van Wagenen Ward (the Hollands' granddaughter), to conserve time, Elizabeth sometimes wrote letters to Vinnie and Emily together. Her practice angered Emily who directed Elizabeth to "Send no union letters," pointing out that "A mutual plum is not a plum. I was too respectful to take the pulp and do not like a stone" (LII 455). Dickinson seemed to think that using the few minutes she could hoard to write letters was a less-than-satisfactory pastime: she preferred to write poems. Surprisingly, her poems remained as strong and wide-ranging as they had been during 1862 and 1863: once she had learned to handle the formal qualities of what would be her characteristic poetry, she drew easily, if carefully, on the strategies she had learned to trust.

Many of her poems from later 1863 and 1864 praise the beauties of the Amherst terrain. Some of these poems are in alignment with each other: a descriptive work like "The Day came slow—till Five o'clock," filled with lush color, fits next to the more definitely shaped "The Angle of a Landscape," observed, in the poet's words, "every time I wake." As the poet notes one "Bough of Apples . . . slanting, in the Sky," she comments carefully on

> The Pattern of a Chimney—
> The Forehead of a Hill—

and she then brings the artifacts in her sight back to their foregrounded landscape, filled with other objects which "never stir at all" (Poems #572 and #578 Fr 571–2, 577–8).

She touches on some of these views in "We see—Comparatively" and she emphasizes the beauty in "The Red—Blaze—is the Morning." In "I am alive—I guess" Dickinson mutes the stress on perceiving beauty so that she can write a narrative (the first line extends to lines

2 and 3—"The Branches on my Hand/ Are full of Morning Glory"), as she also does with "I started Early—Took my Dog." In the latter poem, it is the Sea that the walker visits, personified as a man walking with her (Poems #580, #603, #605, #656 Fr 580, 599, 601, 640). Usually, in Dickinson's nature poems, there are few people. That she manages at times to create a narrative is a rarity. When the poet (or, more accurately, the poet's voice) is linked to the described natural scene, however, the human being takes second place.

Dickinson's nature poems are drawn from the poetic mode she worked to perfect at the start of the 1860s. Many of her best-known poems grew from her diligent attempts to capture nature's beauties. Among the loveliest are "I taste a liquor never brewed," "The Sun—just touched the Morning," "Would you like summer? Taste of our's," "The Day undressed—Herself," and "The Skies can't keep their secret!" She uses separation of words in the latter poem to slow the poem, for example, as lines 5 and 6 break into the quatrains' dominant pace:

> A Bird—by chance—that goes that way—
> Soft overhears the whole . . . .

(Poems #213, #207, #246, #272, #495 Fr 242, 238, 268–9, 290, 505–6). Like many other mid-nineteenth century women writers, Emily Dickinson drew consistently on the surroundings she knew best—the domestic, and often the domestic in conjunction with the natural world. Dickinson combines her visualization of the world around her with the metaphor for her living space in "The Day came slow—till Five o'clock," which closes (in the last stanza, which is set in an Orchard):

> How mighty 'twas to be
> A Guest—in this stupendous place—
> The Parlor—of the Day! (Poem #572 Fr 571).

Specifically evoked is the poet's own domestic scene; as she wrote in "I'm saying every day," Dickinson does not imagine palatial surroundings but instead draws the house that already surrounds her, a structure inseparable from the natural world. This is the middle stanza from this 1863 poem:

> Court is a stately place—
> I've heard men say—
> So I loop my apron—against the Majesty
> With bright pins of Buttercup . . . (Poem #575 Fr 574–5).

Decades later poet Richard Wilbur praises Dickinson's reliance on this domestic specificity, in the guise of metaphor (Wilbur writes "she liked solid and homely detail; and even in her most exalted poems we are surprised and reassured by buckets, shawls, or buzzing flies," 12). Perhaps Wilbur is using her mention of the concrete object in the pattern of William Carlos Williams' admonition that the poet use "No ideas but in things," the modernist caveat that poems should seldom build on only abstractions.

In this Dickinson poem, rather, the poet's use of the concrete comes under the heading of character: only a woman writer would use the sentence "So I loop my apron." The deft movement of physicality—what *is* the motion necessary to "loop" a voluminous apron?—evokes the sheer presence of the woman speaker, unapologetic that she wears the apron, and then in the following line turns the description into the metaphor that fuses the outer world with the interior:

With bright pins of Buttercup.

The domesticity of the "apron" echoes with the poet's choice of "bright pins," a sequence which is swiftly transferred to the natural world with Dickinson's choice of the word "Buttercup." These lines of the poem are placed carefully in juxtaposition with the second line, "I've heard *men* say," making clear the difference between what *women* writers know and what they only hear about.

In its small way, this poem excerpt illustrates the careful detail of critic Aife Murray's *Maid as Muse*: she describes the way Dickinson's life, particularly in the kitchen, placed her to observe the natural world. With the Homestead kitchen spread across the back of the house, two windows on the west and two more in the pantry—and one on the east, Dickinson's garden was visible from some angles. The enormous built-in cookstove provided a kind of table area. Murray quotes from Josephine Pollitt (231) that Dickinson's cooking utensils were kept in one place and that no one else used them: she measured in glass rather than tin, and stirred with silver, not wood. Unlike others in her home, she used round bread pans and dainty rose-shaped jelly molds (Murray 229–30).

As 1863 moves past Dickinson's comfortable reach of subjects for her poems, her work often expands to include larger themes. Her writing of later 1863, a prolific period for successful poems, is marked by many poems that introduce the melange of both disorder and pain, themes that seem to be of new interest to her. She pulls back briefly from that changing emphasis in poem #721, when she defines the many things the word "Nature" might convey:

> "Nature" is what We see—
> The Hill—the afternoon . . .

As the poet segues to a definition of the word that expresses "what We Hear," the reader is alerted to the all-encompassing breadth of the noun; and when the third stanza opens "'Nature' is what We know," the poem becomes one of what Jed Deppman calls Dickinson's "definition poems," of which—he states—there are more than two hundred (Deppman 18) (Poem #721 Fr 686).

More commonly, and probably in tandem with the poet's painful eye illness and her worries about the possibility of losing her sight, Dickinson writes a number of poems later in 1863 that seem overtly pessimistic. She had earlier written some poems that seemed to suggest worries about her health. One, "Before I got my eye put out," was sent in an early group of poems to Higginson. Less fearful than many of her 1863–5 poems, this one describes a bargain she is inclined to take: her eyes in exchange for her possession of the natural wonders she so loves.

> The meadows—mine—
> The mountains—mine—
> All Forests—Stintless Stars—
> As much of Noon, as I could take . . . .
>
> The Motions of the Dipping Birds—
> The Morning's Amber Road--.
> For mine to look at when I liked . . . (Poem #336 Fr 361–2).

Luxurious in her description, Dickinson creates euphoria for this imaginative construct. There is no question about this poem's tone.

During the same period, mid-1862, Dickinson writes, "I like a look of Agony,/ Because I know it's true," as well as "I felt a Funeral, in my Brain" and "'Twas just this time, last year, I died." In a different context, Dickinson's "I'm ceded—I've stopped being Their's" deplores the human need to belong, as "The Soul has Bandaged Moments—/When too appalled to stir" recreates the fear that sometimes strikes a sentient mind (Poems #339, #340, #344, #353, #360 Fr 365-66, 369, 377-78, 385-86). By autumn of 1862, Dickinson caps the sonority of these grim works with "After great pain, a formal feeling comes" and "This World is not conclusion" (Poems #372 and #373 Fr 396–7). Although she still sends copies of most of her poems to Susan Gilbert Dickinson and sometimes to cousins Lou and Fanny, the poet is riding out a period of fear and perhaps of disillusion that seems to weigh permanently on her psyche.

Characteristic of the tonal similarities among much of her late 1862 and 1863 writing is "Delight becomes pictorial/ When viewed through Pain." A brief eight lines, divided into two quatrains, the poem conveys the poet's surprise at the life-altering changes that mark her vision:

> The Mountain—at a given distance—
> In Amber—lies—
> Approached—the Amber flits—a little—
> And That's—the Skies— (Poem #539 Fr 544).

In one of Dickinson's longest poems, "I measure every Grief I meet/ With narrow, probing, eyes," the poet joins with what appears to be much of the human race to question "I wonder if it hurts to live—/ And if They have to try." She then moves among sources of grief (which in this poem does include the war). Acknowledging what she calls "Centuries of Nerve," the poet lists causes for grief in addition to death:

> There's Grief of Want—and Grief of Cold—
> A sort they call "Despair"—

as she combines her knowledge of various griefs ("I could not tell the Date of Mine—/It feels so old a pain") with the physical presence of "others'" sorrows (Poem #550 Fr 552-53).

From the same period, Dickinson has traveled this anatomy of pain to a different kind of expression. "There is a Languor of the Life/ More imminent than Pain--/'Tis Pain's Successor—When the Soul/ Has suffered all it can." In this perfect quatrain, the succinct voice of the poet says plainly that she recognizes the stages of both grief and its acceptance, even if the latter be depression (Poem #552 Fr 554-5). This move to self-searching culminates for a time in two very different poems, one that continues the psychological probing ("The difference between Despair/And Fear—is like the One/Between the instant of a Wreck—/And when the Wreck has been" (Poem #576 Fr 576)) and a second that brings in the all-too-common reliance on religious belief.

In "Of Course—I prayed," the poet dashes the traditional belief in the deity's ability to take suffering away from a human being:

> Of Course—I prayed—
> And did God Care?
> He cared as much as on the Air
> A Bird—had stamped her foot . . .

As the poem continues, the writer concludes that knowing little might be preferable to what she has learned from her own philosophical investigations, a state she names "smart Misery" (Poem #581 Fr 580–1).

To interface these poems from 1863—both before Dickinson was conscious of her eye debility and during the illness's early stages—with the letters she wrote soon after arriving in Cambridge to begin working with Dr. Williams is to see the immense control the poet manifests in her letters home. The despair so evident in many of her poems seems to be erased in comparable letters. For instance, she writes to Vinnie in "about May" of 1864, "I miss you most, and I want to go Home and take good care of you and make you happy every day." She briefly discusses Dr. Williams' care (evidently surprised that she cannot return to Amherst after a few weeks). Then her letter returns to the plaintive tone of her opening paragraph,

> Loo and Fanny [the young cousins] take sweet care of me, and let me want for nothing, but I am not at Home, and the calls at the Doctor's are painful, and dear Vinnie, I have not looked at the Spring (LII 430).

Written in the pencil Dr. Williams prescribed, this letter strikes today's reader as a poised lament.

There are not many letters extant from Dickinson's months in Cambridge, but their scarcity may stem from the fact that she was supposed to use her eyes sparingly. To have jettisoned the shy and fearful poet to Cambridge as she sought a cure for her troublesome eye condition might be seen as a kind of unsympathetic family abandonment. Reassured because the Norcross cousins were also boarding, Edward, Emily, Vinnie, Austin and Sue did not often visit. Nor is there evidence that they wrote. During the 1864 April-to-November stay, Dickinson was apparently left to her own resources. If not steadily miserable, she was visibly sad.

Dickinson was also cut off from her regular correspondents—because her most frequent letters during these years came from the Norcross sisters, with whom she now lived. She did not expect much mail from Elizabeth Holland, and her interchanges with Samuel Bowles were often conveyed within Austin's letters. Charles Wadsworth and his family had recently moved across country to San Francisco; and there seems to have been little mail from either Susan Gilbert Dickinson or Vinnie. Given the fact that Dickinson thought she was about to return home, her family would not have made an issue of circulating her Cambridge address among friends. Even if people had wanted to write to her, doing so would have been difficult. As the summer continues, Dickinson's style in her letters to Vinnie changes. She writes increasingly in third person—speaking of herself as well as the addressee in third. For instance, in a letter dated July 1864, she writes "Emily wants to be well with Vinnie—If any one alive wants to get well more, I would let Him first./ I am glad it is me, not Vinnie. Long time might seem further to Her . . ." (LII 433). In the last letter to Vinnie before returning home in November from the first stay in Cambridge, Dickinson maintains the third-person practice: "Does Vinnie think of Sister? Sweet news. Thank Vinnie. Emily may not be able as she was, but all she can, she will . . . I have been sick so long I do not know the Sun" (LII 435).

Among Dickinson's poems of late 1863 and much of 1864 (described by Franklin as "early" 1864—during her time away from Amherst) are several that embody this physical and spiritual angst, painful with little qualification. Dickinson writes "The hallowing of Pain," in what appears to be a paired relationship with "Deprived of other Banquet,/ I entertained Myself," both poems dated early 1864 and placed in Fascicle 39. Short poems, they lead to a somewhat longer exploration of what the poet terms "The Loneliness One dare not sound," a four-verse poem that explores in stanza two,

> The Loneliness whose worst alarm
> Is lest itself should see—

The writer's admission of such emotional bereavement gains intensity in the third stanza where loneliness is described as "Horror," a condition to be avoided—only "skirted in the Dark—With Consciousness suspected" (Poems #871, #872, #877 Fr 814–15, 818–19).

Such poignant expression comes less than a year after Dickinson is writing poems of exceptional somberness, such as the sober "At leisure is the Soul/That gets a staggering Blow" as well as "Don't put up my Thread & Needle—/I'll begin to Sow." This latter poem describes the persona's inability to see as she sews: "These [stitches] were bent—my sight got crooked—/When my mind—is plain." That second stanza is followed by a fourth more commanding verse,

> Leave my Needle in the furrow—
> Where I put it down—
> I can make the zigzag stitches
> Straight—when I am strong . . . (Poems # 683, #681 Fr 656–8).

Bearable as these more narrative poems are, implying recovery through the poet's choice of imagery, Dickinson works frequently with the concept of physical pain. "Pain—has an Element of Blank," for instance, states

> It cannot recollect
> When it begun—Or if there were
> A time when it was not . . .

Somewhat later, Dickinson writes "Pain—expands the Time" (and in a subsequent verse, "Pain—contrasts the Time") as well as describing a manifestation of that pain,

> I felt a Cleaving in my Mind—
> As if my Brain had split—
> I tried to match it—Seam by Seam—
> But could not make them fit—
>
> The thought behind, I strove to join
> Unto the thought before—
> But Sequence ravelled out of Sound—
> Like Balls—opon a Floor—

In this deftly referential poem, Dickinson captures the scattering essence of her illness. Pain, the cessation of the order she so prized, her unsuccessful efforts to repair that "cleaved" mind—all description leading to the shattered order in lines 5 and 6. With her use of synaesthesia (the sequence somehow ravelled—or, more surely, *un*ravelled—yet coming from Sound instead of Vision) to form the jarring metaphor of the sound of destructive balls rolling "opon a floor." The reader hears the presence of the poet's pain (Poems #760, #833, #861 Fr 719, 785, 812).

A few months before she wrote "I felt a Cleaving in my Mind," Dickinson had expressed a similar kind of fragmented destructive force in "My Life had stood—a Loaded Gun/In Corners—till a Day/ The Owner passed—identified/—And carried Me away." For critic John Cody, this single poem reveals a number of inadequacies he finds within Dickinson. Primary is the conflict between a masculine power—expressed as Dickinson writes her hundreds of expert but sometimes not "ladylike" poems—with the metaphor of the phallic gun taking control of the poem itself (see Cody's close reading, 404–14) (Poem #764 Fr 722–3). Considering the recent deaths of both Henry David Thoreau and Nathaniel Hawthorne, Dickinson may have felt more pressure to create a narrative of morality, rather than the brief noun-oriented poems that inscribed the poet's various reactions to words such as *pain* or *comfort.*

Finding solace in the quantity of her still-expert poems, Dickinson writes much less frequently about the weariness of living in Cambridge, existing separate from her family, and experiencing the long sessions of eye treatments. Once she returns home from her first stay in Cambridge (late November, 1864), she does write a commentary on the treatments she had been given. As Habegger quotes from Dickinson's letter to her cousin Lou: "The eyes are as with you, sometimes easy, sometimes sad. I think they are not worse, nor do I think them better than when I came home.//The snow light offends them, and the house is bright . . . Vinnie [is] good to me, but 'cannot see why I don't get well.' This makes me think I am long sick, and this takes the ache to my eyes" (LII 439, in Habegger 484). Cody's quoting from a different section of this letter supports his analysis that Dickinson felt useless in her home, uncomfortable unless she was separate from her family members while she was upstairs, writing. He quotes her letter saying that for the first few weeks she was back in Amherst, she did nothing but tend her plants and "chop the chicken centers when we have roast fowl . . . . Then I make the yellow to the pies, and bang the spice for cake, and knit the soles to the stockings I knit the bodies to last June. They say I am a 'help.' Partly because it is true, I suppose, and the rest applause. Mother and Margaret are so kind, father as gentle as he knows how, and Vinnie good to me, but 'cannot see why I don't get well'" (LII 439, in Cody 420).

Natural as it was for Lou to wonder how being back in Amherst affected Emily's illness, the question she asked may have been too easily answered. Dickinson's guilt comes through clearly: she cannot help much with the household work, she feels as if her absence of many months has only inconvenienced her family. But a more complete explanation is forthcoming when Dickinson writes to Joseph Lyman, years later:

> Some years ago I had a woe, the only one that ever made me tremble. It was a shutting out of all the dearest ones of time, the strongest friends of the soul—BOOKS. The Medical man said . . . "down, thoughts, & plunge into her soul." He might as well have said, "Eyes be blind," "heart be still." So I had eight (weary) months of Siberia (in Habegger 484).

Any reader of Dr. Williams's book, *A Practical Guide to the Study of the Diseases of the Eye*, published in 1862, would have learned about his deep belief that continuous supervision would eventually cure the illness. That the aching pain becomes worse in the evening, after a day's effort to see, is to be expected—which might be the reason Dickinson tempers her response to cousin Lou: she still feels the irritation in her eyes (Habegger 485–6). After spending the next five months in Amherst, in April of 1865 she returned to Cambridge for another series of treatments. She remained there until October, 1865.

8
Dickinson's Fascicles, Beginnings and Endings

To create an orderly assessment (and, indirectly, a packaging) of her writing, Emily Dickinson drew upon the materials available to her in her Amherst home. Even as she chose among different kinds of paper, Dickinson maintained a steady incorporation of her skills of both sewing and aesthetic arrangement. From the months of creating the first fascicles—probably sometime during 1858—to the demise of that practice, sometime during 1864 in the midst of the stress of dealing with her eye illness, Dickinson was consistent in her practice of dividing her poems into book-length packets, creating a showplace for her achievements and grouping poems with others that explored similar themes.

Numerous critics of Dickinson's poetry have made substantial use of the poet's creation of fascicles. Dorothy Huff Oberhaus, for example, studied the poems in Dickinson's Fascicle 40, the last grouping she created. Oberhaus discusses the poet's close attention to detail both in form and theme proving that the poems so grouped in this collection were drawn from Dickinson's knowledge of, and appreciation for, the Biblical narratives that she often referenced. As Oberhaus states, "throughout F-40 Emily Dickinson draws upon the multiple biblical passages, which she varies, embellishes, and completes, to depict events in the past, present, and future mental life of her protagonist" (13). Oberhaus reads these poems as "a simple conversion. This sequential narrative begins in the recollected past with the sixth poem's debate, when Jesus persuaded her to occupy his 'House,' his earthly kingdom; extends through the fascicle's prevailing present time, when she affirms her chosen way of life as his 'Housewife,' an occupant of his earthly kingdom; and concludes in the anticipated future with the sixteenth poem's imagined meeting with him, when she enters the 'Door' of his eternal house, his heavenly kingdom" (19).

Even as this critic acknowledges that most of the Dickinson fascicle grouping does not provide such a strong narrative, Oberhaus has chosen to concentrate on F-40 so that she can draw comparisons between Dickinson as a moralistic (if not "religious") poet and such works of the English language moralists as Milton; she compares F-40 to *The Temple*, for instance (10).

This chapter explores the way Dickinson created fascicle 25, drawing here on a number of her poems from the summer of 1863 which have already been—if briefly—mentioned. When Oberhaus is able to contend that "The Bible . . . was essential to her poetics, structure, and meaning" as she explores F-40 (11), I rather see the fluidity of Dickinson's arrangement in F-25 as a tribute to her great love of re-creating the beauties, and the complexities which she was always careful to acknowledge, of the natural world.

As R. W. Franklin makes clear, Dickinson never used the term "fascicle" herself; she talked of little books, or sheets of poetry: the groupings represented Emily Dickinson's "own form of bookmaking . . . selected poems copied in ink onto sheets of letter paper that she bound with string" (Franklin 7). After Emily's death, Vinnie found the forty fascicles, which contained over eight hundred poems (of the 1800 poems she had left), along with some loose sheets of her copied poetry, now referred to by critics as "sets." Dickinson's process seemed stable: "when working drafts were copied to a later form, such as a fascicle, the drafts were destroyed" (Franklin 11).

According to the dating and chronology provided by R. W. Franklin in the variorum edition, 20 poems constituted F-25. Many were sent to Susan Gilbert Dickinson; all seem to have been written during the summer of 1863, a period when the poet is at the height of her writing prowess—and just before she begins having painful problems with her eyes. The grouping begins with the description of the artifact of a book, "A precious mouldering pleasure 'tis/To meet an Antique Book," one of the rare poems she wrote about her profession—that of writing, and of making, books. Setting the rarity in distant times—"when Sappho was a living girl"—the poet meditates on the values of accurate, and humanistic, expression (Poem #569 Fr 566–7).

The second poem in the fascicle is "I tried to think a lonelier Thing/ Than any I had seen" and this more philosophical poem introduces the prospect of death (in "Death's tremendous nearness") and the poet's attempts to alleviate its threat. She speaks of "A Haggard comfort" and of her striving to find another such creature as herself—looking for comfort in the company of abandoned griefs (Poem #570 Fr 567–8).

As if orchestrating her readers' reactions to the arrangement of poems in Fascicle 25, Dickinson next places "Two butterflies went out at noon/ And waltzed upon a Farm." It is poems like this that create what critics have called the "comic" Dickinson, and she achieves that comedy through both rhythmic effects and word choice (see Juhasz, Miller, and Smith's *Comic Power*). (Poem #571 Fr 568–9). For Juhasz, Miller, and Smith, three well-established Dickinson critics, the sly (or wry) humor that sometimes marks her poems is a continuation of Dickinson's personal attitudes that her friends and family remembered: her reputation was that of a "noted wit" and her scrutiny of life and death matters often benefits from her tendency toward comedy (Juhasz et al. *Comic Power* 1).

Part of Dickinson's satisfaction with Fascicle 25 stemmed from her pleasure in the next poem (which has been discussed earlier). "The Day came slow—till Five o'clock" is one of her most tactile recreations of the natural world. In the next several poems, however—"It was a quiet way," "I know lives, I could miss," and "I'm saying every day," she leaves the tried and true pattern (that her early biographer George Whicher described as her use of "nouns as collectives," 235) for more voice-oriented narratives. In the first of these three poems, the writer is acted upon by a master figure—*he*—who might be serving as a deity as well as a mentor.

In the possessiveness of the mentor figure ("He asked if I was His"), Dickinson shows the power of an authority which eclipses the normal:

> The World did drop away . . . .
> The Gulf behind was not—
> The Continents were new . . . .

and in "I'm saying every day," the poet figure herself takes on the pride of unexpected shape-shifting—from queen to beggar to singer, always prepared to experience "the surprised Air/Rustics—wear—/ Summoned—unexpectedly—/To Exeter."

This long poem includes the stanza about the apron and its bright pins of Buttercup, another gesture to a person's capacity to change. These two poems are anchored by the brief, middle term, a statement poem Dickinson seems increasingly comfortable with (Poems #573, #574, #575 Fr 574–5).

Poem #576, "The difference between Despair/and Fear," pairs with Poem #579, "The Soul unto Itself" in being abstractly based (Fr 576, 578–9). Between these poems comes Dickinson's highly effective "I went to Heaven/'Twas a small town" ("Beautiful—as Pictures/No Man drew") (Poem #577 Fr 577–8). Grouped with other of her nature poems ("The

Angle of a Landscape" and "We see—Comparatively"), Dickinson then places her outspoken "Of Course—I prayed" just before one of her classically meditative war poems, "I'm sorry for the Dead—Today." This poem is also set in the rural community which laments all losses, even of their own "homely species" (Poems #577, #578, #580, #581, #582 Fr 577–8, 580–2).

The poet interjects "You cannot put a Fire out"—with its comic second stanza, "You cannot fold a Flood—/And put it in a Drawer"—but then continues the fabric of sorrow with the strong "We dream—it is good we are dreaming." Not only the lamenting second line ("It would hurt us—were we awake") but the more visible imagery of death coupled with blood makes the poem difficult to ignore: "Men die—Externally—/ It is a truth—of Blood." Later the poet speaks—unexpectedly—of "the livid Surprise" (Poems #583, #584 Fr 582–3).

The concluding poems of Fascicle 25 may not fit so well as the poems in other segments of Dickinson's grouping. 'If ever the lid gets off my head/And lets the brain away" makes the disorientation of the dreaming-reality paradox entirely personal, as does the cryptic "Some say good night—at night." The concluding section moves briefly upward with "She's happy—with a new Content," which provides a more resolved sense of self:

> She's happy—with a new Content—
> That feels to her—like Sacrament—
> She's busy—with an Altered Care—
> As just apprenticed to the Air—
>
> She's tearful—if she weep at all—
> For blissful Causes . . .

Setting a tone of reconciliation, this poem leads to one of Dickinson's most beloved short works:

> The Heart asks Pleasure—first—
> And then—excuse from Pain—
> And then—those little Anodynes
> That deaden suffering—
>
> And then—to go to sleep—
> And then—if it should be
> The will of it's Inquisitor
> The privilege to die— (Poems #585, #586, #587, #588 Fr 583–85)

In the richness of this representative fascicle—playing upon Dickinson's constant love of the natural world; her awareness of the sorrows of lives and deaths, war and stability; and her capacity to shape poems into structures that express this varying set of emotions so accurately—the reader must be reminded too of critic Dorothy Oberhaus's warning that all of Dickinson's fascicles are integral to her oeuvre. In the critic's words, the content of one fascicle cannot be understood except in the context of all the fascicles—or of all Dickinson's work. As she studies the composition of Fascicle 40, Oberhaus concludes that "the mediator— who is represented as the author and protagonist of all forty fascicles . . . celebrates the present way of life she has chosen" (Oberhaus 10). Such a statement applies equally well to these closing poems of Fascicle 25, with the poet-speaker satisfied with what she terms her new "Content" and with her willingness to acknowledge the stages of life's acceptance—pleasure, excuse from pain, anodynes that deaden suffering, sleep, and finally—death.

Oberhaus makes another point about Dickinson's art, that all her poems are "interdependent . . . the referent for one poem's pronoun is frequently found in another" (Oberhaus 11). To have created this interlocking system—of nouns and pronouns, themes and subthemes— moving through the 1800 extant poems that comprise Dickinson's oeuvre is to signal a kind of comprehensive and tactile philosophy that may not ever be succinctly expressed. (Also see Eleanor Heginbotham's *Reading the Fascicles of Emily Dickinson*.)

When Sharon Cameron wrote her second book about Dickinson's poetry, it was prompted partly by various studies of the fascicles. She makes the point that "It is not that Dickinson couldn't publish or that she chose not to. It is rather than she couldn't choose how to do so" (Cameron 54). In the larger view, Cameron gives a positive reading of what she terms Dickinson's "choosing not choosing," a more complicated assessment than just thinking about ambivalence. This is Cameron:

> What I shall call Dickinson's "not choosing" is exceptional. It is exceptional, however, not because it is not choosing, but rather the presumption that not choosing is necessary is contested by the representation of not choosing; for in the poems the choice of particular words implied by the lyric frame to be imperative is rather shown to be impossible. Thus if there is an inclusive "or" and an exclusive "or," Dickinson's poems seem to exemplify the latter situation (this but not that) while in fact representing the former situation (this as

well as that). Thus not choosing in Dickinson's poems is different from not choosing in Whitman's (Cameron 23–4).

To add in Helen Vendler's expansion of what she had originally called Dickinson's chromatic seriality (as in "I'll tell you how the Sun rose"), is to see that Cameron's approach differs but that both critics are creating a different grid for Dickinson's poems.

Vendler notes, confronted as she is by many of these poems from Fascicle 25, that Dickinson's practices changed with her expanding ideas. When she discusses "The Heart asks Pleasure—first," Vendler contends that the order of elements has changed and that the tone is much more anxious (Vendler 67). The need for order has given way to the rush of different emotions, different kinds of information: Dickinson, she says, is experiencing a "confusing multiplicity" and therefore she sacrifices "the neatness of the serial" and lets the poem "lead her in unforeseen directions" (Vendler 70).

To illustrate these changes, Vendler chooses "After great pain, a formal feeling comes" and "I felt a Cleaving in my Mind," commenting on what she sees as the reasons for the changes: "The great crisis in Dickinson's work arrives when her instinctive practice of serial 'filled up' chromatic advance encounters unavoidable fissure, fracture, rupture, or abyss. This is the crisis that any writer wedded to serial chromaticism would be bound to face" (Vendler 71).

The relationship between Dickinson's poems of the very early 1860s and these of the inordinately prolific years 1862, 1863, and a bit of 1864, also must come into consideration. The choosing, to use Cameron's trope, that Dickinson was able to perform when she wrote only a few poems a week or a month changes dramatically when she produces almost a poem a day.

Dickinson has also begun seriously defining herself as poet in much more expansive ways: she has learned her craft, she has made her work into the carefully-stitched or bound books, and she has just as carefully discarded poems and drafts that she has not included there. Emily Dickinson has become an accomplished poet.

9
The Painful Interim

Once back at the Homestead in late November, 1864, Dickinson—as we have seen from her letter to her cousin Lou—does not experience a visible recovery. Some of the mystery of Dickinson's eye ailment may be explained in part by Lyndall Gordon's contention that the illness that the poet had long experienced was epilepsy rather than consumption, and that some manifestations of the effects of light and brightness on the eyes could be connected with that systemic weakness (Gordon 127–30). Medical science in the 1860s was moving slowly toward understanding the full effects of one diagnosis or another; most of Dickinson's biographers note that the poet felt that she had disappointed her family by her slow return to health. There is a tone of disappointment in the latter pages of her letter to Lou: she clearly plans a return to Boston: "what it would be to see you and have the doctor's care—that cannot be told . . . when I dare I shall ask if I may go, but that will not be now" (LII 439).

Feeling as if her family is creating unnecessary tasks so that she can see herself as useful, Dickinson misses what she had expected—fitting back into the family's life with urgency. While she was living in Cambridge, returning home had undoubtedly taken on the auspices of sheer promise. For the poet, being so long (and so painfully) separate from the Homestead, the Evergreens, and her life contained within those boundaries was true exile. Once back in her inviolate room, she was free to resume what biographer Jerome Loving called her "secret career . . . She would not publish, of course, but she would expose enough of her work to become known as a poet" (Loving 60). As she had written in "Publication is the auction," the conscientious writer's role is to "reduce no Human Spirit/To Disgrace of Price" (Poem #788 Franklin 742). It is clear that Dickinson has been considering her options. That process, too, has come to a halt in the immediacy of her worries about her possible loss of eyesight.

One of Dickinson's late 1863 poems that speaks with definite foreboding is the moving "All but Death, Can be adjusted." Her choice of the word "adjusted" signals the personal control she was already using to stay calm in what appeared to be adverse circumstances—as a contributing member of Edward Dickinson's well-placed family, if his older daughter were to become seriously handicapped, she could predict ways the family life would necessarily change. Like other family members, Dickinson was investing much hope and love in the young child, Ned, and his promising infant life: if "All but Death, Can be adjusted" reflects a consideration of the Dickinson family in relation to her own health, the poem "Growth of Man—like Growth of Nature" reflects her wise meditation on Ned's incipient place in that family (Poems #789 and #790 Fr 742–4).

The shorter of the two poems makes a statement as the poet thinks of "Dynasties repaired—/Systems—settled in their Sockets—/Citadels—dissolved." The recovery of the Dickinson family reputation, begun by Edward after his father's move to Ohio and then continued, impressively, by Austin—a man with great charisma to add to his father's steady righteousness—was a given for both family members and the town of Amherst. Being so integral her father's daughter/or son, Dickinson was privy to those dynastic dreams—as the existence of the two manor-like homes made clear to all of Amherst.

In that light, the promise that Ned's birth in June, 1861, encapsulated for the family was clear. That Dickinson often wrote about his antics, and that she wrote a formal letter to him from Cambridge—on his third birthday, June 19, 1864—showed how clearly her life had been changed by his existence. In the third-birthday letter, she referred to his "braided gown," made for him by the family dressmaker. But she also wrote a paragraph that suggested the playful aunt-nephew connection that dominated their lives: "Emily knows a Man who drives a Coach like a Thimble, and turns the Wheel all day with his Heel—His name is Bumblebee. Little Ned will see Him before//His Niece" (LII 432). Because her letter had begun with the phrase "My little Uncle," she is reversing gender roles here, as well as relationships, so that Ned understands that she is "a Hundred miles" away—or else she would be there for his birthday. Impacted already by Dickinson's choice to refer to herself in third person, and by her frequent use of the male gender self-referentially, any reader would see this brief note as compelling evidence of the existing aunt-nephew intimacy.

When she writes in "Growth of Man—like Growth of Nature/ Gravitates within," she is presuming a connection between the "All but Death, Can be adjusted" and this poem. This longer statement-poem explores the way the poet comes to knowledge ("Through the solitary prowess/Of a silent Life"). After its admonitory third stanza

> Effort—is the sole condition—
> Patience of Itself—
> Patience of opposing forces—
> And intact Belief—
>
> Looking on—is the Department
> Of it's Audience . . . .

Once Dickinson has had her eye examination in Boston, early in 1864, several poems before she leaves for Cambridge—and during her months in Cambridge—speak to her absence from home. One of the most effective is "Away from Home, are They and I—/An Emigrant to be," a two-quatrain poem in which Dickinson speaks about acquiring "The Habit of a Foreign Sky" (Poem #807 Fr 762). The poem forces readers to identify the poet's commonplace activities—one envisions Dickinson always surrounded by the natural world, and understands now how distant from her customary surroundings her life becomes in an urban city, which she calls "a Metropolis of Homes."

Another of her early 1864 poems that relates to her living far from the Homestead is "A nearness to Tremendousness—/An Agony procures." In these few stanzas the poet recounts the "Boundlessness" of "Affliction," claiming that Affliction cannot exist in "Contentment's quiet Suburb" and, therefore, as one result, "It's Location/Is Illocality" (Poem #824 Fr 779–80). Densely convoluted, image set against image, this poem is a distillation of Dickinson's pain, both physical and emotional, as she drifts through the hot summer and into the autumn loveliness of the Boston locale.

Taking a somewhat retrospective stance, the poet in "I learned—at least—what Home could be" confesses that she is drowned by Memory.

> What Mornings in our Garden—guessed
> What Bees—for us—to hum—
> With only Birds to interrupt
> The Ripple of our Theme

As the poem wends its way through seven quatrains—and one single line appended to the fifth "And then Return—and Night—and Home"—its distilled message is that "Home" becomes a "Place," "Where Dawn—knows how to be" (Poem #891 Fr 828). Less directly stated is Dickinson's "All forgot for recollecting" in which during the third stanza she describes "Home effaced—Her faces dwindled—/Nature—altered small." In this poem, the speaker is described as "a timid Pebble," facing a "bolder Sea" (Poem #827 Fr 781–2).

Mixed with these poems are several that seem directed to Susan Gilbert Dickinson, the usual recipient of Dickinson's poems. Following her birthday letter to Ned, Dickinson writes an enigmatic letter to Susan (dated June 1864 and using the third-person address). "Thank Susan for the effort, I shall not mind the Gloves—I knew it was the Bell, and not the Noon, that failed . . ." (LII 432). Intimate in ways only Susan and Emily recognized, it seems clear that from the early days of Ned's existence, Dickinson was thinking of Susan and her son as paired. For example, in a letter to Mary Bowles written spring of 1862, Dickinson describes "Sue—draws her little Boy—pleasant days—in a Cab—and Carlo—walks behind, accompanied by a Cat—from each establishment—" (LII 406). The vivid description of the households' cats and Carlo, Emily's dog, places the baby—not yet a year old—in the midst of the Dickinsons' love. Her note continues, "It looks funny, to see so small a man, going out of Austin's house."

Problematic as Susan's life had become after the birth of her son, with numerous difficulties caused by the wrong, or an inferior, baby nurse, she had managed generally to be available to Emily. There were periods when the poet's feelings were damaged by Susan's inability to comment on her poems—or on her life—and one of those periods comes clear when Susan wrote Emily a note of apology:

> I have intended to write you Emily to-day but the quiet has not been mine. I send you this, lest I should seem to have turned away from a kiss—If you have suffered this past summer I am sorry . . . .When I can, I shall write (Hart and Smith 101).

Using the Hart and Smith collection (*Open Me Carefully*), with correspondence and poems arranged as they were in the handwritten fair copies, provides a different kind of information about the relationship between the two women. For example, a poem that follows the one above reads,

> Sweet Sue,
> There is
> no first, or last,
> in Forever—
> It is Centre, there,
> all the time—
> To believe—is enough
> and the right of
> supposing— (Hart and Smith 102).

As critic Betsy Erkkila noted, "the centrality of this relationship is the text of Dickinson's life and work" (Erkkila 41). Habegger, who agrees with this assessment, too sees Dickinson's return home in late November, 1864, as a harsh reminder that any previous relationship with Susan had changed. Habegger notes that Dickinson's "letters to Sue . . . are highly wrought literary objects, enameled, glittering, succinct to the point of obscurity." What he refers to as "charged messages" reminds the reader that much of the commerce between Susan Gilbert Dickinson and Emily Dickinson had always been "private," even if it was written on paper. Sue was "the animating presence in Emily's writing" (Habegger 487–8).

Of Dickinson's 1864 poems, "Wert Thou but ill—that I might show thee/How long a Day I could endure" is a testimony to the poet's constant patience and love. It moves through sequential quatrains that allow proofs of the writer's acceptance, always stately, always impassioned, and closes with a simple declaration of unquestioning love:

> No Service hast Thou, I would not achieve it—
> To die—or live—
> The first—Sweet, proved I, ere I saw thee—
> For Life—be Love (Poem #821 Fr 777).

Another so identified is Poem #816, "I could not drink it, Sue,/Till you had tasted first" (Fr 770–1). In a section about Susan Gilbert Dickinson's great pain (unnerving pain, in effect) upon the death of her second sister Harriet Gilbert Cutler, Habegger links this poem and another, "Unable are the loved—to die," with Dickinson's note to Susan:

> You must let me go first, Sue, because I live in the Sea always and know the Road. I would have drowned twice to save you sinking, dear, If I could only have covered your Eyes so you wouldn't have seen the water (LII 441, Habegger 464–5).

Harriet's death comes just a few weeks before Dickinson is due to return to Cambridge, in April of 1865, so nothing about her loss—including Susan's almost complete breakdown over the news—was in place to affect the poet's months at home.

What does affect those months are two occurrences: first seems to be Dickinson's realization that, in her absence, tending to the fascicles (and incorporating her Cambridge poems into the massive quantity of materials that remained in Amherst) was an impossibility. Biographers and critics accept the fact, somewhat cryptically, that Dickinson stopped collecting her work into fascicles sometime in 1864; Fascicle 40 is thus the last of her completed booklets. Second is the unutterable fact that the Civil War continues, seemingly unabated. Even as Austin had bought someone to serve in his place soon after Dickinson had first gone to Cambridge, the relentless losses of thousands of men in the military scarred everyone's consciousness. For Dickinson, following accounts of the war through the *Atlantic Monthly*, Higginson's essays in that periodical (some, excerpts from his journal; again, entire essays about military practices, as in his "Regular and Volunteer Officers," pp. 348–57 of the July, 1864, issue) created a more personal bond with the sometimes distant "war news."

In the "Regular and Volunteer Officers" essay, for example, Higginson insisted that the US government must "pay . . . honest earnings." Any soldier who serves, African American or white, must have the confidence to know that "his wife and family are not to be cheated of half his scanty earnings by the nation for which he dies" (356). He continues, "an administration which orders its Secretary of War to promise a black soldier thirteen dollars a month, pay him seven, and shoot him if he grumbles" should be punished. His essay then turns to the praise of Rufus Saxon (under whose command Higginson may have served in South Carolina), connecting the events of the military in 1863 and 1864 with the "President's Proclamation on New Year's Day," which he calls our contribution to "the great series of historic days . . . permanent festivals of freedom" (357).

Higginson's essays continued through the *Atlantic* issues of October, November, and December, 1864. His commentaries are not isolated in these issues: in the March, 1864, issue, for example, Mrs. Furness comments on the condition of soldiers in hospitals ("Our Soldiers," 364–71) and Lt.-Col. B. L. Alexander describes "The Peninsular Campaign" (379–88, March, 1864). Dickinson would also have read these issues because many of them included stories by Rebecca Harding Davis—though she was not identified by name but was rather described as "The Author of

Life in the Iron-Mills"—as well as fiction by Harriet E. Prescott and poems by Alice Cary. Louis Agassiz also published a number of essays there during this time.

Dickinson writes a few poems in the 1863–5 period that clearly relate to war, poems such as "I many times thought Peace had come/ When Peace was far away" and "Midsummer was it, when They died—/ A full, and perfect time." In the latter work, she gives the dead the supremacy of eternity as they "leaned into Perfectness—/Through Haze of Burial" (Poems #737 and #822 Fr 698 and 778). Following the lead of Dickinson's biographer Alfred Habegger, many critics read one of her later poems, "Further in summer than the birds," as a poem of both war and personal loss. The biographer calls it an "elegiac meditation" and reads the eventual four-stanza version. Dickinson had originally written seven quatrains, sending this version to Gertrude Vanderbilt, who was recovering from having been shot by her maid's rejected suitor. In the later version, the reader identifies with the quiet acceptance of the pervasive cricket song ("So gradual the Grace/A pensive Custom it becomes/Enlarging loneliness"). In the original longer version, some effective lines clarify the description that opens the poem:

> The Earth has many keys—
> Where Melody is not (Poem #895 Fr 831–5).

Equating the cricket's song with Earth's "elegy" brings the poet to rest in that almost soundless resonance. In Habegger's words, "Some songs propose to release us from loneliness; this song merely enlarges it . . . It is the chant of acceptance, not Christian but Druid, leaving behind a keener sense of nature and solitude, a recognition that everything is different from what one thought and hoped, and that one has already begun to live with that" (Habegger 491–3).

Dickinson had barely returned to Cambridge and to her doctor, when General Robert E. Lee surrendered to General Ulysses S. Grant at Appomattox Courthouse, Virginia, effectively ending the Civil War. Five days later, on April 14, 1865, President Lincoln was assassinated. Had Dickinson reason to lament her return to what she saw as a painfully ostracized place, more than a hundred miles from her beloved Homestead, the national mourning for Lincoln would have provided that reason. Even though in retrospect Dickinson had found that her return home was less joyous than she had expected, and many of the poems she had written early in 1865 suggest a terrible sense of stasis, of resignation to her life as it was going to be, none of the patterns of her existence in Amherst had prepared her for the immense lament that blanketed the United States.

In the commemorative *Atlantic Monthly* essay about Lincoln written by historian George Bancroft (published to close the June, 1865, issue), he recounts the 1500-mile funeral procession from Washington, DC, to the middle States, borne "through continued lines of people." He emphasizes that "the sincerity and unanimity of grief were such as never before attended the obsequies of a human being."

Giving much space to the history of slavery in America, and to praising the *Emancipation Proclamation*, Bancroft concludes with his tempered view that both the *Proclamation* as well as Lincoln's assassination illustrate the former's "great principles of speech and action, freedom of government, through ever-renewed common consent—will undulate through the world like the rays of light and heat from the sun." Bancroft concludes, "There can be no spot in Europe or in Asia so remote or so secluded as to shut out its influence."

Chary in her letters home, Dickinson makes a comment to Vinnie about their father's behavior once Jefferson Davis, President of the Confederacy, was captured May 10, 1865—Lou says "no one but He [Edward], can do it Justice" (LII 442). There are also comments about her daily living, and about worrying over Sue—still bereft after her sister's death. Most importantly, she conveys news about her eyes, "The Doctor says it must heal while warm Weather lasts, or it will be more troublesome." Otherwise, Dickinson communicates little about national news, and part of this reticence may stem from the fact that she knows that her family in Amherst is also reading the *Atlantic Monthly*, and experiencing the same kinds of things she is. Life in Cambridge seems full: Dickinson assures Vinnie that "I have more to say than I can" (LII 442). A few months earlier, she had written similarly to Lou: "I have so much to tell I can tell nothing, except a sand of love" (LII 439).

She returns home this time in October. Soon, in letters to Elizabeth Holland (November 1865), Dickinson writes that she has "lost" Margaret O'Brien (addressing Elizabeth as "Dear Sister"}. Her comments are the expected tone of cryptic irony rather than sentiment—after all, the maid Margaret has been an immense help to Dickinson while she writes, and while she is absent from the Homestead and its housekeeping. Dickinson writes, "Besides wiping the dishes for Margaret, I wash them now, while she becomes Mrs. Lawler, vicarious papa to four previous babes . . . . I winced at her loss, because I was in the habit of her . . . but to all except anguish, the mind soon adjusts" (LII 444). Later to

Elizabeth, she notes—even more cryptically, "'House' is being 'cleaned.' I prefer pestilence. That is more classic and less fell" (LII 453). One does not question Dickinson's deep sorrow when Carlo, her companion dog of more than 15 years, dies on January 27, 1866. Although she mentions the loss to Higginson, the rest of her correspondence from early 1866 maintains its normalcy. In fact, a letter to Elizabeth Holland includes a comment of pure joy, understated here because Dickinson knows that her friend will realize its import: "Friday I tasted life. It was a vast morsel. A circus passed the house—still I feel the red in my mind though the drums are out" (LII 452).

10
To Define *"Belief"*

In most studies of nineteenth-century American literature (perhaps more to the point, literature which is being theologically considered), the reader thinks first of the author's religious propensities. Given the fact that Emily Dickinson throughout her writing career tended to use the prosody of the hymnal stanza, her use of words and ideas associated with hymns—all kinds of praises to God—would be almost automatic. In her case, however, Dickinson's adolescent years of deciding whether or not to convert to church membership had shaped her belief system differently: as we have seen, Dickinson was the only member of her family (and almost the only one of her friends) who did not convert. In the Amherst, Massachusetts, of the mid-nineteenth century, she was an anomaly.

Although Dickinson grew up in an atmosphere that was, in critic Roger Lundin's words, a "curious mix of Whig republicanism and evangelical morality," she was influenced visibly during her adolescence by the teachings of geologist–paleontologist Edward Hitchcock, then president of Amherst College (Lundin 19). The comparatively heavy emphasis on science throughout Dickinson's years at Amherst Academy (where she consistently took courses in chemistry, algebra, physiology, botany and biology) probably resulted form Hitchcock's influential presence in the area—although much of the American world was flooded with a fascination with science. When in 1850—several years after Dickinson had gone to Mount Holyoke for a year—Hitchcock published *Religious Lectures on Peculiar Phenomena in the Four Seasons*, she and her family absorbed the further attention to his methods and, in this case, to the natural world as it changed dramatically, season by season. Both Lundin and Robin Peel agree that Dickinson learned her scientific methods of careful observation and apt recording from studying Hitchcock's work (Lundin 31–5, Peel 17, 78).

For Hitchcock as scientist, however, religious belief was enhanced through science. He "sought to reconcile orthodoxy and the new geology by arguing that the long history of the earth was merely one more evidence of the constancy and glory of God" (Lundin 32). Between Dickinson's immersion in Amherst's educational milieu and her vexed year as a student of Mary Lyon's at Mount Holyoke, Lundin contends that she had early developed her "disenchanted understanding"; he quotes from "I dreaded that first Robin, so" in illustration:

> I could not bear the Bees should come,
> I wish they'd stay away
> In those dim countries where they go,
> What word had they, for me? (Poem #347 Fr 372–3)

This sentiment echoes the latter part of Dickinson's "I felt a Funeral in my brain," which includes the lines

> Then Space—began to toll,
>
> As all the Heavens were a Bell,
> And Being, but an Ear,
> And I, and Silence, some strange Race
> Wrecked, solitary, here— (Poem #340 Fr 365–6).

There are many such illustrations of Dickinson's conflicts about religious belief, especially in her poems from 1861 and 1862.

Peggy McIntosh and Ellen Louise Hart consistently warned readers that "religious terminology in her poetry does not indicate that she held orthodox religious beliefs." Pointing out that Dickinson was "in turn satirical, skeptical, awed, reverent, speculative, outraged, tantalized, ironic or God-like herself," the reader must beware: the poet will align herself personally with "divinity, sometimes as Jesus, sometimes as co-creator" (McIntosh and Hart 2973). Of course, nineteenth-century culture was impacted with conflicts that evolved from religious beliefs—or the lack of those. Religious philosopher Laurie Maffly-Kipp states that the century is filled with "commentaries on officially-sanctioned religious attitudes," which in number "far outweigh accounts about people's actual beliefs." In this critic's view, Dickinson's expressions about religion suggest that she be grouped with Angelina and Sarah Grimke, Jarena Lee, and even Harriet Beecher Stowe—with questioning (if not outright critique) firmly expressed. About Dickinson,

Maffly-Kipp states, "her poetry reveals a perceptive and critical religious sensibility, one keenly tuned to a spiritual world removed from the Calvinism of her upbringing. Much of her verse is overtly anticlerical and anti-institutional, depicting a God hidden from the lives of humanity" (755–6).

What Lundin referred to as Dickinson's "struggles over whether to join the church" (49) surface in each of the poet's biographies. Richard Chase devotes much space to her discomfort as she is first attracted to the beliefs Mary Lyon instills, and then flees from them. Chase describes a late-night meeting Mary Lyon had called, inviting women who were undecided about conversion: the meeting was directed at "all those who had today felt an uncommon anxiety to decide." Seventeen women came, including Dickinson. "The evidence indicates that this was the crisis of the poet's religious life. The clear and momentous fact is that she definitively drew back from the final commitment" (Chase 54–5). Chase continues that Dickinson was influenced in two aspects: the first was that her father—at that time—had not converted and the second was that "she seemed to think becoming saved would mean giving up 'the world'" (Chase 56–7). He also cites the similarities he finds between Dickinson's attitudes and those of Herman Melville, that accepting Christianity "has come to represent passivity, spiritual surrender, and mediocrity" (Chase 59). His assessment is somewhat parallel to Charlotte Nekola's comment that this strange stubbornness on Dickinson's part suggests that the poet equates religious conversion with marriage, and that both signal—in her mind—"the subordination of self to another" (Nekola 151).

In Chase's view as well, Dickinson's attitudes toward conversion may reflect her dislike of what he calls "township society." Admittedly, Amherst was a small town, and as we have seen, the philosophy of separate spheres was much in evidence there. For Dickinson, who understood that she was gifted intellectually, and had the opportunity to become an accomplished poet, *belonging* socially as most unmarried women did would have deprived her of the mental activity that was so significant to her. By choosing differently, Dickinson was avoiding the town's "emotional tenuousness, its cultural isolation, and its heavy uniformity of manner, sensibility, and opinion. In her work, she sees that the 'majority' comes near to having the power of life and death over the spirit of man" (Chase 18).

In agreement with Chase, Joan Kirkby reads much of the poet's work as a dialogue between "earthward" tendencies as opposed to what the poet viewed as "heaven." By choosing not to convert, Dickinson "refrained, celebrating her attachment to the earth" (Kirkby 110). The critic chooses to use the poem "Some keep the Sabbath going to church/ I keep it staying at home" in illustration, and one might add to that "I cautious, scanned my little life," for in this earlier poem Dickinson spells out her allegiances with "the little Barn/Love provided Thee" rather than with any "Deity." Calling herself/persona "A Cynic," she draws on the negative nineteenth-century concept of the unbeliever, but in this poem, that cynical questioner is clearly positive (Poems #236 and #175 Fr 259 and 209–10).

As if she were reading Professor Hitchcock, Dickinson—says Kirkby— uses her nature poems "to bring the self into alignment with the processes of . . . mutability that inform nature" (Kirkby 117). Some of this concept colors the critique of Inder Nath Kher, who sees Dickinson as a religious poet—a "profusely mythic and religious" poet whose aim is to "break through the surface of existence. She shows no faith in an established, institutionalized form of prayer, and has no respect for doctrines and dogmas" (Kher 30). To this, Dickinson admitted in an 1859 letter to Mrs. Joseph Haven the fact that she had not yet met the Reverend Seelye, who had the Sunday before "preached in our church . . . upon predestination." Dickinson then explains, "but I do not respect 'doctrines' and did not listen to him, so I can neither praise, nor blame" (LII 346).

At this point, the need for definition accrues: quoting from Northrop Frye, Kher insists that Dickinson's poems must be read collectively, as an oeuvre, rather than being separated by themes. Considering her body of work as dealing with "the human predicament and destiny," Kher finds that the poet was writing "one long poem of multidimensional reality" (Kher 2). That reality, in many cases, included her religious, or semi-religious, beliefs: this critic says that Dickinson's use of "church is interchangeable with the human heart . . . It is the center and circumference of reality" (Kher 52). Biographer Connie Kirk underscored this sense of questioning omnipresence as she states that Dickinson "pondered the concept of immortality and other spiritual questions all her life" (Kirk 34).

For George Whicher, religion in the poet's work is buried under what he calls Dickinson's "loneliness and her isolation," traits which gave her a personal metaphor for "the individual's defeat by circumstance" (Whicher 307). His comment foreshadows the approach Robert Weisbuch took in his important 1975 study, that the "extraordinary tension" existing between tenor and vehicle in Dickinson's poems shows the ambiguity she herself experienced. For Weisbuch, Dickinson "combines a self which is powerful, autonomous, and godlike with a self that is all-vulnerable, limited, and victimized" (Weisbuch xi–xii).

Some of this ambiguity as it relates to formal religious belief is questioned by contemporary writer Joyce Carol Oates, who states "Though 'God' is frequently evoked in the poetry, one is never quite certain what 'God' means to Dickinson. A presence? An experience? An outdated tradition?" (Oates 187). Critic James McIntosh categorizes Dickinson's expressions of faith as "nimble believing," a consciousness more akin to ecstasy than to reason (2). He associates her work—and what seem to be her varied belief systems—with those of Emerson, Melville, and Thoreau, saying that they all "searched for a world in which one accepts the instability of thought" (McIntosh 21). He also claims that Dickinson's philosophies stemmed from her "lifelong reading in the Bible," and her almost constant use of figures from the Bible in her poetry (McIntosh 5).

Dickinson's 1974 biographer, Richard B. Sewell, after stating that Dickinson "had no respect for doctrines" (651), discusses her work as showing her reliance on "a healthy amount of Puritan didacticism, coming vicariously from her family training, from the Biblical 'I say unto you' vein, from the hymns and sermons of the First Church of Amherst, and certainly from the late-Puritan, New England literary climate" (711).

Separating Dickinson from her nineteenth-century milieu is, of course, impossible: she was an intellectual *of* her times, and religion was a significant element of those times. Sewell accordingly discusses her poems in relation to those of the British and American writers she would have read. He points out that her poetic form "is not from Donne or Herbert or Vaughan or Quarles, but from that hymnologist to New England Congregationalism, Isaac Watts" (713). He continues that Dickinson "was far less positive" than either Emerson or Thoreau, and should be recognized as "the poet of the passing insight, the moment of vision, the unitary experience." He adds that she "had no social or political program and was inclined to smile at those who did" (714).

It fell to Elisa New, writing in *The Regenerate Lyric: Theology and Innovation in American Poetry*, to remind readers of the historical times. New states that poetry was "the religious center of an already religio-centric literature . . . fueled by an experimental Calvinism not so easily dislodged by Unitarian, Transcendentalist, or Romantic forces" (New 2). As if echoing David S. Reynolds in *Beneath the American Renaissance*, New confirms that writers' religious beliefs were discerned through their works, their words. And in Reynolds' explication of Dickinson's "subversive" writing, he points to what he calls "the collision between the old and new sermon styles" that he finds operative in her work (Reynolds 31).

One of the difficulties in any consideration of Dickinson's religious aesthetic—specifically in the ways in which this concept appears in her poetry—is that she uses the hymn stanza so integral to religious rite as the structural basis of most of her writing. In an early vituperation of Dickinson's work, for example, Ivor Winters seems offended by the fact that she chose to use the prosody of the hymn stanza even though she was not speaking of appropriate topics. Between such condemnatory words as "abominable," "unpardonable," and "countrified eccentricity," Winters admitted that some of Dickinson's poems were "great." He admired the continuing theme she wrote from, that of "the inexplicable fact of change," but he was highly critical of her uses of prosody throughout (Winters 149–50, 160). For Allen Tate, also, although he compares her work with that of John Donne, he objects to the ways Dickinson takes liberties with the reader's expectations. He notes that she confuses the reader by perceiving abstraction and thinking "sensation"—"Her poetry is a magnificent personal confession, blasphemous and, in its self-revelation, its honesty, almost obscene" (Tate 289, 298).

Today's reader is not accustomed to such harsh language being used to describe Dickinson's poetry. The jarring gap for a critic who reads the hymn-like prosody and then finds the personal revelations that connect Dickinson's work to twentieth-century poetry was unique in the critical practice of assessing poems. In the Tate essay, admittedly, his strong opinions are set against a historical overview that links Dickinson's work with the poet's rebellion at Mount Holyoke, which Tate describes as "a theocratic state" (Tate 283). To clarify his reactions to her achievement, he compares Dickinson with Edgar Allan Poe, stating that "there is no other American poet whose work so steadily emerges under pressure of certain disintegrating obsessions, from the framework of moral character . . . The poet *is* the poetry" (Tate 285).

When in 1989 Joanne Dobson considers Dickinson's work—reflecting on the fact that the influential Tate essay was written in 1928—she stresses that the poet was writing as a female, a woman caught in the machinations of the separate sphere ideology in which she lived. Dickinson walked carefully around the important social issues of her time—"abolition, the oppression of the Indians, women's rights, the plight of the working poor"—and she did not overtly express her views on those subjects. What was left for her to record was the presence of morality, of religion per se, and so that theme occupied a good deal of her writing. As Dobson concludes, women writers—including Dickinson—almost had to use their art as "cultural reinforcement . . . affirming society's preconceptions" (Dobson xi, 59).

Parallel with Dobson's apologia, Jane Donahue Eberwein has termed one of Dickinson's poetic modes her "habit of renunciation." Because she writes so often about the spiritual (rather than various orthodoxies), Eberwein creates a category of what she calls Dickinson's "prayer poems" (Eberwein 137–8).

The most inclusive criticism on this theme has recently been published by Linda Freedman. Her *Emily Dickinson and the Religious Imagination* (2011) forces readers to think beyond Christian boundaries, as she points out that the mid-nineteenth century was a time of interest in comparative religions. She traces some of Dickinson's use of sun imagery, for example, to her knowledge of world religions (i.e., the sun god), and expands the notion of what religion must have meant to Dickinson's aesthetics (Freedman x).

This critic says, to start, that she follows Elisa New's critique: "I do not think that poetry became Dickinson's secular way of being religious or that poetry replaced religion in Dickinson's thought" (Freedman 2). But she admits early on that Dickinson's feelings about religion were—and remained—"ambivalent," and that what she frequently expressed in her poems was "her deep preoccupation with different attitudes toward the unknown" (Freedman 4). Viewing her study as one based in epistemologies—those of poetry and those of religion, Freedman presents a different way of thinking about this critical dilemma.

Some of the discomfort critics have felt with Dickinson's art has stemmed from what readers might see as the lack of fit between prosody and theme. For instance, among the many comments about her use of the English hymn tradition stands that of James Olney, who says that the poet "adopted and adapted the traditional meters" so that what most readers would have seen as a tight, restrictive poetic format became a vehicle for showing—in many cases—"a very large element of play" in Dickinson's work. He insists that the poet sets "her rhythm off against, and filters it through, certain highly traditional metrical forms, thereby radically reconstituting these traditional meters and, as it were, commenting on them" (Olney 5, 27).

In any larger scheme of assessing Dickinson's poetic practices, Olney points to the fact that "This strategy of containing explosive emotional content within quite strict formal bounds, thereby paradoxically increasing its potency while simultaneously diminishing its danger, is common to Dickinson" (Olney 128). Whicher calls Dickinson's prosody "lyric" but expands that category to include the "psalm or hymn." He notes that "She accepted it [this form] as unquestioningly as she accepted the alphabet" (Whicher 227). (See Victoria N. Morgan's *Emily Dickinson and Hymn Culture* for an exhaustive discussion of this problem.)

One of the premises of Clark Griffith's analyses of Dickinson's poetry is what Whicher implies, the disjunction between form and content. Griffith concludes that "her desire for stability [is] in conflict with her recognition that all seems chaos; her quest for the orderly and intelligible" struggles against ways the poetry can contain that struggle (Griffith 83). Earlier, Emily Stipes Watts had leavened her suggestion that Dickinson saw God as a "swindler" (see Poem #711 Fr 679) by stating that the poet "accepted an unhappy cosmos, but at the same time . . . found and celebrated the available joys" (Watts 134, 136).

Vivian R. Pollak coalesces several of the thematic emphases the reader confronts in deciphering Dickinson's poems about belief and religion per se. She notes that "Dickinson asks us to confront some of the most enduring issues of American life and of life anywhere: for example, the problem of death, the problem of God, and the problem, too, of love" (Pollak 4). Because Dickinson had lived her life already immersed in both the actuality of death or the fear of it, many of her religious poems meditate upon the existence of death. Yet reading criticism of the poet's work, and aligning critical commentaries with one another, are slight tasks compared with assessing Dickinson's poems on any given theme. For instance, Dickinson wrote between eighty and a hundred poems that use the words "death," "dying," "died," and related nouns in their titles or their titular sentences. Impossible as it seems to make a stable pattern out of the poems of this thematic group, many of these are among her best known: "Death is the supple suitor," "Because I could not stop for Death," "All but death can be adjusted," "I heard a fly buzz when I died," "A word is dead when it is said," "It is not dying hurts us so," "The dying need but little, dear," "Till death is narrow loving," "There's been a death in the opposite house," "She died—this was the way she died," "We wear our sober dresses when we die," "Unable are the loved to die," "The distance that the dead have gone," "To die takes just a little while," "The frost of death was on the pane," "It was not death—for I stood up," "Not all die early dying young" . . . Reading just a few of this group proves that there is no single pattern, no single tone, and that many

100

of the poems that appear to be "about" death are really about either love or living.

In several of Dickinson's best-known "death" poems written in summer and fall of 1862, for example—"It was not Death—for I stood up" and "Because I could not stop for Death"—she personalizes both the abstraction of "death" and the poet-persona. Both poems are unusually active: the poet creates momentum from the relationship between the figure of death and the figure of the speaker. At six quatrains, both poems are relatively long. Both are narratives, though fanciful ones. Perhaps most significant, both speak to the experience of dying as positive because, in one case, the speaker reaches "Eternity" and in the other—a poem which appears to end in Chaos—the poet also remembers the tranquility of her own orderly burial. The juxtaposition Dickinson uses in this poem ("It was not Death, for I stood up") links the peacefulness of the speaker's apparent denial with a later recognition of that same speaker's journey to ostensible "Despair."

At her best when she can use the hymnal stanza to create a narrative that moves easily, Dickinson does not err at all in "Because I could not stop for Death." Identifying the usually fearsome spectre as "kindly," she joins the speaker and Death from the start of the poem within the carriage, surrounded with thoughts of Immortality. As the conveyance moves through recognizable images of life, the tone of reminiscence softens—"the School, where children strove/At Recess—in the Ring" and "the Fields of Gazing Grain." Then comes "the Setting Sun," with one of Dickinson's spritely qualifications ("Or rather—He passed Us"). Energetic and wry, the poet's qualifying correction breaks into the sentimental look back at childhood. Stanza four complains of the poet's too-light clothing; stanza five depicts a "House that seemed/A swelling of the Ground," not some magisterial (and perhaps sanctimonious) "Father's House." The last stanza creates a feeling of satiety. The speaker has finished the journey: time has stopped, or the speaker has realized that time has become irrelevant:

> Since then—'tis Centuries—and yet
> Feels shorter than the Day
> I first surmised the Horses' Heads
> Were toward Eternity (Poem #479 Fr 492–3).

Whereas the poet in "It was not Death, for I stood up" uses the same stanza pattern, the rhythms of this poem are less fluid. The inherent contradictions (between what the poet expects and the "reality" of life) create lines that break and jostle. The poem moves through negative disclaimers:

> It was not Death ....
> It was not Night ....
> It was not Frost, for on my Flesh
> I felt Siroccos—crawl—
> Nor Fire—for just my marble feet
> Could keep a Chancel, cool—

By the fourth stanza, which begins the break from the poet's seemingly erroneous readings, Dickinson has changed rhythms. These solid quasi-depressing lines are her forceful reply to the earlier dialogic expectations:

> As if my life were shaven,
> And fitted to a frame,
> And could not breathe without a key,
> And 'twas like Midnight, some— (Poem #355 Fr 379–80).

Dickinson's versatility in crafting her poems strikes any reader: "pattern" in a critic's lexicon as he/she deals with Dickinson's work does not suggest the predictable.

A contrasting Dickinson poem, dating from 1865, consists of only two quatrains. "The dying need but little, dear" tells no story but its softer awareness (suggested by the added word "dear") gives the reader a sense of the complete picture of loss. It begins conversationally, defining what "little" will be necessary ("A Glass of Water's all,/A Flower's unobtrusive Face") but the latter four lines create a world of bereavement:

> A Fan, perhaps, a Friend's Regret
> And Certainty that one
> No color in the Rainbow
> Perceive, when you are gone— (Poem #1037 Set 7 Fr 918).

Here are three Dickinson poems, all expressing laments connected with death, yet so differently constructed, leaving the reader with a sometimes sharp, sometimes nostalgic, sense of both acceptance and loss.

The reader is reminded of the second part of James Olney's caveat about Dickinson's greatness as a poet, a principle that has to do with her language choices. Olney states that the best poets employ "a personal use of the language, a personal formation or deformation of the language, to an extraordinary degree—what I will term 'making strange' with the language" (Olney 4). Just as Dickinson created her own rhythmic form from the hymn stanzas readers were so familiar with, in her choices of diction, in her locution, she proved herself a different kind of genius.

11
1865, The Late Miracle

Even though Dickinson spent another long period of months in Cambridge—from April of 1865 to October, she once again managed to write hundreds of consistently good poems. This total does not represent the flood of writing that 1863 had given her, with the poem count close to 300, but after a decline in 1864 to 98 poems, her production in 1865 continued on that same path. Aife Murray counts Dickinson's total in 1863 as 295; in 1864, 98; and for 1865, 229 (Murray 80). Murray also quotes from contemporary poet Robert Creeley's comment that Dickinson's production here—already increased tremendously by the events of the war—was prompted by her eye condition. This is Creeley, "that's when she goes for broke and writes Higginson. That's when the authority of her ability must have utterly been possessed, possessive . . . And that's of course the time too when she begins to make decisive changes in her whole proposal of herself to the world" (in Murray 81).

Few other critics of Dickinson and her poetry have brought to their assessment this startlingly emotion-based connection. Of course Dickinson knew she was writing beyond her previous abilities. Adrienne Rich also saw the fact of this remarkable production as Dickinson's recognition of her own genius. Writing in what was to become her seminal 1975 essay, Rich stated

> I have a notion that genius knows itself; that Dickinson chose her seclusion, knowing she was exceptional and knowing what she needed. It was, moveover, no hermetic retreat, but a seclusion which included a wide range of people, of reading and correspondence. Her sister Vinnie said, "Emily is always looking for the rewarding person." Given her vocation, she was neither eccentric nor

103

quaint; she was determined to survive, to use her powers, to practice necessary economies" (Rich 160).

Dovetailed with these insightful comments by two fine contemporary poets is Murray's scholarly assessment, which relates Dickinson's precipitous decline to come (from 1866 through 1870, years averaging only 11 poems yearly) to the fact that the Dickinson's full-time maid, Margaret O'Brien, married in October of 1865, and that the household had no other consistent help for the next three and a half years. Murray elaborated, "Emily did not adjust. This was a crisis . . . A dependable maid and understanding sister were a winning combination. They had made possible 'a course for the breakaway'"—and now the poet was to spend "long hours in the kitchen." In Murray's words, Dickinson "was effectively silenced" (Murray 82–3).

Even as Murray discusses what she calls Dickinson's "formidable . . . powers of concentration," as a woman critic herself, she understands the niggardliness of counting costly effort, the insistent demands for attention that arise hour by hour, day by day. The sweep of Dickinson's almost unimaginable creativity had grown to its height in 1863 and then it resumed briefly in 1865. But Murray noted that, for Dickinson, "The return of a writing practice coincided with Margaret Maher's firm establishment in the Dickinson routine"—an event that did not occur until 1870 (Murray 78, 83).

Dickinson was writing at home in Amherst during her hiatus from her Cambridge treatments—that meant from January through March of 1865 and into April. With the death of Susan Gilbert Dickinson's sister Harriett just before Emily's return to the Boston area, and Susan's breakdown following that death, Dickinson's writing would have stumbled. Like the rest of the United States, Dickinson also had to absorb the assassination of President Lincoln; she also had to recognize that the end of the Civil War might not mean an immediate return to normalcy. But once she was back in Cambridge, undergoing more eye treatments, she could then resume her writing: she had lived here before; she knew the routines; she knew that she had the full attention and support of her beloved Norcross cousins.

It is also spring, Dickinson's beloved season. As she writes in Poem #948,

> Spring is the Period
> Express from God—
> Among other seasons
> Himself abide

> But during March and April
> None stir abroad
> Without a cordial interview
> With God— (Fr 869).

In the less didactic "Always Mine!" (Poem #942) she writes in the second line, "No more vacation!" a choice of words that suggests a parental admonition she may have heard as she went upstairs to write. If being at home in Amherst was to be seen as a "vacation" for her, she might have viewed her return to Cambridge as the opportunity to resume her work. In Cambridge, no one interferes with her choices. Instead, "Every Dawn, is first" (Fr 865).

Content in her boarding house room, Dickinson sends short missives back to Susan Gilbert Dickinson, always commiserating with her about the impact of her sister's death. "The Overtakelessness of those," "Absence disembodies—so does Death," "As one does Sickness over"— Poems #894, #904, and #917 Fr 830–1, 898, and 848)—limn their congruent despair. Later in the year, Dickinson's note to Susan after the latter has gone to Geneva, New York, reads "I am glad you go—It does not remove you—I see you first in Amherst, then turn my thoughts without a Whip—so well they follow you," a note that accompanies the poem "An Hour is a Sea" (Poem #898 Fr 838). Another effective poem on this theme is "That is solemn we have ended," which includes the lines about "a leaving Home, or later,/Parting with a World" (Poem #970 Fr 842).

As the year wears on, Dickinson's poems on the pervasive theme of death grow longer—whether she is thinking of Lincoln or of family members or of friends. One of the most moving is the seven-stanza "The last Night that She lived," this one marked as having been written later in 1865 and placed in what by this time Dickinson is calling "Set 6c" (the other poems mentioned here were placed in "Set 5." Critics explain that while the poet no longer was creating her customary fascicles, she did arrange her poems on long sheets of paper, and continued to number their groupings.) One interesting element of "The last Night that She lived" is that Dickinson includes the dying woman's family in the narrative:

> We waited while She passed—
> It was a narrow time—
> Too jostled were Our Souls to speak . . . (Poem #1100 Fr 958–9).

The conclusion of the poem speaks to those mourners who remain, thinking of what will be their "awful leisure . . . Belief to regulate." No explanations suffice, even as (in an earlier stanza)

> We noticed smallest things—
> Things overlooked before
> By this great light opon our minds
> Italicized—as 'twere.

In the rhythmic narrative Dickinson creates, she suggests a possible illumination through the loss of the loved one: why else give readers a moment-by-moment description of the process of first witnessing, and then accepting, death?

A similarly wide-reaching poem is "We outgrow love, like other things" (Poem #1094 Fr 951). A brief quatrain, the poem recounts the way the outgrown love is put away in a drawer and then, when later found, is compared with "Costumes Grandsires wore." The most famous of Dickinson's poems of loss is perhaps "The Bustle in a House/ The Morning after Death" (Poem #1108 Fr 966). Brief in its moving description, the poem emphasizes "The sweeping up the Heart/And putting Love away" as if coalescing images from the two previously discussed poems.

As these last several poems suggest, during 1865 Dickinson seems to be turning toward a simpler language. Two poems not connected with death as theme show this tendency clearly: "A Door just opened on a street" shows the poet-persona "lost" (in both stanzas of the poem, the description of the persona the only connecting link); "A man may make a Remark" also undercuts any incipient drama through its terse, non-descriptive language. In the latter poem, the speaker qualifies in line two, "In itself—a quiet thing" and then continues into a more abstract second stanza:

> Let us divide—with skill—
> Let us discourse—with care . . . (Poems #914 and #913 Fr 845–6).

as the poem joins other of Dickinson's admonitory works from 1865. Several of these are also very well known today: "The Poets light but Lamps," "Finding is the first Act," and "If I can stop one Heart from breaking" all illustrate the way Dickinson has gained proficiency in creating the sense of a maxim without relinquishing her careful ambiguity with language choices. In the first poem, Dickinson erases the writer's ego that she understood so well:

> The Poets light but Lamps—
> Themselves—go out—

The second tercet praises the construct of the poem itself ("vital Light// Inhere as do the Suns"). The poem concludes

> Each Age a Lens
> Disseminating their
> Circumference (Poem #930 Fr 855).

Critic Judy Jo Small points out that Dickinson's breaking expected rhythm is a means of emphasis. She would term this one-word ending a "closural suspension" because it does not resume the poem's earlier pace but instead ends emphatically (Small 175).

Just as "Finding is the first Act" narrates a schema of the counting poem, this one ending in complete disillusion ("Finally, no Golden Fleece/Jason, sham, too"), so "If I can stop one Heart from breaking" opens Dickinson to the unusual charge of didacticism (Poems #910 and 982 Fr 844 and 889). During this year, she wrote a number of single-quatrain poems, as if underscoring the principle of the maxim—wise lines which could be remembered, whether published or not.

Literary historian Emily Stipes Watts points out that during the mid-nineteenth century, people wrote poems suitable for children's reading, regardless of how that work was described. Many of Dickinson's short poems might well have been considered appropriate for children and their instruction. In Watts' words, the poems were not differentiated (135); she comments on Poems #59, #9, and #274 and to those early works, drawing from 1865, one could add poem #970, "The Mountains sat opon the Plain" (a clear exercise in personification); poem #908, "They ask but our Delight;" Poem #1008, "How still the Bells in steeples stand;" Poem #944, "A Moth the hue of this," and several of the aphoristic poems already discussed, perhaps "Finding is the first Act" (Fr 882, 843, 903, 866). For Dickinson to modify her usual aesthetic focus as she wrote might well be a commonplace gesture, since so much of her personal interest was focused on Ned, her nephew, and the community's small children that she was learning to know through association with him. (Her subsequent letters to Elizabeth Holland and others mention the little boy, describing his attempts to use humor in his language choices: "Ned tells that the Clock purrs and the Kitten ticks. He inherits his Uncle Emily's ardor for the lie" (LII 449.))

Significantly, some of Dickinson's longer poems from 1865 are among her most effective. Whatever kinds of experimentation she was devising, partly demanded by her absence from the Homestead and her comforting upstairs room, did not change the remarkably consistent quality of such poems as "Crumbling is not an instant's Act" or "When they come back—if blossoms do." Both poems work hard against any tendency toward a happy ending (Poems #1010 and #1042 Fr 903–4 and 921). "Crumbling is not an instant's Act" is a rigorous prolegomenon of dissolution: it moves through various "organized Decays" from "a Cobweb on the Soul" through "Elemental Rust" to expedite what the somewhat innocent word "crumbling" truly implies. As the terse last quatrain states, "Ruin is formal." The speaker's mood in "When they come back—if Blossoms do—" is much more tentative and personal. The speaker admits that "I always feel a doubt" and, in the next stanza, "I always had a fear." She is not saying that blossoms can never come back—only that she is apprehensive that they may not.

Linking these two impressive works with such other briefer poems as "Not to discover weakness is," "We learn in the Retreating," and "Best Things dwell out of sight," the reader finds a tone of nostalgic solemnity—if not relinquishment. As "Best Things dwell out of sight" completes its initial comment with its second line—"The Pearl—the Just—Our Thought"—Dickinson in even these comparatively short works draws from the pithy intellectualized sense of maxim (Poems #1011, #1045, #1012 Fr 940, 922–3, 905). There is an urgency about the poet's need to express the hard truths, which she does even more emphatically in "There is a finished feeling/Experienced at Graves." (Poem #1092 Fr 949–50). In the longer and more layered poem, "As imperceptibly as Grief," Dickinson uses eight quatrains to spell out the mourning over a summer that cannot last:

> Departed was the Bird—
> And scarcely had the Hill
> A flower to help His straightened face
> In stress of Burial—
>
> The Winds came closer up—
> The Cricket spoke so clear
> Presumption was—His Ancestors
> Inherited the Floor . . . (Poem #935 Fr 858–61).

For Small, this poem illustrates the tendency she classifies as Dickinson's use of something unexpected—"Into the Beautiful" is not only esoteric, it feels somewhat imprecise (Small 212). "As imperceptibly as Grief" is also one of the poems Wolosky includes in her wide-ranging commentary, saying that Dickinson concentrates on the deaths of the personal life (and the natural) as well as the deaths in war as a means of facing the blurred and imprecise issues of "immortality" (Wolosky 42). As Dickinson ponders what seems to be both inescapable and inexpressible in these several hundred poems written during 1865, her focus moves from the war—or from themes that clearly express the disastrous effects of war—to the personal, though without her use of the personally-inscribed narratives that appear to draw on real experience.

A rare example of the above that comes from Dickinson's work in 1865 is "A narrow fellow in the grass/Occasionally rides." Published on February 14 of 1866 in the *Springfield Daily Republican*, the poem (titled "The Snake" in the newspaper) has great popular appeal—it could be directed toward child readers as well as adults. Famous for its concluding four lines, the poem describes both the natural beauty of the "fellow" and his awe-inspiring effect:

> But never met this fellow
> Attended, or alone
> Without a tighter breathing,
> And Zero at the bone (Poem #1096 Fr 952–3).

Excepting this poem, which fits more easily with her poems from several years earlier, the general direction of Dickinson's proficiency—and mood—during 1865 appears to be dismay, an unflinching recognition of what most of life has to offer. Or in the words of Alfred Habegger,

> If the more than six hundred poems that Dickinson wrote in 1863, 1864, and 1865 are read against those of 1861 (an experiment made possible by the new variorum edition's refined dating), certain directional tendencies stand out with such clarity it is unlikely her work can ever again be seen as somehow not developing—not building on her experience. Proportionally, we find an increase in the number of poems on abstract themes and a corresponding decrease in the number of first-person narratives . . . . Of course, many things did not change (Habegger 471–2).

12
Maintaining Urgency

The years in Dickinson's life from 1866 through 1870 seem to pause, creating a subdued shadow in what has up to this time been a relatively frantic battle to *accomplish*. The pace of her life was changing. It was only earlier in 1865 that she had written to Lou, from Amherst, urging the younger cousin to take a brief vacation trip, "Life is so fast it will run away, notwithstanding our sweetest *whoa*" (Lll 439).

When Dickinson next returned to Amherst in October, 1865, at least partly to absorb some of the housework that Margaret O'Brien's departure occasioned, she intended to resume the writing life that had previously fulfilled her. Yet although Habegger titles his chapter dealing with the years 1866 to 1870 "Repose," the poems and letters that Dickinson wrote suggest, rather, a mode of uncertainty, unrest. Not only was she facing the household work she did not enjoy, but she was also bearing the grief—a few months after her return—of Carlo's death. The poet's bereavement was genuine.

The few poems that date from the 1866–7 period suggest a grim acceptance of these conditions. "There is a strength in proving that it can be borne/Although it tear" opens Poem #1133, a statement that is followed in lines 3 and 4 with sentiments equally despondent:

> What are the sinews of such cordage for
> Except to bear . . . (Fr 986).

The imagery of bearing weight, pain, unpleasant physical duress is new to Dickinson's work. The reader does not attribute her second couplet to her creating rhyme (in "tear/bear"); most of Dickinson's rhymes are slant or *off* in some way. In her relatively few complaints to friends about life without a full-time maid, there is usually a gloss

110

of humor that undercuts her actual words. Here, no humor softens these lines.

This poem, and what seems to be its pair poem ("We do not know the time we lose—/The awful moment is") supports the tempered and wistful qualities of even Dickinson's nature poems. Usually diverse in tone, sparked with revealing imagery, her nature poems build from a scaffolding of pleasure. But during 1866 and 1867, nature appears to have lost its excitement. "The Lightning is a yellow Fork," for example, focuses on what Dickinson describes as "The Apparatus of the Dark" while "inadvertent fingers" drop "awful Cutlery" (Poem #1140 Fr 990). "The murmuring of Bees, has ceased" provides a similar reassessment, leaving only a few remaining friends to populate the poet's world. The reader is also told within that poem that "Nature's Laugh is done" and, perhaps as a result, the writer comments on "thoughts we will not show" (Poem #1142 Fr 991–2).

A poem dated 1866 is even more ominous. "The Frost of Death was on the Pane" in one way continues Dickinson's 1865 interest in providing a range of views of nature, but this poem is the darkest of that group. "'Secure your flower,'" is the admonition in line two, and then the reader sees that in this poem Dickinson's flowers are less joyful than they are "passive." Line 17 expresses what might be the poet's response to the vicissitudes of this narrative:

> We hated Death and hated Life
> And nowhere was to go—
> Than Sea and continent there is
> A larger—it is Woe (Poem #1130 Fr 981–4).

Perhaps what appears to be the most dramatically somber poem from these years ("The Sky is low—the Clouds are mean") moves back in time to Dickinson's wry surprise structure. She here shapes the plaintive initial quatrain to create a tone that reminds the reader of some earlier nature poems. The poem, however, concludes

> A Narrow Wind complains all Day
> How some one treated him
> Nature like Us is sometimes caught
> Without her Diadem (Poem #1121 Fr 975).

Accompanying one of her 1866 letters to Elizabeth Holland, prefaced with a comment that helps the reader—as well as her friend—relate the poem to the poet's changing circumstances, is the more characteristic "I cannot meet the spring—unmoved/I feel the old desire" (Poem #1122 Fr 976) (LII 449).

To underscore how little time Dickinson can now spend on her writing, Franklin in the variorum edition takes careful note of the way these poems are written. Scribbled on the backs of letters or of merchants' advertisements, or on scraps of used paper, these poems seem—in some cases—to have been early drafts instead of the carefully copied and re-copied poems included in, first, Dickinson's fascicles and then, during the years of her eye difficulties, the long sheets of paper called "sets." Some of her poems from the later years of the 1860s feel unfinished. For instance, the dramatic "There is a strength in proving that it can be borne" juxtaposes two sets of couplets that leave no question about their sober intent, but then these four lines are followed by a third couplet that differs in both rhythm and tone. The poem ends

> The ship might be of satin had it not to fight—
> To walk on seas requires cedar Feet.

Franklin notes that "seas" in line six was originally the word "tides," which might create a more difficult task for the speaker/ship. The mixture of tones here, specifically the choice of the word "satin," undercuts the direction of the first four lines—as well as refusing to maintain the long-short patterning of those lines—and leaves the reader wishing for the poem to end with one of Dickinson's apt metaphors. Again mentioned in Franklin's notes is the fact that this poem was written "in pencil on a fragment of wrapping paper." Such details contribute to the reader's sense that this poem—and perhaps others from this period—never reached the level of completion that many of Dickinson's earlier poems had attained.

When Vendler remarks that Dickinson's later poems are less effective, that there is "a falling off" or "a regression, sometimes, to earlier and easier formulations," agreement or disagreement becomes difficult. For the reader to move from the body of Dickinson's most effective poetry—that written between 1862 and 1865, amounting to over 600 poems—to these years when, at best, the poet managed to write less than a dozen poems each year creates an imposing difficulty in itself. (Before the Franklin variorum edition, determining when poems were written was almost impossible.) There is also the problem that most readers and critics of Dickinson's poetry are accustomed to placing the poems very generally—saying, for example, this is probably a poem from the war years; this poem relates to Dickinson's illness of the eyes—so that distinguishing between poems from 1864 and 1867 was not a primary critical occupation. Vendler bases her assessment of changing merit in Dickinson's writing on the writer's techniques: she is interested in the ways the poet finds closure, saying that Dickinson often shapes conclusions that "baffle closural arrest" (Vendler 83). She ascribes this practice to the fact that in her later years, Dickinson "becomes aware that life has no foreseeable or neat ending." The poet is thus "Unable to think any longer that endings are either predictable or pleasant" (Vendler 85).

Critic Greg Johnson too defends the fact that Dickinson's work changes as she ages. He calls it "a more discernible pattern of development . . . than has heretofore been acknowledged," claiming that even if her poetic themes remain constant, Dickinson's "emotional and psychological attitudes toward these themes increase in complexity" (Johnson 6).

For Joyce Carol Oates, recognizing that Dickinson was and remained a lyric poet, the surprise comes in the fact that her intensity never lessened. Oates discusses the aesthetic of Dickinson's art, comparing it with religious belief, stating that the "motive" for her poetry lies in "the poet's interior experience. Improvisation and impersonation, submitted to a rigorous method of revision; the braiding together of disparate fragments jotted down over a period of time—even years: the task is to make of the finite, infinity; and of the self's dying, immortality" (Oates 174).

> What is remarkable about Dickinson's career is the fact that, living so fierce an interior life as Dickinson did, with virtually no stimulus apart from human relationships of a domestic or social kind, and what she might have read, or heard, of the larger world, she did not burn herself out as so many lyric poets have done . . . She wrote fewer poems, but the quality remains (Oates 175).

Dickinson's return home late in 1865 was to her a kind of closing off of possibilities. In her various answers to Higginson's suggestions that she come to visit Boston, with its active literary scene, the reader sees the poet's recognition of her (probably) permanent location—Box 207, Amherst, Massachusetts. In the spring of 1866, for example, she replies to his suggestion, "I am uncertain of Boston," continuing

> I had promised to visit my Physician for a few days in May, but Father objects because he is in the habit of me (LII 450).

Much of this letter from Dickinson concerns "A narrow fellow in the grass" and the fact that the poem had appeared in the February 17, 1866, *Springfield Republican*. Higginson perhaps never had realized that his Amherst poet friend was on intimate terms with both Samuel Bowles, the paper's publisher, and Josiah Holland, who served as its literary editor. As Dickinson wrote, "I had told you I did not print," and it may be that her embarrassment over the poem's having been published led to her refusing any further publication during her lifetime.

In her June 9, 1866, letter to Higginson she explains further, "I must omit Boston. Father prefers so. He likes me to travel with him but object that I visit" (LII 453). She then invites Higginson to visit her in Amherst.

It is not until her letter to him dated June of 1869 that Dickinson writes one of her most familiar prose sentences, "I do not cross my Father's ground to any House or town" (LII 460). Here the immediate image of seclusion—Dickinson entrenched behind fences, an embattled figure who pretends she does not walk across the lawn to Austin and Susan's Evergreens—intensifies when she compounds the word "House" with "town." The reader sees her emphatic choices: no more shopping trips with Vinnie, no more appearances—even if fleeting—at Amherst College Commencements, and (without Carlo) no more walks outdoors.

By the time of this letter (summer of 1869), the reader also envisions Dickinson in her white dress. Even as Aife Murray points out how easily laundered—and bleached—the white cotton dresses would have been, compared with the difficulty of keeping clean more fashionable fabrics such as wool, linen, silk and merino, there has been much speculation about Dickinson's choice of the plain white garment. Jean Mudge describes one of the late examples of this attire as "made of men's formal shirting fabric of embossed cotton" (Mudge 179). For all the speculation about the appeal of the simple white fabric to Dickinson (ranging from the fact that Balzac wore white robes when he wrote, to her avoiding the print fabric of the lower-class "housedress"), Murray suggests, "White was a sign of the absence of labor; cleanliness of dress was equated with a virtuous mind." It was also what Murray called "a threshold marker," to indicate Dickinson's high class as well as her untouched virtue (Murray 170–2).

To connect Dickinson's gradual adoption of this quasi-uniform with her recognition of her ever more confining circumstances is not difficult. Her life has hemmed her in, but she has not relinquished making choices. She still chooses to write and send letters to her beloved

Norcross cousins, to Elizabeth Holland, to Susan Gilbert Dickinson, and—intermittently—to Higginson. She still chooses to read as avidly as her time away from cooking and housekeeping allows. Because of these time limitations, too, she may have turned increasingly to reading the later books of the Bible, long a private source for her of both sustenance and narrative. It is, in fact, in the book of Revelation that the notion of her wearing white may have begun. Revelation is the book of the reader, of course: "Blessed is he that readeth" (l:3). The text also admonishes the reader to become a writer: "I am Alpha and Omega, the first and the last: and, what thou seest, write in a book . . . Write the things which thou has seen, and the things that are, and the things which shall be hereafter" (I:11, 19). In book 3, Revelation admonishes the listener to "buy of me gold tried in the fire . . . and white raiment, that thou mayest be clothed" (3:18). By the fourth and later books, all the respected elders ("four and twenty") and the angels are "clothed in white raiment." The book of Revelation closes with this coda,

And to her was granted that she should be arrayed in fine linen, clean and white: for the fine linen is the righteousness of saints (Rev. 19:8).

Perhaps closer to home and to her embodiment of what qualities constitute that home, this Biblical admonition may have carried greater weight than the customs of European writers. Even if Dickinson thought ironically about her passing into sainthood, there would be no reason to defy one or another of its basic principles.

Murray also points to the fact that Dickinson's wearing white cloth was another means of her being transgressive—Murray's term is "class trespass" and she sees Dickinson as finding ways to defy social codes. When the poet had written years before (1860) to her cousins, "My sphere is doubtless calicoes," Dickinson was already voicing that defiance; and when she thanked the cousins for sending her a brown cape, she announces, "at present I wear a brown dress with cape if possible browner" (Murray 170–1).

For Murray, too, Dickinson's adopting one kind of dress for all her waking hours was symbolic of the unifying experiences of her life: "By wearing a housedress for all of her activities, she made gardening, cooking, visiting, and writing seamless and redefined all of them as women's household work" (Murray 172).

The early work of critic Jean Mudge concentrates on Dickinson's changing attitudes to her role within the Homestead (and, one might add, to her increasing confinement there—whether because of Edward

Dickinson's attitudes or her own). Mudge contends that from 1864 on (following the poet's first stay in Cambridge and then her return), she had realized that what she thought of as "the Mansion" was to provide permanent incarceration. For Mudge, this acceptance becomes what she calls Dickinson's "third stage of reacting" to her home. "The fleeting, unsystematic, but recurring quest for home" recurs in a number of Dickinson's mid-1860s poems (Mudge 187, 195). She also views the fact that Edward Dickinson had built his daughter's conservatory on the east wing, facing south, a mixed blessing. Important as it was for the poet—as a place to nurture both her plants and her poems—it was another means of confining her to the building her family had created (Mudge 147).

More consistently than most of Dickinson's critics, Mudge locates the language of the search for home in Robert Browning's books of poetry; he writes often about the house as well as the home, with a kind of self-consciousness that would have been unusual in mid-century poetry. There are reviews of his 1864 collection, *Dramatis Personae*, in both *The Springfield Republican* and *The Atlantic* (where this book is discussed as illustrating the "peculiarity" of all his work, p. 644, November issue). She also comments that both Susan Gilbert Dickinson and Emily owned a copy of this collection by Browning (Mudge 123).

Soon after Dickinson returned to Amherst, her thoughts were focused on two life-altering events: the first was the death of her beloved dog, and she immortalizes Carlo in a "letter-poem" written to Higginson, much on the order of many of her poem-letters to Susan. The second was her awareness of Susan's second pregnancy—news which may have reached her early in 1866 (Martha, the Dickinsons' second child, would be born November 29, 1866). It could well be that both of these happenings would have taken Dickinson away from her usual mind-set as she approached her poetry. As Habegger notes, rather than thinking of Dickinson's changed output as a sign of her sheer emotional exhaustion (after writing more than 600 poems during the previous three years), the critic might well see deeper reasons for change. Her few poems written from 1866 to 1870, according to her biographer, are not Dickinson's usual "first-person poem recapitulating or reflecting on her past. The writer who had lavished herself on acts of memory, exploring her history, her singularity, her starved triumphs, her hard-won mastery, had for the time being stopped trying to tell her story" (Habegger 499).

There is little question that her loss of Carlo was a devastation. She breaks a year-long silence to Higginson with the brief note—"Carlo died—" followed by her signature and then her repeated question, "Would you instruct me now?" (LII 449). More representative of her unyielding grief is her June 9, 1866, letter to him, and here she arranges lines as if they were poetry. She admits outright to missing her dog ("I wish for Carlo") and then adds a quatrain of her poetry. But the actual poem occurs next, taking Higginson from images that he would connect with her life with her dog into her pervasive religious impulse:

> Still I have the Hill, my Gibraltar remnant.
> Nature, seems it to myself, plays without a friend.
> You mention Immortality.
> That is the Flood subject. I was told that the Bank was the safest place for a Finless Mind. I explore but little since my mute Confederate,
> yet the "infinite Beauty"—of which you speak comes too near to seek.
> To escape enchantment, one must always flee.
> Paradise is of the option.
> Whosoever will Own in Eden notwithstanding Adam and Repeal (LII 454).

Signed "Dickinson" with no given name or initial, this letter fuses her life with Carlo (joined in the longest segment, "I explore but little since my mute Confederate,") with her seemingly higher poetic themes—signaled by immortality, infinite Beauty, enchantment, paradise, and finally Eden—with *Adam* as the place holder rather than *Eve*.

With this letter-poem that commemorates her relationship with Carlo, she includes four poems that are all, even if obliquely, related to grief: "Blazing in Gold," "Ample make this Bed," "To undertake is to achieve," and the poem she had worked over thoroughly, "As imperceptibly as Grief." As she said in her letter responding to Higginson's query about immortality: "This is the Flood subject." What other topic will immerse her emotions and her skills to the extent that the theme of death and what follows it can.

Drawing from her thick sheaf of early 1860s poems to place "Blazing in Gold—and /Quenching in Purple," Dickinson begins her grouping with a paean to the death of a day,

> Then—at the feet of the old Horizon—
> Laying its' spotted face—to die! (Poem #321 Fr 338)

There is a glory in this expiration, whether or not the viewer equates this lush description with Carlo.

More directly related to the beloved animal's death is "Ample make this Bed/Make this Bed with Awe," especially because the third line extends the concept of honored repose: "in it, wait till Judgment Break." The sonority of the poem's ending also suggests reverence:

> Let no Sunrise' Yellow noise
> Interrupt this ground (Poem #804 Fr 759).

The third poem she sends, "To undertake is to achieve," links with "As imperceptible as grief"—abstract, aiming to create some depth of emotion in an effort to cover, and possibly color, the existence of the enormity of loss. Although "To undertake is to achieve" misses the thrust of the direct statement of the latter poem, it still coasts on the emphatic "fortitude of obstacle" and "fine suspicion" (Poem #991 Fr 894). Not so soft as "As imperceptible as grief," it still makes the reader understand *effort*, even if that effort is not immediately equated with pain.

Less directly stated throughout 1866 is Dickinson's concern with her beloved sister-in-law's pregnancy. Part of her involvement with the growth of this second child stems from her immense love for little Ned, soon to be five years old and the true apple of the Dickinson family's eyes. There is also the indescribable bond of gender that Dickinson realizes through countless poems, and countless years, with Susan Gilbert Dickinson. Susan's pregnancy is crucially important to the poet as well because her experience of being at odds with her own mother (or at least of seeing her own mother as far different from herself) has made her interested in maternal bonding—or non-bonding.

Several of Dickinson's best poems before she is aware of Susan's pregnancy reflect on this gender-bond between women. (As Habegger points out, Dickinson sends most of her best writing to Susan; he counts 73 poems, using Franklin's dating process, which Dickinson sent to Susan from 1863 to 1865, Habegger 467.) One of these earlier poems is the magisterial "The largest woman's heart I knew—" where its immense properties (being able to "hold an arrow, too") are joined with those of the poet's own heart, "I tenderer, turn me to" (Poem #532 Fr 546). Moving from 1863 to 1865 to Dickinson's "I am afraid to own a Body," the poet here fuses "body" with "soul" and terms them both "Profound—precarious Property/ Possession, not optional" (Poem #1050 Fr 925). This latter is a rarity among Dickinson's works, because the physicality of the female transcends the abstract nomenclature of the soul. Between these two poems Dickinson writes a number of what Hart and Smith have called "letter-poems," such as

> Sister,
>   We both are
> Women, and there
> Is a Will of God—
> Could the Dying
> confide Death,
> there would be no
> Dead—Wedlock
> is shyer than Death.
> Thank you for
> Tenderness . . . (Hart and Smith 137).

A few months earlier, from Cambridge, Dickinson had written to Susan so that at the center of her prose—here defined as poetry by the editors, and quoted from their text—was a loving description of little Ned:

> It would be best to
>   see you—it would
> be good to see the
> Grass, and hear the
> Wind blow the wide
> way in the Orchard— . . . .
> Love for Mat, and
> John, and the
> Foreigner—And
> kiss little Ned
> in the seam in
> the neck, entirely
> for Me— . . . (Hart and Smith, 132).

Shrouded in the secrecy of Susan's privacy—who but the couple expecting would give voice to any mention of their incipient child?— Dickinson wrote no poems during 1866 that speak of birth, of the developing of a child, of the roundedness of her beloved Susan's body. Instead, she writes about Ned—to almost all her correspondents. To Elizabeth Holland she describes Ned's having been ill "for a week, maturing all our faces. He rides his Rocking-Horse today, though looking apparitional" (LII 449). To Kate Anthon, a new friend who was a former classmate of Susan's,

> Sue's little boy rides by with a long stick in his hand, beating imaginary beasts.—He is fond of Hens and other Songsters, and visits a colt in our barn demi-daily (LII 451).

In August, while Susan and Austin are at the seashore, Dickinson writes to Susan: "Ned is safe—Just 'serenaded' Hannah, and is running off with a Corn Leaf 'tail,' Looking back for cheers. Grandma 'hoped' characteristically 'he would be a very good Boy.' 'Not very dood,' he said, sweet defiant child" (LII 454).

One of the few full letters that Dickinson sends by mail to Susan, this one ends with a litany of closings:

> Do not fear for Home—
> Be a bold Susan—
> Clara sold the tobacco, and is good to Ned—
> Dreamed of your meeting Tennyson in Ticknor and Fields—
> Where the Treasure is, there the Brain is also—
> Love for Boy— (LII 455).

Dated August, 1866, this letter reflects Dickinson's deepest concerns—for Susan in her pregnancy, for the care of little Ned, for her and Susan's literary lives, and for the child not yet born (expressed here as "Boy," sending her aunt love to him).

Dickinson writes nothing but brief messages once Susan and Austin have returned. In fact, there are comparatively few letters—and even fewer poems—dating from 1866. One fragment written by Dickinson to Lou Norcross—undated—may refer to Susan's lying in. Here the poet says, "Every hour is anxious now, and heaven protect the lamb who shared her fleece with a timider, even Emily" (LII 456). (Habegger provides a different gloss for this message.)

Dickinson's year of returning home from Cambridge, from her pursuits of life outside her family's Amherst, was filled with not only housekeeping, but also with both mourning for her dog's loss and the exhilaration of the arrival of a new, healthy Dickinson child.

13
Colonel Higginson, Appearing

As Austin and Susan's family grew, it became clear to the Dickinson family that the children's best care-giver was Aunt Emily. Dickinson's role with Ned, Mattie, and their friends is described lovingly by MacGregor Jenkins, who played with the Dickinson children, living nearby in the pastor's house; his father officiated at the funerals of both Edward Dickinson and Emily. In his *Emily Dickinson, Friend and Neighbor*, Jenkins draws a differently nuanced picture of the "exquisite, vibrant life" the poet led. Seen from her bedroom window as she lowered a basket of gingerbread to the waiting children, Aunt Emily was "a joyous person," ready to help them build gypsy camp sites, providing news about the neighborhood to them (speaking of herself in third person), and sending notes to Mac's parents addressed to "Mr. and Mrs. Clergyman" or "Mr. and Mrs. Pastor" (Jenkins 35, 45, 58, 83). Jenkins recalled that Ned and Mattie's aunt "was not shy" with the children and their friends (21).

He recalls getting the gingerbread in its basket as a memorable experience. Dickinson saw to it that the basket was "slowly lowered. I can see it now, jerking its way down from what seemed to us then an incredible height. We saw two delicate hands playing out a much knotted cord, and framed in the window above a slender figure in white and a pair of laughing eyes . . . The basket always contained gingerbread . . . not like any gingerbread I had ever seen before or have ever encountered since . . . long, oval cakes, crisp and brown on the outside, but within a light brown or yellow and delicately sweet and gummy. The flat tops were hard and shiny" (Jenkins 40).

Jenkins recounts a gift Dickinson had sent his mother (after the family had moved to Pittsfield to minister there). She often sent flowers but this time, several pussy willows was the offering. The poet's note said, characteristic of her tendency to joke, "Nature's buff message—left for you in Amherst. She had not time to call. You see her Father and my Father were brothers. –Emily" (Jenkins 120–1).

He also remembers the fact that Aunt Emily and Ned sometimes spoke in a private language, a dialect made up of references to characters and books, as well as—later—allusions and phrases from Dicken's novels (Jenkins 25).

The poet loved the spring, Jenkins remembered, and she loved her garden, where she was often to be found standing or kneeling on an old red army blanket when the ground was damp. In his concluding words, "She had created for herself a spiritual solar system in which she lived and everything in it was important and full of meaning" (Jenkins 136).

Few critics have been interested in Dickinson's relationship with children, her family's and her neighbors', but her poems—as well as her letters—speak to her interest in them, and her contentment in being with them (no matter how reclusive other parts of her life seemed). In an 1867 poem, for example, Dickinson writes of "The Merchant of the Picturesque,"

> . . . To Children he is small in price
> And large in courtesy—
> It suits him better than a check
> Their artless currency . . . (Poem #1134 Fr 986).

Seldom included in commentaries about Dickinson are some of the famous family recipes—rice cake, for example, or the vaunted gingerbread—but as Aife Murray says, "Moving among piano and pie crusts and paper—because 'there is no boundary line to art'—Emily could have spent all day meditating on the cricket, hammering out an original tune on the piano, gazing from the pantry-window until she was poised to set the poem down on the page" (Murray 108).

A further element of the life Dickinson returned to after Cambridge was her music. When Edward arranged to buy his older daughter the rosewood piano from Hallet Davis and Company of Boston, she was only fourteen. She helped to choose the pedestal type piano stool with its luxurious red velvet top. She practiced at least two hours every day and was an accomplished composer and innovator, as guests remember her inventing comic and witty songs at gatherings.

As a student at Mount Holyoke, Dickinson had one-half hour of singing and one hour of piano practice daily. According to Carolyn Cooley, she included among her "portfolio" many difficult works—Beethoven

Waltzes, an assortment of salon music, and "The Bird Waltz," "Aurora Waltz," "Sliding Waltz" (some of the slides she mastered featured nine notes to a beat; others, seven) (Cooley 11–18). As she more and more often chose writing and reading over her music, the piano became a piece of furniture; no one else in the family played it. (For a time, Vinnie was also studying the piano, but whenever the sisters tried out pieces for four-hands, Vinnie lost patience.)

It was not a boring life, there in the Homestead, marked by the 280 Main Street address—but it was no longer a teeming life of excitement or literary promise. Bracketed by two poems from these years, Dickinson's existence meandered as it tried to answer the immediate and sometimes emergency calls for fresh bread, a suitable pudding for supper, a clean kitchen floor: no one noticed if days went by without writing time, or energy for either reading or music. As Dickinson had written in an 1865 poem, "And this, of all my Hopes . . . the silent end/Bountiful colored, My Morning rose/Early and sere" (Poem #975 Fr 885). Correspondingly, her 1867 "There is another loneliness/That many die without" replicates the mood of those 1866 poems discussed earlier (Poem #1138 Fr 988–9). Speaking of the loss of friends, the poet here remains staunchly loyal to

> . . . nature, sometimes, sometimes thought,
> And whoso it befall
> Is richer than could be revealed
> By mortal numeral.

It was a physically quiet life, however. As Roger Lundin observes, stemming partly from the close of the war, Dickinson experienced a "definitive turn in her life." She never left home again; in fact, "she stopped making any trips at all off the grounds," even to go to the "other house" (Lundin 132).

More likely to show continued dependence on Susan Gilbert Dickinson, then, the poet had come to realize that she would not receive from her beloved Susan the kind of omnivorous attention she wanted. Now there was another baby, with more conflicts with new baby nurses, and a five-year-old who was demanding in his own ways. As John Cody noted, beginning around the time Dickinson had written "Your Riches taught me—poverty!," her yearning for not only Susan but Susan's full life was unmistakable. Cody states that Susan came to represent everything Dickinson was missing: "For Emily, Austin's home was a constant reminder of all she lacked" (Cody 393). That realization, in itself, might keep Dickinson within the Homestead's perimeters. For his sister's need to remain at home, occupied with her various sorts of work, it was Austin who was most sympathetic: "like her, he loved solitude and was subject to attacks of melancholy anxiety" (Lundin 88). Austin saw Emily's life as perfectly natural. After all, he had been aware of her poems for decades, even if intermittently. And as she had written in 1862

> To put this World down, like a Bundle—
> And walk steady, away,
> Requires Energy—possibly Agony (Poem #404 Fr 428).

Emily Dickinson had long had in mind the direction she would eventually choose.

Susan Gilbert Dickinson, however, felt put upon. She could not continuously fight against that tendency to depression that sporadically invaded Austin's make up, nor could she respond with alacrity to Emily Dickinson's needs. In Polly Longsworth's assessment, "It isn't hard to understand how Sue easily and often injured both Austin and Emily . . . she gave intelligent, respectful attention to Emily's poems, but could not cope with the inordinate love that sponsored them" (Longsworth 116). Again, Betsy Erkkila reinforces this understanding: she calls Dickinson's love of and dependence on Susan Gilbert Dickinson "the central relationship in the text of Dickinson's life and work . . . It was Dickinson's intense, passionate, and sometimes troubled love relationship with Sue and not her relationship with the Master—or any of the various men who have been proposed to play that role—that was the central and enduring relationship of her life" (Erkkila 41).

Hart and Smith connect a famous Dickinson poem, "The Soul selects/ her own Society" with Susan Gilbert, commenting that on the back of her short poem appears a new stanza. They quote it this way, as if it were a poem,

> Love reckons by
> itself—alone—
> "As large as I"—
> relate the Sun
> To One who never
> felt it blaze—
> Itself is all the
> like it has— (Hart and Smith 133).

Repeatedly, Dickinson points her poems toward Susan, whether or not she sends a work to her sister-in-law, or uses her name.

Much of the busyness of Dickinson's life between 1866 and the early 1870s related to her father. More financially profitable than he had ever been, Edward figured his net worth during the postwar years as $28,700 in 1866, $32,600 in 1867, and $47,800 in 1869. The two Dickinson lawyers moved into new offices during 1868, and Edward worked hard—often behind the scenes—to bring the Massachusetts Agricultural College to Amherst. (That institution eventually became the University of Massachusetts at Amherst.) In Austin's judgment, as he brought Frederick Law Olmstead into the mix, the landscaping of that college's grounds was unequaled (Habegger 505).

Dickinson herself did not feel that her life was leisurely. During one of Vinnie's absences, Emily wrote to Susan Gilbert Dickinson, "I am so hurried with Parents that I run all Day with my tongue abroad, like a Summer Dog" (in Habegger 518). But she did keep her literary and quasi-literary actions active.

It was obvious that Dickinson's only professional correspondent remaining after her months away in Cambridge was Thomas Higginson. Her interaction with Samuel Bowles occurred mainly through Susan and Austin, and her correspondence with the Hollands was directed to Elizabeth, not Josiah. Besides her Norcross cousins, no one else in New England was writing to Emily Dickinson.

Her only letter to Higginson during 1867 was a two-line missive seemingly responding to his *Atlantic Monthly* essay, "A Plea for Culture," which appeared in the January, 1867, issue (LII 457). Wineapple notes that the *Atlantic* had paid him $1000 for a series of ten essays (he accepted the fee and wrote those essays in 1867 but turned down the same offer the following year). She notes that he had hoped to edit Thoreau's journals, but he was not given that assignment; neither did he become editor of the *Atlantic Monthly*, a plum task that went to William Dean Howells (Wineapple 170, 176).

By 1869, with no subsequent letters between Dickinson and Higginson, there is finally a fulsome exchange (letters may have been lost but nothing exists to suggest that there were other letters). Dickinson writes in reply to Higginson's invitation (evidently in May, 1869, asking her to come to specific events in Boston)—turning him down once more but responding carefully, and with genuine emotion, to his cheery letter. He closes that letter, "Write & tell me something in prose or verse, & I will be less fastidious in future & willing to write clumsy things, rather than none." Implicit in that comment is his apology for not replying to her earlier letter. His signature, "Ever your friend," is encouraging (LII 462).

Dickinson's June, 1869, letter is a true response. She uses as greeting, "Dear friend," and comments (in response to his use of the word *Immortality* years earlier),

> A Letter always feels to me like immortality because it is the mind alone without corporeal friend. Indebted in our talk to attitude and accent, there seems a spectral power in thought that walks alone— I would like to thank you for your great kindness but never try to lift the words which I cannot hold.

She discusses the possibility that he may come to Amherst, ending that thought with her disclaimer: "your letters always surprise me. My life has been too simple and stern to embarrass any."

It is in this letter that Dickinson uses the phrase "I do not cross my Father's ground," but her writing covers much more content: "Of our greatest acts we are ignorant—" appears near the end of the writing, and is followed by the mysterious paragraph (few commentators have any reference for this statement):

> You were not aware that you saved my Life. To thank you in person has been since then one of my few requests. The child that asks my flower "Will you," he says—"Will you"—and so to ask for what I want I know no other way (LII 460).

Unlike most of her letters, this one she signs "Dickinson."

By the following summer, Higginson plans to visit Dickinson after he has come to Amherst in connection with the death of his older brother, Stephen. Although he told her he would arrive a day before he did, the meeting eventually took place. According to Brenda Wineapple, the day Higginson entered the Homestead, he found his books—*Out-door Papers* and his novel, *Malbone*—on the library table, and then he heard what might have been "a child's step rushing in the hall. Then an airy, slim form appeared: Emily Dickinson, her dress white, her shawl blue, her hair Titian red, parted in the middle and pulled back. She carried two daylilies in her hand, which she placed in his. 'These are my introduction' she whispered. 'How long will you stay?'" (Wineapple 164).

Wineapple provides her reader two additional commentaries. About *Malbone*, which was serialized in the *Atlantic* during the first six months of 1869, she notes that its hero—Philip Malbone—is based loosely on

Higginson's nephew, Storrow, and his dream lover is named "Emilia." She also includes information about Higginson's marriage, and his painfully ill wife Mary. "Virtually paralyzed, her fingers so stiff she turned the pages of a book with a wand, she sat in her chair day after day, forgivably querulous and upset. His home had become a hospital, he confided to his diary, and Mary, crying for the pain he was powerless to relieve, begged him over and over not to leave her . . ." (Wineapple 162). Setting the stage for a romantic gloss to color Higginson's meeting with Dickinson, the biographer of Higginson in his literary role creates a tension that seems unavoidable. She also provides the full text of the letter Higginson writes to his wife Mary from Amherst, after he has spent time with his elusive poetess.

Segments of Higginson's letter are often quoted. His views expressed to Mary are in themselves disjointed, separated by shifts in recollections of things Dickinson has said: "I find ecstacy in living—the mere sense of living is joy enough" she says at one point. "Truth is such a rare thing it is delightful to tell it." "How do most people live without any thoughts. There are many people in the world (you must have noticed them in the street) How do they live. How do they get strength to put on their clothes in the morning." Without any recording device, Higginson is carefully tracking not only what Dickinson says but the way she says it. He also includes a question he has asked, about her possible need for employment, or of "going off the place & never seeing any visitor" to which quandary she answers simply, "I never thought of conceiving that I could ever have the slightest approach to such a want in all future time" (& added) "I feel that I have not expressed myself strongly enough."

Higginson is also attempting to place Dickinson. He describes the Dickinson place as "A large country lawyer's house, brown brick, with great trees & a garden" (Higginson Heath 1957 ff). For him the central space is the parlor ("dark & cool & stiffish,") and once Dickinson appears, he comments that in her "soft frightened breathless childlike voice" she told him

Forgive me if I am frightened: I never see strangers & hardly know what I say—but she talked soon & thenceforward continuously—and deferentially—sometimes stopping to ask me to talk instead of her—but readily recommencing. Manner between Angie Tilton & Mr. Alcott—but thoroughly ingenuous & simple which they are not & saying many things which you would have thought foolish & I wise.

When he steps outside, he calls the home "a lovely place, at least the view Hills everywhere, hardly mountains." He is quite interested in Edward Dickinson (and has commented originally on the fact that the family members appear to lead separate lives—his seeing no one except Emily during his visit, which ran from 2 p.m. to 9 p.m.). The following day he does see Edward, and describes him as "thin dry & speechless," adding "I saw what her life has been." He retells the story of Austin and the sisters' hiding *Kavanagh* under the piano cover—and the punch line, that once their father found it, he was displeased. And one of Edward's students was amazed that he had not heard of Lydia Maria Child, "& used to bring them books & hide in a bush by the door." After her reading the first of these books, Dickinson "thought in ecstasy, 'This then is a book! And there are more of them!'"

When he discusses Dickinson's baking, he adds her description: "She makes all the bread for her father only likes hers & says '& people must have puddings' this very dreamingly, as if they were comets—so she makes them." Again, to his listing of what he remembers of her commentary: "Women talk: men are silent: that is why I dread women." "My father only reads on Sunday—he reads lonely & rigorous books." "When I lost the use of my Eyes it was a comfort to think there were so few real books that I could easily find some one to read me all of them." And, one of the most famous of his reconstructions of her language: "If I read a book [and] it makes my whole body so cold no fire ever can warm me I know that is poetry. If I feel physically as if the top of my head were taken off, I know that is poetry. These are the only way I know it. Is there any other way."

Among her other quoted topics, Higginson lists, "Could you tell me what home is," "I never had a mother. I suppose a mother is one to whom you hurry when you are troubled," "Is it oblivion or absorption when things pass from our minds?" and her story about fearing her father: "I never knew how to tell time by the clock till I was 15. My father thought he had taught me but I did not understand & I was afraid to say I did not & afraid to ask any one else lest he should know." Appended to this story is Higginson's comment, "Her father was not severe I should think but remote."

As he prepares to leave, he cites Dickinson's telling him, "Gratitude is the only secret that cannot reveal itself." She also reprimands his saying that he would come again in a year, or, in his phrasing, *some time*. She said "Say in a long time, that will be nearer. Some time is nothing."

To Mary, Higginson adds in confidence, "I never was with anyone who drained my nerve power so much. Without touching her, she drew from me. I am glad not to live near her. She often thought me *tired* & seemed very thoughtful of others." In a similar account to his sister, he called Dickinson "my singular poetic correspondent."

Critics may have complained about some of Higginson's phrasing in this account—making an issue of the same kind of condescending tone that male writers and critics have for decades employed as they comment on the writing—or the personae—of women. But it is Higginson's deft and ample reciting of this hours-long meeting with Emily Dickinson that brought a sense of her and her mind into both literature and history.

14
1870–1873

Higginson's summer visit seemed to provide a nexus of stability for Dickinson. Not only does her writing of poems increase dramatically in 1870 but the tone of her letters during 1870, 1871, and 1872 has changed. She becomes not only calm but pleasantly retrospective. Of paramount importance during these years is her correspondence with Elizabeth Holland, the Norcross cousins, and Higginson himself. Weeks after his visit to Amherst, Dickinson writes him one of her most substantial (and in some ways) intellectual letters. Dated September 26, 1870, her letter opens with images of "sweetness," comparing her surfeit after his visit with her aimlessness beforehand: "I remember your coming as a serious sweetness placed now with the Unreal" (LII 479). She compares her satiety with that lack of hunger expressed by "the man of the Revelations" (see Revelation 7:16).

She furthermore compares the relationship she feels with Higginson to that between a vein and, in his role, an artery. She speaks as well of "her solemn indebtedness" and then breaks abruptly to state, in two brief sentences:

> You ask great questions accidentally. To answer them would be events . . .

In an earlier sentence, she reported calmly, "I thought and went about my work." In this non-declamatory way, she surely implied that his visit had brought her health, and in that peace of mind she is able to work well. Later in the same letter, Dickinson discusses literary matters which Higginson had mentioned during his visit—Marie White Lowell's poems, for example, and Higginson's own essay on the subject of women's rights. Rather than describing herself as his equal, however, she apologizes: "If I ask too much, you could please refuse." That comment is followed by prose that has the reach of poetry: "Shortness to live has made me bold" (LII 480).

Signed, once more, "Dickinson," this correspondence is followed by her second letter, dated only "about October." Referring to the "Riddle" she shares with him, she returns to his previous interest in the subject of "Immortality." Interspersed with excerpts from poems, Dickinson's prose also divides into lines. For example,

> I was much refreshed by your strong letter—Thank you for Greatness—
> I will have deserved it in a longer time! (LII 482)

She asks him what "inspiration" means. She asks him about Emerson. She asks him about his returning to Amherst. Then, there is a year's hiatus before the correspondence resumes. Dickinson's next letter to him is dated November, 1871.

Dickinson's letters to Higginson after 1870 may well be considered the beginning of what poet Aliki Barnstone sees as the poet's last formulation—a style that creates a fusion of prose in poetry. Barnstone traces Dickinson's having finished with the production of her fascicles to this more insistent, and later, involvement with letters. As this critic suggests, Dickinson's later "poems were gathered from scraps of paper and letters. Work that has been deemed 'prose' [by critics] scans and rhymes. She sent poems as prose to some friends; sometimes she sent the same pieces as poems to others" (Barnstone 117).

Barnstone points out too the ways all Dickinson's missing letters complicated this process of definition. Some of what she calls Dickinson's later "poems [might be] shut up in the prose that has been classified as letters. In the extant letters, there could be many unlineated poems that in other letters—now missing—Dickinson sent as lineated poems."

The impact of changes in Dickinson's poetics may well be that she is developing what Barnstone calls a "relational poetics that was connected with the world, a world of specific readers." In her satisfaction with this mode, she adds to what Barnstone describes as her "lifelong refusal to reject her earthly attachments in order to gain entrance into God's heaven" (217; see also William Shurr along with Anna Dunlop and Emily Grey Shurr).

Many of Dickinson's letters to Higginson feed into the symmetry Barnstone finds: they also parallel her achievements in prose as she writes to such an intimate as Louise Norcross. Treating Dickinson's letters from a historical perspective, Barnstone includes in her thinking the three "Master" letters—as if they were written much later in the poet's canon. Barnstone provides lineation for the last of those letters in much the same way Hart and Smith do for Dickinson's notes to Susan Gilbert Dickinson (Barnstone 116). It is in the rigorous work of Paul Crumbley, as well as in the lineation that Hart and Smith perform in their *Open Me Carefully* that critics have grown familiar with the concept of Dickinson's prose being read poetically (Crumbley Pen 171–2).

Critics chart a number of what they describe as changes once Dickinson's writing of poems dwindles to a comparative trickle during 1866 and 1867. James McIntosh points to what he sees as her lessening use of "dramas of love." When later Dickinson resumes writing about representations of nature, he notes that these poems of description are "frequently imaged at a distance" (McIntosh 37). Critic James Guthrie echoes what he sees as "her overall trend toward abstraction" (Guthrie 151). He attributes some of Dickinson's changes in style to her tendency to protect her eyes, noting that she redefines "the notion of a place according to states of being rather than sense evidence" (Guthrie 80).

With the four poems which Dickinson sent to Higginson in her letter dated November, 1871, she resumed her earlier practice. The letter itself cajoled him about his respect for Joaquin Miller; she in turn mentioned positively Helen Hunt's and Robert Browning's poems. Three of the poems she included were recent work, and all illustrated the critics' comments above—abstract in their focus, they yet employed familiar sentiments in their two-quatrain format. Poem #1227, "Step lightly on this narrow Spot—/The Broadest Land that grows," in fact, anticipates the poet's praise for her beloved country—replete with patriotic imagery in the second verse, all in the service of her aim, a "deathless syllable." (Fr 1058–9). Another poem dated 1871 is "The Days that we can spare/ Are those a Function die" (Poem #1229 Fr 1060–1). Dickinson had some difficulty getting her numerical or her economical terms aligned, and changed lines five and six from their original meaning ("Our Estimates forsook/Our affluence a Whim") to a more definite couplet. The second stanza in her revision, then, runs

> Our Estimates a Scheme—
> Our Ultimates a Sham—
> We let go all of Time without
> Arithmetic of him—

One of the works that critic Gary Stonum finds both representative and illustrative of Dickinson's long-term interest in mathematics, ratio, economics, and (one might add) architecture, "The Days that we can spare" condenses terminology from wider fields into a typically cryptic poem of intentionality: human figuring cannot compete with the Deity (or at least with a mentor) who creates his own "arithmetic," of which Time is an image. Note that it is the human being who fails: "*Our Estimates . . . . Our* Ultimates . . . " (Stonum 133–4).

The third of Dickinson's enclosed new poems is "Remembrance has a Rear and Front." The second line compares the abstraction, "remembrance," to a House, complete with Garret and Cellar. At her best mixing the concrete with a familiar abstraction, Dickinson relates Poem #1234 to others of her works that are physically, and linguistically, poems about structures (Fr 1063–4).

It is interesting that Dickinson reaches back in time for Poem #594, which was originally written in 1863. Perhaps she includes it because it has been greatly revised, and its more optimistic ending fits well with this grouping. "When I hoped I feared/Since I hoped I dared" refers to a structure that is said to be a church; and the enervation that is suggested in both "Remembrance has a Rear and Front" (in the first version, "Leave me not ever there alone" appears as line 7, but it has been dramatically changed for the final copy) and this poem, in which the spirit world gives the speaker reason to rejoice ("He deposes Doom").

Rarely does Dickinson move a poem out of its dated boundaries. In this case, she seemed eager to comfort a reader: "Spectre cannot harm—/ Serpent cannot charm" begins stanza two, where the power resides in the figure who, even in his humanity, or perhaps *because* of his humanity, "deposes Doom" (Fr 591–2).

By the time of Dickinson's next letter to Higginson, mid-March, 1872, she encloses three poems—again, all recent. But in this brief letter of condolence over the death of his brother, Dr. Francis John Higginson, she has assembled wry, even quasi-comic, poems. The opening of the letter itself is somewhat brisk, sentences arranged in three separate lines as if part of a poem:

> I am sorry your Brother is dead.
> I fear he was dear to you.
> I should be glad to know you were painlessly grieved—

Addressed to "Dear friend" and signed "Dickinson," the letter seems to exist primarily to convey poems to Higginson's attention (LII 494).

Of these three poems, two are dated 1872, and they relate to each other. Poem #1266 begins with a more outspoken first line than the work

Dickinson sends to her mentor: "He preached about breadth till we knew he was narrow" is modified to become "He preaches opon 'breadth' till it argued him narrow" (Fr 1091–3). Leaving some part of interpretation— both of the sermon and of the poem—to a good reader, Dickinson slams the speaker (proclaimed "a Liar," yet named ironically "so learned a man"). The speaker has no simplicity nor does he speak truth.

Similarly, "The Sea said 'Come' to the Brook," Poem #1275, recasts the measure of power and powerlessness. Even though the Sea demands possession of the small Brook—not wanting it to grow into another Sea—he cannot stop its increase in size, so the dialogue concludes being an interchange between the original "Sea" and the newer "Sea," the latter saying, "'Learned Waters—/Wisdom is stale to me'" (Fr 1099–100).

For the third inclusion, Dickinson moves back to an 1871 poem "To disappear enhances," a poem about a man who runs away, and thereby avoids "the extatic limit/Of unobtained Delight" (Poem #1239 Fr 1070–1). From her writing of 1871 and 1872, Dickinson might have chosen any number of poems that treat the appearance of "fame" or prominence—"The Stars are old, that stood for me," "The Clover's simple Fame," "The show is not the show," and particularly "What we see we know somewhat/Be it but a little" as well as "Tell all the truth but tell it slant—/Success in Circuit lies," (Poems #1242, #1256, #1270, #1272, and #1263 Fr 1074–5, 1083–4, 1095–7, and 1089–90). Had she gone back further in time, she might have chosen poems from 1870, the year of Higginson's visit, (the remarkable poem #1186, "Oh Sumptuous moment/Slower go") or even further back in time to some striking poems written in 1869 (for example, #1155, "The Snow that never drifts—/The transient, fragrant snow") or from 1868, poem #1149, "After a hundred years/Nobody knows the place." But as Murray points out, it was not until 1870–1 that Dickinson once again wrote with finesse and confidence, and in quantity. Murray attributes the poet's revitaliza- tion—moving from the average of 11 poems in both 1868 and 1869 to 28 poems in 1870 and then 48 in 1871—to the placement of Margaret "Maggie" Maher as full time maid for the Dickinson family. Her place- ment was contentious, in that another family was trying to lure her away, but once Dickinson felt comfortable with Maggie's decision, she could once again set up a schedule for her writing (Murray 79).

1870 is the date most observers of Dickinson's life consider the start of her visible "withdrawal" from community. Whicher states, "By 1870 her seclusion had become a conscious resolution," a statement he tempers by claiming that "her retirement had no anti-social implications" (Whicher 135, 137). It began gradually, Whicher says; he did not find her practices "abnormal" (Whicher 134). Longsworth supplements this belief by noting that by Dickinson's early twenties, she was avoiding Sewing Circle and other similar groups (Longsworth Amherst 31). For Aliki Barnstone, the poet's "withdrawal . . . was never absolute . . . her isolation was compromised by her family, her reading, her abundant correspondence, and by her poems," which often draw on popular culture (Barnstone 5). Earlier critics, however, thought Dickinson's near-invisibility striking—evidence of mental states that were far from the expected. John Cody, for example, describes the poet's seclusion "that was almost airtight as far as the neighbors and Amherst social life in general were concerned" (Cody 443). Even Cody, however, admits that "she seems to have remained accessible to some of the neighborhood children and to Austin's children." And Murray would posit that Dickinson's relationships with the various Irish immigrants who worked intermittently or full time for the Dickinsons were fulsome, involving, and satisfying (Murray 116–18).

Contemporary poet Susan Howe provides an intellectual context, explaining Dickinson's withdrawal as a result of 'her fractured sense of being eternally on intellectual borders" (Howe My Emily 21). She notes the irony of Dickinson's choice—to avoid society so that she might "shut herself inside her childhood family constellation," creating a "self-imposed exile, indoors" (Howe My Emily 13). When as late as Higginson's 1870 visit, Dickinson speaks of having had no mother, and the critic himself had assessed her father as distant and severe, one wonders at her insistence in staying within that family-dominated space.

For Albert Gelpi, Dickinson's escape from society was her means of denying the influence of that society. He writes, "No pessimist knew the power of blackness more deeply than Emily Dickinson" (Gelpi 36).

To recognize the more stable plateau that Higginson's visit had contributed to Dickinson's life is to agree with Alfred Habegger—in Higginson, Emily Dickinson thought she had found her master (Habegger 553). Through the years of their acquaintance, however, he consistently disappoints her and she eventually "seems to have realized she could not be Higginson's kind of writer, and that the social, serious responsible voice he called up in her was less vital than her own voice" (Habegger 555). As her letters written during the early 1870s show, however, she remained respectful of his opinions about literature, even as she sometimes bantered with him—often reminding him of Shakespeare's greatness.

15
The Beginning of the Calendar of Deaths

The 1870s began the cycle Dickinson was hoping to avoid: she wrote on July 27, 1872, to the Norcross cousins, "Little Irish Maggie went to sleep this morning at six o'clock, just the time grandpa rises, and will rest in the grass at Northampton tomorrow. She has had a hard sickness, but her awkward little life is saved and gallant now. Our Maggie is helping her mother put her in the cradle . . ." (LII 496). The Dickinsons' new maid, Maggie Maher, was doing her work of bridging elements of the community with the occupants of the Homestead, and while Dickinson's somewhat patronizing tone (speaking of the teenager's "awkward little life") offends today's reader, the diminution of the young woman's body can be forgiven. It was a practice of sentimental writing to equate women's lives with their childhoods: the trope of *innocence* was the aim. In this case, the daughter of James and Ellen Kelley was dead at 17.

A year earlier, Dickinson had written to Lou and Fanny about her father's ill health, suggesting that her worries about him "made a little creature of me, who thought myself so bold":

> Father was very sick. I presumed he would die, and the sight of his lonesome face all day was harder than personal trouble. He is growing better, though physically reluctantly. I hope I am mistaken, but I think his physical life don't want to live any longer. You know he never played, and the straightest engine has its leaning hour. Vinnie was not here. Now we will turn the corner (LII 486).

Edward Dickinson was sixty-eight in the year 1871. Whereas he was soon to step down as treasurer of Amherst College, he had been elected to the General Court of Massachusetts. Later he would serve another term in the state legislature (Hart and Smith 148–9). During the early

1870s, Edward "was an active shareholder in the Hampden Cotton Manufacturing Company," even though that business was declining. He invested in "the private, toll-charging Sunderland Bridge." And even though he was less active in the First Church, "he continued to take a keen interest in the Northampton Lunatic Asylum" (Habegger 504).

When Edward relinquished his role as treasurer at the College, he was reasonably sure that Austin would be elected to take his place. The father-son combination had worked well as a legal team, but outside the office there was conflict. Even after Austin got the college books in order (the repetition of son tidying up after his father—as Edward had after Samuel—did not go unnoticed by the elder), Austin felt that his whole demeanor rubbed against Edward's giving priority to conventional behavior: Austin valued his own "romantic, exuberant nature" but his father remained "disciplined, relentlessly rational" (Longsworth Amherst 18).

One of the areas of difference between father and son was Austin's seeing himself as an arbiter of the arts: Austin and Susan's Evergreens showcased their collection of contemporary European and American painting. The collecting had begun with the Pre-Raphaelites, and then Austin moved to paintings done by members of the Hudson River School. He owned *Autumn Evening in the White Hills* by Sanford Gifford and *Sunset with Cows* by John Kensett. He had acquired a number of lesser-known works, including Hans Frederick Gade's *Landscape: Norwegian Scenery, with Bears* and two paintings by Gottfried Johann Pulian. Eventually the walls in the formal areas of the Evergreens were filled with the layered paintings, two and three levels high (Longsworth Amherst 44).

The Everglades itself was a strikingly different house, incongruous to some extent, placed as it was so near the Homestead. The architecture was taken from A. J. Downings' recently published *Architecture of Country Homes*, designed and built by Northampton architect William Fenno Pratt. The house sat on a plot that occupied one third of an acre: Austin was as involved in landscaping as he had been in designing the house, and he scoured the area for years searching for plants and bushes to incorporate in his grounds (Longsworth Amherst 37).

In private, Edward always mentioned that he had spent $5500 on building the Evergreens. Biographers have pointed out that Austin was to repay his father $3000, but there is no evidence that he ever did so. Given the constant state of his usually depleted finances, there is no reason to think he would have ever had the funds available (Longsworth Amherst 56).

The two households managed to co-exist, even without much commerce between them. Sue still responded to her sister-in-law's notes and poem pieces; but Ned and Mattie provided connecting cables of love and enjoyment, and not only for Aunt Emily. During the early 1870s, Ned was turning ten and Mattie was an independent and somewhat self-righteous little girl: Dickinson's correspondence is full of notes to her first-born nephew. With the constant help of Maggie Maher, the Homestead was running simply but effectively. And Dickinson once more had hours of private time when she could return to her upstairs room and think about writing both poems and letters. Even with the household help, however, the poet wrote less.

It was as if Dickinson was not written *out* (which many critics have since claimed—amazed as they have been by the six hundred poems she wrote during the early and mid 1860s) but in some respects, perhaps, Dickinson was written *over.* She was physically emptied. She had experienced illness of the eyes; the pain had seldom left her. She had experienced a life of looking on—seeing her father's life diminish, realizing that little zest for going on remained; she had seen her mother's life come trembling to a near standstill. She knew what the flurry of energy in Austin's demeanor meant: he would find more paintings to purchase, even though he knew as well as his father did that the Dickinsons' coffers were once again close to empty.

The poet indicates the tenor of the Dickinsons' lives in several of her 1871 poems. Thinking of her father's health, she fictionalizes his illness in "'Twas fighting for his Life he was . . . ." The second stanza of that poem is dramatically effective,

> It aims once—kills once—conquers once—
> There is no second War
> In that Campaign inscrutable
> Of the Interior (Poem #1230 Fr 1061–2).

In "The harm of Years is on him/The infamy of Time," she laments the loss of "his Morning Forces" as she covers a range of emotion in these spare eight lines (Poem #1215 Fr 1872). Less directly, "So much of Heaven has gone from Earth/That there must be a Heaven" reprises the move from earth to distances unknown, carrying Dickinson's usual cryptic warning in the third stanza: "Too much of Proof affronts Belief" (Poem #1240 Fr 1073). Perhaps most poignantly, a set of two tercets (Poem #1224 Fr 1056):

> Are Friends Delight or Pain?
> Could Bounty but remain
> Riches were good—

> But if they only stay
> Ampler to fly away
> Riches are sad.

Judging from Dickinson's extant letters, in 1871 she would have voted for a positive view of "Friends"—many of her letters to Elizabeth Holland, the Norcross cousins, Mary Bowles, Susan, Mrs. Henry Hills, and Perez Cowan express nothing but loving thoughts and hopeful wishes. She mourns with Elizabeth when she must have her eye removed; she laments with Lou when she sees her beau marry someone else; and she thanks Mrs. Henry Hills for her kindnesses to Vinnie. Yet even as her correspondence offers a transparent view of her assumed happiness, some of her poems from 1872 speak of caution.

"We like a Hairbreadth 'scape," along with "Had I not seen the Sun" and "If my Bark sink," posits success for the poet-speaker (Poems #1247, #1249, #1250 Fr 1078–9) in that the adventure of taking on what needs to be accomplished fuels personal strength. "If we had ventured less/The Gale were not so fine," Dickinson writes in her aphoristic style. Pitting the human speaker against a range of obstacles, each of these 1872 poems is confirming the spirit of accomplishment, if not exactly of adventure.

Dickinson's 1872 letter to Higginson shows that this theme of meeting, and conquering, obstacles is important to her. In a letter dated "late 1872," she begins with the consideration of friendship: "To live is so startling, it leaves but little room for other occupations though Friends are if possible an event more fair." She thanks him for "having been to Amherst" and she asks him to return. She signs the letter with a couplet that suggests boundlessness,

> Menagerie to me
> My Neighbor be (LII 500–1).

And she uses as signatory, "Your Scholar."

The reader assumes that she had no response from Higginson, for in 1873 she writes on a card, "Could you teach me now?" and then on a sheet of stationery, "Will you instruct me then no more?" (LII 511–2). Within this envelope, she sends three more poems. "Longing is like the Seed," a poem about Constancy in which the last seed "Believing if it intercede/It shall at length be found," and "Dominion lasts until obtained/Possession just as long," a poem that goes on to speak about Eternity and Permanence, both poems dated from 1873 (Poems #1298 and #1299 Fr 1125–6). The third poem is from several years before.

"Not any higher stands the Grave" is a tightly controlled and less personal work (Poem #1214 Fr 1871–2). There is still no letter from Higginson, but in early December, he does visit Amherst. Hired to present a lecture at Amherst College on woman suffrage, Higginson pocketed his hundred dollars and went to see Dickinson. There is no transcript of this visit; he evidently had not written his wife about the encounter, though he did write to his sisters that he saw Dickinson briefly (she, who goes nowhere and admits very few visitors). Again dressed in white and carrying a flower, for this occasion a Daphne odora, the poet once more asked him how long he could stay (Wineapple 192–3).

Four weeks later, December 31, 1873, he wrote Dickinson a "New Year greetings" letter, making reference to their pleasant time and explaining to her,

> Each time we seem to come together as old & tried friends; and I certainly feel that I have known you long & well, through the beautiful thoughts and words you have sent me . . . (LII 519).

He ends that paragraph with something of a declaration when he says, "I will try to speak the truth to you, and with love."

Higginson then talks about the snowy beauty that surrounds him, and mentions a gift just sent, "some field lilies yellow and scarlet, painted in water colors." He also tells her that Helen Hunt is wintering in Colorado. He signs this letter, "Your friend."

Perhaps the warmest letter Higginson has ever written to her, this truly personal expression—coupled with his second visit to her home—may have been frightening to the reclusive woman. Dickinson was clearly more comfortable writing than she was talking face to face. Her January reply tries to echo his warmth, beginning "Thank you dear friend" and then continuing with a kind of metaphoric disavowal, "I always ran Home to Awe when a child, if anything befell me."

Dickinson then creates several definite poemlike intervals in the letter. The first occupies six lines, though they appear to be prose. Their enigmatic message exists between the separate lines:

> Of your flitting Coming it is fair to think.
> Like the Bee's Coupe—vanishing in Music.
> Would you with the Bee return, what a Firm of Noon!
> Death obtains the Rose, but the News of Dying goes no further than the Breeze. The Ear is the last Face.

We hear after we see,
Which to tell you first is still my Dismay (LII 518).

In her hurry to explain the ways she may choose to process information, Dickinson gives the palm to hearing/reading—she distances
communication. And toward the end of the letter she uses a quatrain,
the last line of which—"Was it you that came?"—returns the reader to
the "flitting Coming."

> "Field Lilies" are Cleopatra's "Posies."
> I was re-reading "Oldport."
> Largest last, like Nature.
> Was it you that came? . . . .

The letter is signed "Your scholar."
As is her usual practice, Dickinson includes a poem in this missive.
"Because that you are going/And never coming back" is one of her
saddest and longest (as well as most stolidly paced) works. Originally
arranged in eight-line stanzas, the final version reverts to quatrains (and
is ten quatrains long). Although the poet reminds her reader that "Death
is final," she also describes their understanding of each other in the lines

> Significance that each has lived
> The other to detect . . . (Poem #1314 Fr 1135–40).

Although this poem veers off into stanzas that appear to question
Biblical wisdom, Dickinson may have completed her thinking in this
particular poem in a later round of writing; see Poem #1318 (Fr 1143):

> Our little secrets slink away—
> Beside God's shall not tell—
> He kept his word a Trillion years
> And might we not as well—
> But for the niggardly delight
> To make each other stare
> Is there no sweet beneath the sun
> With this that may compare.

The reader has only to compare and contrast these lines with those
that Dickinson had written to her cousins during the spring of the
previous year. In April of 1873, she burst out in apparent joy, "Spring is

a happiness so beautiful, so unique, so unexpected, that I don't know what to do with my heart . . . Life is a spell so exquisite that everything conspires to break it . . ." (LII 506).

Defeating the possibility of another spring rhapsody in 1874, again recorded in her letters to the cousins, is this awareness: "Father is ill at home. I think it is the 'Legislative' reacting on an otherwise obliging constitution" (LII 529). Dickinson writes this in February, 1874, and Edward Dickinson's diary notes that he is absent from the state legislature (to which he had been elected in early November, 1873) from late in February through early March.

In late May, 1874, Dickinson again writes Higginson. This time she responds to his Memorial Day poem, "Decoration," which appeared in a recent issue of *Scribner's Monthly*. She notes "You have experienced sanctity." She also explains that she has little to send him because "Existence has overpowered Books." She then comments on the fact that although Higginson has visited her twice (what she actually writes is "Twice, you have gone—Master") neither her brother nor her "sisters," evidently including Susan Gilbert Dickinson in her count, has seen him. On that premise, she asks him to return. (LII 525). This letter is unsigned.

With Edward Dickinson's returning to Boston for a session of the state senate in mid-June, the lives of the Dickinsons at both the Homestead and the Evergreens were nearly destroyed. By the evening of June 16, 1874, Edward is dead. So capacious had been the father's responsibility, so involving had been his interest in the activities of his three children and, to a certain extent, of his wife that his absence was deafening, blinding, horrifying.

After a weekend in Amherst, Dickinson had returned to his Tremont House room. On the morning of June 16, he spoke to the assembly about appropriations for the Troy and Greenfield Railroad (his election to represent the Fourth District of Hampshire County led to his being seated on the Special Committee of the Senate and the House on the Hoosac Tunnel line of railroads). Boston was melting down in a heat wave: Edward felt ill and returned to his hotel for lunch. When he talked with his physician, he was told he was apopleptic and was prescribed morphine. Austin later said that was what killed him; his father could never tolerate that drug (Wineapple 200).

Emily Dickinson's summer letter to the Norcross cousins tries to describe both her mental state and her all-encompassing sorrow. She speaks of not being able to "recall" herself, even though she had originally been "strongly built." In one brief paragraph she describes Austin's entering the house, holding the telegram that tells them of Edward's illness. The horses are being readied to take Austin and Vinnie into Boston, but then the second telegram arrives, announcing their father's death. In the next of her paragraphs, Dickinson wanders in her writing just as she did—after Edward's death—throughout the Homestead:

> Father does not live with us now—he lives in a new house . . . He hasn't any garden because he moved after gardens were made, so we take him the best flowers, and if we only knew he knew, perhaps we could stop crying.

She closes, "I cannot write any more, dears. Though it is many nights, my mind never comes home . . ." (LII 526).

This letter parallels and yet differs appreciably from her July, 1874, letter to Higginson. That focuses more definitely on Edward Dickinson. She writes, "His Heart was pure and terrible and I think no other like it exists. I am glad there is Immortality—but would have tested it myself—before entrusting him" (LII 528).

Dickinson opens this letter with the touching memory of her spending the weekend afternoon with her father—before he returned to his work in Boston.

> The last Afternoon that my Father lived, though with no premonition—I preferred to be with him, and invented an absence for Mother, Vinnie being asleep. He seemed peculiarly pleased as I oftenest stayed with myself, and remarked as the Afternoon withdrew, he "would like it to not end."

Similarly, in a letter to Mary Bowles, Dickinson retrieved her memory of Edward's being his caring and careful self: "The last April that father lived, lived I mean below, there were several snow-storms, and the birds were so frightened and cold they sat by the kitchen door. Father went to the barn in his slippers and came back with a breakfast of grain for each, and hid himself while he scattered it, lest it embarrass them. Ignorant of the name or fate of their benefactor, their descendants are singing this afternoon" (LII 662–3).

Clearly, Dickinson had become her father's daughter—or even her father's son—and her mourning for his loss was intense, long-lasting, and life-changing. Even though she had often felt that she could not please him, his influence radiated through her life and its choices: no other man could replace him, no other mentor could influence her. It seems likely that Edward Dickinson's influence was as great on all the other members of his household, but in his older daughter's poetry the record is described at its sharpest.

There is no mention in Dickinson's writing of her father's funeral. She did not attend it. She did not speak with any of the mourners who came to pay respects. Instead, she remained in her room upstairs, leaving the door ajar so she could hear what was being said downstairs and, with her windows open, outside. In the words of Theodora Van Wagenen Ward, "The foundations of Emily's life were severely shaken" (Ward 101).

The town of Amherst mourned Edward Dickinson. Stores closed on the Friday of his funeral, which was held in the packed entrance hall of the Homestead, "with ranks of settees on the front lawn for the overflow." According to Habegger, the Dickinsons—especially young Mattie—were "stunned by the intensity" of Austin's grief (Habegger 562). The service was starkly modest: only white daisies from the Dickinson garden were used, and his coffin was carried on the shoulders of college professors and businessmen, from the house to the grave (Murray 191). Similarly, for the memorial service on June 28, held in First Church and officiated by Reverend Jenkins, their neighbor, Emily again was absent. Samuel and Mary Bowles attended; Bowles had written the obituary that appeared in the *Springfield Republican*. One of the great men of Amherst was gone.

16
Surviving Death

A different stage of Emily Dickinson's writing life began in 1874. Despite the poet's genuine emotional involvement with the losses of war, with the bereavements of the families of the consumptive friends and acquaintances, with the disappointments of her often competitive nature, there was no loss like that of her father. As Roger Lundin summarizes, "The equilibrium that Dickinson had established by the mid-1870s was shattered when what she called the 'Dyings' began. Between the passing of her father in 1874 and her own death in 1886, she was to lose every person of importance to her, save her brother, sister, and sister-in-law . . . The death of her father . . . was the first great loss of many, and in some ways it proved to be the hardest" (Lundin 224).

In James McIntosh's critique of Dickinson's writing, after 1874 "her poetry reflects her awareness of the deaths of many closest to her and her contemplation of her own death" (McIntosh 37). During both 1874 and 1875, there are frequent groups of her poems that seem to memorialize her father, as well as the sudden and devastating circumstances of his death. Most of these poems are somber, although there is one comic effort: "Floss won't save you from an Abyss/But a Rope will" speaks with the acerbic tone familiar to earlier Dickinson poems. She discounts the physical charm of the Rope, she notes that the prices for both are "reasonable," but she points out the risks a person faces: "I tell you every step is a Trough—/ And every stop a well" (Poem #1335 Fr 1155). More often, Dickinson's poems are reflective, as in "The Pile of Years is not so high" (with its mention of using her Heart to enable her to reach what is valuable), or "Time does go on" and sometimes, writing that becomes abruptly descriptive:

> From his slim Palace in the Dust
> He relegates the Realm,

> More loyal for the exody
> That has befallen him (Poem #1337, Poem #1338, Poem #1339
>   Fr 1156–7).

In some poems, the poet figure's bereavement is the text, as in "Whether they have forgotten." Here the speaker protects herself from what might be indifference, but finally in the second stanza, has to admit

> Miseries of conjecture
> Are a softer wo
> Than a Fact of Iron
> Hardened with I know . . . (Poem #1334 Fr 1154–5).

Dodging the bullet of grief, Dickinson manages to keep writing as "Without a smile—Without a throe" and "As Summer into Autumn slips" tell her readers (Poem #1340, Poem #1341 Fr 1157–60). ·Both point toward "To flee from memory/Had we the Wings" and the more direct "Not with a Club, the Heart is broken/Nor with a Stone" (Poem #1343 and Poem #1349 Fr 1161–2, 1165). Had Dickinson had a shorter period of writing behind her, any reader might have thought these sentimental poems: instead, they are clear expressions of what she cannot bring into words in her living grief.

During 1875, Dickinson achieves more variation in her laments. "That short—potential stir/That each can make but once—/That Bustle so illustrious" then moves to definition, that "Bustle . . . Is the éclat of Death." This poem gains power when it is set against the mournful "Escape is such a thankful Word." (Poems #1363 and #1364 Fr 1184–5). In the latter poem, the middle stanza achieves the threatening soul-wrenching abyss:

> Escape—it is the Basket
> In which the Heart is caught
> When down some awful Battlement
> The rest of Life is dropt—

With her usual unexpectedly forceful word choice, Dickinson then continues to a third quatrain,

> 'Tis not to sight the savior—
> It is to be the saved—
> And that is why I lay my Head
> Opon this trusty word—

Dickinson's art is saving her . . . although what occurs within the Homestead may not show her grief ameliorated. As she had written in Poem #1353 (Fr 1174), "To pile like Thunder to it's close/Then crumble grand away/While everything created hid/This—would be Poetry//Or Love—the two coeval come."

Among her most impressive poems during this heavy period of almost unrelieved grief is "That sacred Closet when you sweep/Entitled 'Memory'" (Poem #1385 Fr 1209). Often referenced as a great poem about memory itself, it is frequently anthologized. It is another example of what surprises most critics, that Dickinson's grief did not bury her for long.

Part of her personal resilience may have come from hearing the good news that Susan and Austin were expecting their third child. Susan, at forty-four, was a conundrum: why had she chosen to carry a third child? Because Edward Dickinson had died intestate, Austin was truly mired in finding all the parts of the Dickinson estate. Perhaps the months-long responsibility had made him anxious about his own branch of the Dickinson family; only he and Susan had produced children and, bright and independent as both Ned and Mattie were, perhaps their parents should continue developing the family. (Habegger describes the indefinite situation that Edward's having left no will created. Emily Norcross was in no condition to become the legal executor. Austin, as the oldest child and the male, was accordingly in charge. What Austin did was, after securing the signatures of his sisters and his mother in early August, leave all legal matters unsolved for the next 20 years. He "did nothing to settle the estate by dividing it among the heirs . . . It was by *not* making a will that Edward gave Austin the means to take protective custody of his mother and sisters without anyone's interference," 563–4.)

There was no visible discomfort among Emily Norcross or her daughters, but perhaps more friction and anxiety existed than was apparent. Three hundred and sixty-four days after Edward's death, Emily Norcross had a severe stroke—and though she lives more than six years longer, she was at least partially paralyzed all that time. Immediately, Vinnie, Emily, and Maggie Maher took over her nursing.

It is at that point that Dickinson resumes her letters to Higginson. Dated "mid-June" 1875, her first note to him reads, "Mother was paralyzed Tuesday, a year from the evening Father died. I thought perhaps you would care." Signed "Your Scholar," the letter prompted a quick reply from Higginson. She then continued in a letter dated July, 1875, to assess her mother's improvement ("She was ignorant at the time and her Hand and Foot left her") and to explain why she deceives her parent—Dickinson does not tell Emily Norcross that she has had a stroke; she does not explain why Edward does not come to visit. About herself, Dickinson says quietly "Home is so far from Home, since my Father died" (LII 542).

In a letter to Elizabeth Holland a few months earlier, she had thanked that friend for her affection and her attention, saying "It helps me up the Stairs at Night, where as I passed my Father's Door—I used to think was safety." In other letters, she speaks of nightmares. Here, at the start of this letter to Elizabeth, she announces, "My House is a House of Snow—true—sadly—of few—" and describes "Father—in the Masked Bed—in the Marl House. . . . When I think of his firm Light—quenched so causelessly, it fritters the world of much that shines." (LII 537).

On August 1, 1875, Thomas Gilbert Dickinson is born. He will be known as "Gib," and beloved in ways that the Dickinson's first-born, Ned, could only envy. Emily's note to Sue says simply, "Emily and all that she has are at Sue's service, if of any comfort to Baby—Will send Maggie, if you will accept her—" The note is signed "Sister" (LII 543).

In later correspondence with Higginson, Dickinson does not mention Gib's birth. She instead offers him books which her father had purchased for her, and which she therefore felt she could not open. One was George Eliot's poem collection and the other, Frothingham's *Theodore Parker.* Higginson evidently owned the latter so in Dickinson's attempting to send him the Eliot book, several mishaps occurred (requiring three subsequent letters). The important elements of this January 1876 letter is that Dickinson enclosed five strong, recent poems. Of these, "The Heart is the Capital of the Mind" may be somewhat representative—abstract, aphoristic, and, in some respects, coping. The poet declares that "The Heart and the Mind together make/A single Continent" and then continues to urge the reader to recognize greatness in him/herself (Poem #1381 Fr 1201–3). Just as Dickinson has moved her grieving self back into her writing room (she later replies to Higginson's inquiry about what she is doing, "Little—wayfaring acts—comprise my 'pursuits'—and a few moments at night, for Books—after the rest sleep," LII 548), so she is now writing a kind of practice poem, carefully phrased. By 1877, her work has regained its power.

In the analysis of John Cody, Dickinson was so affected by Edward's death that she would probably never regain her earlier, hard-won autonomy. Because of her father's sheer force—and his disrespect of the feminine, an attitude that played out in his behavior toward her mother—she would never find a replacement for him, and to earn his love, she had herself become masculinized (Cody 101–2). In feminist analysis, Cody's psychological profile grew malignant: Wendy K. Perriman's lengthy treatise that pictures Dickinson as an incest survivor draws from psychoanalytic theory of recent decades, and explores Dickinson's shyness, her sleep problems, her inability to leave the house, her eating patterns and above all her reticence about sexuality in light of incest patients' reactions. *A Wounded Deer: The Effects of Incest on the Life and Poetry of Emily Dickinson* draws mainly from Dickinson's earlier poems, supporting Habegger's contention that Dickinson stopped trying to tell her own story after 1867 and 1868 (Perriman 169). The author also draws from the best of existing psychiatric analyses, so that her premises are reasonably well supported. She is particularly interested in what Jay Leyda calls "the missing center" of Dickinson's poems, the sudden shifts away from topics, the "gaps," and Dickinson's use of the child as speaker (Perriman 16–61).

Perhaps not recognized by many critics as *unnormal* behavior (a coined word to differentiate it from "abnormal") is Dickinson's correspondence with Mary Higginson. When Higginson's wife lost her father, Dickinson reached out—sending a note along with rosebuds. Begun in early 1876, this series of letters extended until Mary Channing Higginson died in 1877 on September 2, and seemed to exist separate from Dickinson's familiar correspondence with Higginson himself (in her letters to him she referred to his ailing wife as "his friend"). In Dickinson's spring, 1876, letter to Mary Higginson, she explains,

> The tie to one we do not know, is slightly miraculous, but not humbled by test, if we are simple and sacred. Thank you for recollecting me. I have now no Father, and scarcely a Mother, for her Will followed my Father, and only an idle Heart is left, listless for his sake.
>
>   I am sorry your Hand harms you—is it easier now? Mr. Higginson told me you loved the Buds—You should own my own, but the Orchard is too jocund to fold and the Robins would rob the mail. Who knocks not, yet does not intrude, is Nature . . . (LII 555).

Writing easily, with her family-oriented "joke" coming at the end of the second paragraph, Dickinson yet shares with Mary Higginson what she thinks is important for the similarly bereaved woman to know about her new correspondent.

By the holidays, there is even more familiarity in Dickinson's letters. A note dated Christmas 1876 opens, "Dear friend./I wish you were strong like me."

Interspersed with her letters to Mary Higginson are Dickinson's letters to Higginson himself: she seldom fails to mention Edward or the fact of Edward's death. In a spring, 1876, letter, for example, she comments, "When I think of my Father's lonely Life and his lonelier Death . . ." (LII 551). In her August, 1876, letter, she juxtaposes good wishes for Mary with her axiomatic commentary:

> I hope Mrs. Higginson is no more ill. I am glad if I did not disturb her. Loneliness for my own Father made me think of her. Always begins by degrees (LII 558).

In a June, 1877, letter, once more, Dickinson writes, "Summer is so kind I had hoped you might come. Since my Father's dying, everything sacred enlarged so—it was dim to own" (LII 583).

After reading that Mary Channing Higginson had died, Dickinson wrote the bereaved husband two short notes, offering her help: "If I could help you?" begins the second letter, closing "Did she know she was leaving you? The Wilderness is new—to you. Master, let me lead you" (LII 590).

In a longer letter that same month, Dickinson notes, "We must be less than Death, to be lessened by it—for nothing is irrevocable but ourselves. I am glad you are better" (LII 591). More poignant is her second "early autumn" note: "Danger is not at first, for then we are unconscious, but in the after—slower—Days—" (LII 594).

It will be another several years before Dickinson writes anything of an intimate nature to Higginson, and then she admits, "I am sorry not to have seen your 'Hawthorne,' but have known little of Literature since my Father died—that and the passing of Mr. Bowles, and Mother's hopeless illness, overwhelmed my Moments . . ." (LII 635).

17

"Mother's Hopeless Illness"

When Samuel Bowles died, Dickinson felt that another blow had landed squarely on both her heart and on the Dickinson family's collective well-being. Early in 1878, his funeral attended by Vinnie and Austin, the Dickinsons were still able to rejoice that Austin had survived his two-months of malaria more than a year earlier; and that Ned was learning to cope with what had clearly become his chronic attacks of epilepsy. In Dickinson's rushed world of caring for her mother and the various members of Austin's family, the years passed as if they were months.

The existence of the Dickinson family in both its locations—the Homestead and the Evergreens—had become centered fully on the care of its children, and the care of its aging. Many households had been so organized in this focus for their whole existence. The Dickinsons, however, had usually pictured themselves as much more integrated into the community. The life of Amherst was in many respects the life of the Dickinsons.

Embedded in the profile of the Dickinson family, housed so prominently in its two comparative mansions, was the tradition of success (and in nineteenth century America, that success would be determined by the male members of the family). When Ned was taken by his first epileptic seizure during a mid-February night in 1877, and then experienced a second seizure the following morning, in the doctor's presence, the family felt only dismay. The family doctor, Dr. Fiske, feared that the fits were connected to the rheumatic fever Ned had had in 1874 (Gordon 133).

As Gordon summarized the family's response, "Ned's seizures were unpredictable, though Austin records after one attack: 'I noticed his eyes an hour before bedtime last night as very black and bright'" (Gordon 135).

"Ned was not told he had epilepsy. He'd wake in the morning with no sign beside a sore tongue and sometimes a headache, which Sue would treat with 'fomentation.' It could happen that a headache preceded an attack and heavy breathing might follow. Some seizures were mild enough for Ned to go to classes the next day. Some were so violent they shook the house" (Gordon 135).

This critic then summarizes the entries from a diary that Austin kept during 1880, in which he recorded Ned's illness patterns when he was 19 and attending Amherst College. He had eight seizures that year, all "at night, about one hour into sleep. . . . At any sound, Austin would leap over the rails at the bottom of the bed he shared with Sue and rush upstairs. It was always Austin who went and he never got used to the groans from Ned's room, the foaming mouth, the spasms of mouth, neck, and chest, and the strained breathing that followed convulsions [which he called] 'distressing to see'" (Gordon 135).

Given the dramatic nature of Ned's episodes, perhaps the quiet languishing of Emily Norcross Dickinson in the house next door deserved little description: long-lasting as it was, it was little changing as the aging woman continued to wear away. There is one fall in which she breaks a hip, which means she does not walk again; but her consciousness is so blurred that she seems to have no preference for caregivers—sometimes Vinnie attends her, sometimes Emily, sometimes Maggie. Just as Emily was probably going through menopause during her mother's being bedfast, so her mother's threat to her well-being as a woman became of less importance. Betsy Erkkila points out that once menopause had occurred, "motherhood no longer represented a threat to the poetic work she [Dickinson] had already pursued on her own terms" (Erkkila 48). This critic further discusses the fact that Emily Norcross was in many ways, during this long illness, herself childlike. Dickinson describes her mother's health to Elizabeth Holland, in early 1878, as "tranquil, though trifling. She reads a little—sleeps much—chats—perhaps—most of all—about nothing momentous, but things vital to her—and reminds one of Hawthorne's blameless Ship—that forgot the Port—" (LII 604).

By the time of their mother's stroke, both the daughters knew that Vinnie was in charge of the Homestead. Throughout Dickinson's letters, her reliance on her younger sister is a consistent emphasis; as early as 1859 she wrote to Mrs. Joseph Haven, "Vinnie has been all, so long, I feel the oddest fright at parting with her for an hour, lest a storm arise, and I go unsheltered" (LII 346). In 1873, Dickinson thanks Elizabeth Holland for her kindness to Vinnie, saying "She has no Father and

Mother but me and I have no Parents but her" (LII 508). And after their mother's stroke, Dickinson notes, "Brave Vinnie is well—Mother does not yet stand alone and fears she never shall walk, but I tell her we all shall fly so soon, not to let it grieve her, and what indeed is Earth but a Nest, from whose rim we are all falling?" (LII 648).

Vinnie as household manager apportioned the menial duties, which included caring for Emily Norcross, and oversaw the men who helped with the grounds and flowers; Maggie Maher; any one else hired temporarily to aid Maggie; and herself and Emily. When Aife Murray considers the close bond that developed between Maggie and Dickinson, leading the latter to ask Maggie to keep her fascicles in Maggie's room, stored in her trunk, she also comments about Vinnie's relationship with the servants. In fact, she makes clear that Maggie worries about the amount of work Vinnie takes on, particularly after her mother's debility (Murray 203–4).

Two new strands of activity begin to appear in Dickinson's letters and poems. Starting in the fall of 1877, both Higginson and Judge Otis Phillips Lord had become widowers: while Dickinson had long been communicating with the former, her contact with her father's friend, Judge Lord, a conservative Whig who shared Edward's political stands, had been largely familial. Judge Lord had visited the Dickinsons at their Homestead several times, usually bringing his wife Elizabeth with him. Chosen to become a justice in the Supreme Court of Massachusetts late in 1875, he and his wife visited the Dickinson family in October of 1876—just before Austin's contracting malaria. By December of the following year, Mrs. Lord was dead. Even as Judge Lord had worried about Emily's health, he and his wife assumed she had ailments connected with aging, not cancer. (See Walsh's *Emily Dickinson in Love*, 2012, for a different version of this relationship.)

A second connection that stemmed, at least partly, from Higginson was the rekindled friendship between Dickinson and her childhood friend, Helen Hunt—a well-known writer of both fiction and poetry. Through Higginson, Helen Hunt urged Dickinson to publish; much of their subsequent correspondence deals with that topic. Rather than a friendship like the one between Dickinson and Elizabeth Holland, Helen Hunt (later Helen Hunt Jackson) reminds the reader of a very limited, and pesky, acquaintance.

In the autumn of 1880, Judge Lord makes three visits to the Dickinsons. The first includes his family of in-laws; the second, his niece, a woman Dickinson had enjoyed on previous visits. The third visit he comes alone—as he will frequently do over the next several years. For Christmas of 1880, he brings the *Concordance to Shakespeare* for Dickinson. As both Habegger and Wineapple clarify, the drafts of letters from Dickinson to Lord that appear in the three-volume *Letters* are misdated. Although there was correspondence between Dickinson and Judge Lord for some years, these fragments of what appear to be love letters would not have existed until after Mrs. Lord's death. They probably were written in 1881 and 1882 (Habegger 587, Wineapple 221). Because Vinnie destroyed the personal letters Dickinson had received after her death—at the poet's request—and because her letters to Lord are also missing, what remains are the notes and earlier versions of some of Dickinson's letters to him. At one point in their courtship, they wrote letters to each other every week (the Judge continued to live in Salem); to have lost this correspondence leaves a serious gap in the narratives of both their lives.

For critic Brenda Wineapple, the fragments and drafts of Dickinson's letters to Judge Lord should be categorized along with the earlier "Master" letters, written from 1859 through 1862, and perhaps unsent. She describes the "Lord" letters as filled with "passion, subtlety, and wit," and yet, because they are drafts, perhaps mislead the reader. They may "tease the reader rather than illuminate the relationship between Dickinson and a man eighteen years her senior" (Wineapple 222). When John Cody assesses the relationship, he concludes that Dickinson "thought of Judge Lord as a paternal, benign, loving parent. He, however, did not regard her primarily as a daughter" (Cody 100). In John Walsh's recent book, he gives an account of a love that began decades before Elizabeth Lord's death.

Dickinson's poems that date from 1877, 1878, 1879, and 1880 tell the reader a widely varied story. Fewer of these works center on loss. It is as if in the poet's grieving over the death of her father in 1874, and exploring his absence in the strong poems of 1875 and 1876, she has found a different cast for her emotional—and poetic—energy.

In 1876, she is still elaborating on the theme of mourning, as in Poem #1398:

> Gathered into the Earth,
> And out of story—
> Gathered to that strange Fame—
> That lonesome Glory
> That hath no omen here—but Awe— (Fr 1220).

Strangely contemporary in Dickinson's emphasis on the ending of "story," this poem draws again on the concept of "Awe," a many-faceted noun for her that she has used in the place of Sun: a radiating power, a force that seems to incorporate the observer's psyche as well as the source itself.

Grouped with the poems of nature she was increasingly returning to, such as "The Worthlessness of Earthly things/The Sermon is that Nature sings" and "Touch lightly Nature's sweet Guitar," "Gathered into the Earth" is part of what becomes an expressive foundation for the poet's years-long grief (Poems #1400 and #1402 Fr 1221–3). "In many and reportless places/We feel a Joy" fuses these elements: the poet once again draws on both the beauties and the cyclic patterns of nature for her metaphors (Poem #1404 Fr 1224).

In some poems, this metaphoric equivalence is literal:

> Summer laid her simple Hat
> On it's boundless shelf—
> Unobserved a Ribbon dropt—
> Snatch it for yourself!
>
> Summer laid her supple Glove
> In it's sylvan Drawer—
> Wheresoe'er, or was she—
> The demand of Awe? (Poem #1411 Fr 1228–31)

Relying on the staple of the all-significant "Awe," this poem connects with the poetry of lament written earlier. In other poems, the descriptive lines are truly metaphoric: "How fits his Umber coat," "Trust as the stars," "These held their Wick above the West." (Poems #1414, #1415, #1416 Fr 1234–6).

By 1877, along with her impressive poems of nature comes a series of "larger" poems such as

> How much the present moment means
> To those who've nothing more . . . (Poem #1420 Fr 1239).

and "What mystery pervades a well!" (Poem #1433 Fr 1253–5). It is in August of this year that Dickinson sends a group of four poems to Higginson (after many months without such a submission). It is as if the critic in the poet knows that her energy as writer has returned. According to Murray, whereas Dickinson wrote only 31 poems in 1876, there are 42 poems dated 1877 (Murray 79).

One of the most original of Dickinson's later poems is "It sounded as if the streets were running/And then—the streets stood still." Several variants of the poem exist, most of them using the word "air" instead of "streets." The concrete noun makes the reader pay attention: macabre in its imaginative pull, this surreal image gives wider dimension to lines three and four, which introduces the concept of "Awe" again, and this time links that noun with "Time."

> Eclipse was all we could see at the Window
> And Awe—was all we could feel—

In a striking closing metaphor, Dickinson once again personifies her true subject:

> Nature was in an Opal Apron—
> Mixing fresher Air (Poem #1454 Fr 1272–4).

Set in stark contrast to "It sounded as if the streets were running" is the slowly paced "I have no life to live/But lead it here" (Poem #1432 Fr 1251–2). Again, Dickinson takes this two-quatrain poem through several versions, beginning with these opening lines,

> I have no Life but this—
> To lead it here . . .

Similarly, whereas the several early versions end with the lines "The love of you" and "The loving you," this final copy has as its closing "The Realm of you." Notes suggest that this poem was intended for Samuel Bowles (to whom Dickinson had years before sent those enigmatic "wife" poems), and that when Dickinson sent it to Higginson—with the closing line using "Realm," she described it as "Word to a Friend."

A third 1877 poem was more conventional in both content and form. "She laid her docile Crescent down" (with the male pronoun later replacing the "She") included other changes. The second line has a word replaced: "And this *mechanic* Stone" becomes "And this *confiding* Stone." The poem invokes sorrow for the person who has died ("she" in earlier versions and "he" in the final) (Poem #1453 Fr 1270–2). Like this third poem of the group, "After all Birds have been investigated" (the fourth poem) Dickinson includes revised versions—"Birds" dates originally from several years before. In this carefully paced poem, the poet reverts to the long line followed by, and accented by, a shorter:

> After all Birds have been investigated
> And laid aside

> Nature imparts the little Blue Bird—
> Assured

While establishing what becomes a voiced emphasis, Dickinson here continues the sentence that "Assured" starts,

> Her conscientious voice
> Will soar unmoved
> Above ostensible vicissitude . . . (Poem #1383 Fr 1204).

This steady yet accented pace continues in several of her poems from both 1878 and 1879—"I thought the Train would never come," "The Road was lit with Moon and star," "A Chilly Peace infests the Green" and the rigorously honest "Your thoughts don't have words every day" (Poems #1473, #1474, #1469, #1476 Fr 1286–7, 1289–91). This last poem pairs with "Oh, honey of an hour," a shorter poem found in a letter draft to Judge Lord. The two collectively set up Dickinson's aesthetic—and explains in part why she is so diligent about her work with words.

> Your thoughts don't have words every day
> They come a single time
> Like signal esoteric sips
> Of the communion Wine
> Which while you taste so native seems
> So easy so to be
> You cannot comprehend it's price—
> Nor it's infrequency.

Compared with "Oh, honey of an hour," the elements that echo are the unveiling of either passion or skill. The latter poem focuses more definitely on the marriage rite, when Dickinson speaks of "my minutest dower," in the search for being deserving (Poem #1477 Fr 1291–2).

Suggesting that other of these works were intended to be a part of a letter, the note that accompanied "A Chilly Peace infests the Grass" read "Nature, the sweet parishioner, trust *her*." Similarly, late in 1878, Dickinson's "We knew not that we were to live" was directed to Higginson, after she had read of his engagement to Mary Potter Thacher in the *Springfield Republican*. Her preface to that eight-line poem reads, "Till it has loved—no man or woman can become itself—Of our first

Creation we are unconscious." Wineapple, for one, was sure that Dickinson's disappointment upon reading about her friend's engagement made her lean more favorably toward the suite Judge Lord was pressing (Wineapple 219). It is true that the frequency of Dickinson's letters to Higginson diminished appreciably.

18
Courtships

All the Dickinson acquaintances knew that Vinnie was the daughter who would marry—she was pretty, she was vivacious, she was far from shy. During the early years of their mother's illness, both Vinnie and Emily seemed to be encouraging suitors—Vinnie was courted visibly by a Northampton banker (Longsworth Amherst 67), and we have seen that, after months of hesitation, Dickinson seemed to encourage Judge Lord. It will be several years later before Austin brings an unexpected scandal to the pristine Dickinson name, when he falls in love with the young wife of Amherst College's new astronomer. The consequences for not only the Dickinson family, but for the efforts to preserve Emily Dickinson's work, are far-reaching.

Vinnie does not marry. Neither does Emily. Both women are struggling to maintain their mother's health along with their own: Maggie Maher attests to the tremendous burden the care of Emily Norcross has become, and Murray quotes the words of two of Maggie's great-grandnieces, 70 years after her death, that she was "working much too hard there at the Dickinsons." (Murray also notes that "Austin and Sue had both a cook and a maid, as did most of the Dickinson's peers," 115.)

To the suggestion that Emily Dickinson liked the alternation of physical and kitchen work with her writing, one might disagree: we have seen how distraught she became once Margaret O'Brien married and left their household. Added to what was already a busy house then, their mother's illness was hardly inconsequential. In Dickinson's words, "The responsibility of Pathos is almost more than the responsibility of Care. Mother will never walk. She still makes her little Voyages from her Bed to her Chair in a Strong Man's Arms—probably that will be all" (LIII 675). About the same time Dickinson writes to the Norcross cousins, "Mother's dear little wants so engross the time,—to read to her, to fan her, to tell her health will come tomorrow, to explain to her why the grasshopper is a burden, because he is not so new a grasshopper as he was,—this is so ensuing, I hardly have said 'Good-morning, mother' when I hear myself saying 'Mother, good-night.'" In this period, Dickinson tells Lou and Fanny that Maggie's brother has been killed in the mine, "and Maggie wants to die, but Death goes far around to those that want to see him. If the little cousins would give her a note—she does not know I ask it—I think it would help her begin, that bleeding beginning that every mourner knows" (LIII 678). It is occasions like this, plentiful as they are in Dickinson's correspondence, that leads Roger Lundin to describe what he calls Dickinson's "self-styled ministry of consolation" (Lundin 243).

The following year, Josiah Holland dies after a sudden heart attack, and Dickinson's constant flow of letters to Elizabeth illustrates the importance she herself finds in consolation. Of the first of the half dozen letters written in the month after his death, Dickinson laments, "We read the words but know them not. We are too frightened with sorrow. If that dear, tired one must sleep, could we not see him first? . . . Our hearts have flown to you before—our breaking voices follow. How can we wait to take you all in our sheltering arms?" (LIII 712).

A few weeks later, Dickinson's letter opens, "After a while, dear, you will remember that there is a heaven—but you can't now. Jesus will excuse it." As she often does in these letters of consolation, Dickinson asks about the circumstances of Dr. Holland's dying, "I am yearning to know if he knew he was fleeing—if he spoke to you. Dare I ask if he suffered? Some one will tell me a very little, when they have the strength . . . Cling tight to the hearts that will not let you fall" (LIII 713). And one of Dickinson's most poignant letters to Elizabeth recalls her last sight of Josiah, linking this memoir to the fact that she has just stored his recent essays away in her cabinet drawer,

> It shall always remain there—nearest us—in the Room to the East Father loved the most, and where I bade the Doctor Good Night, that November Morning—He put one Hand on Vinnie's Head and the other on mine, and his Heart on your's, as we both knew, and said that the Sunshine and the Scene he should always remember (LIII 718).

In Dickinson's greatest poems, and in her continuous relationships with her friends, the power of anecdote—of characterization, of form, of aesthetic conveyance—shone through.

As Murray summarized about this time in Dickinson's life, here at the start of the 1880s,

> The tight family unit came undone. Two friends the poet held dear passed from the scene: Josiah Holland died in October 1881 and was followed in six months by Charles Wadsworth. Emily's mother was buried that fall of 1882 to be followed a year later by her eight-year-old nephew Gib. She coped with her maid's bout with typhoid, and her brother's attack of malaria. Recovered from the malaria but not the loss of his son, Austin leaped headlong into his torrid affair with Mabel Todd the month after Gib's burial . . . Four months later, in March 1884, Otis Lord passed away (Murray 202).

Not to suggest that such a sorrowful chronology holds mysteries about Dickinson's art—or her ability to keep producing that art even in the midst of such losses—but it is a commonplace of such expert critics as Richard Gray to combine death and love and aesthetics in his assessment of Dickinson's achievements, poems that "ignite awareness." He speaks of the value in recognizing "the sense of the circumscriptions imposed on the isolate self . . . her condition and subject was isolation . . . her 'self' was 'a prisonhouse' and her poetic mission 'was to explore the dimensions of her call: to find out what could be felt or known, what surmised or guessed at . . . The result is a poetry that manages to be at once passionate and sly, visionary and ironic" (Gray 111–13).

Perhaps Otis Lord thought more modestly about Dickinson's poems, when in 1863 she mailed to him a copy of "The Judge is like the Owl." Emphasizing his wit as well as his wisdom, the poem describes his acerbic, sometimes tough, humor (demeanor Wineapple calls "hotheaded, gruff, and arrogant," 221). In the poem's second line, Dickinson links "the Judge" with her father ("I've heard my Father tell"), and concludes that she asks from him, the Judge-Owl, in exchange for her poem, "a Tune/ At Midnight" (Poem #728 Fr 691–2).

As explained earlier, the misdating of drafts of letters from Dickinson to Lord, and the sheer absence of a correspondence that likely ran for several years, handicaps any biographer's recreation of the relationship between the widower judge and the younger, never-married poet. Guthrie sees the relationship as compatible, saying, in fact, that Dickinson's concept of "heaven" grew into a state bound by physical bodies. "Having been made acutely aware in middle age both of the transitoriness of earthly experience and of the rarity of physical, passionate love, Dickinson could no longer countenance a heaven with physical substance, either of the earth or of the flesh" (Guthrie 115). He reads what remains of their correspondence with attention to patterns that he terms "erotic play" and "coded" references. Any critic must realize, of course, that what occurs in Dickinson's drafts may not have been included in the letters actually sent. But even without the actual texts, Guthrie's assessment that Dickinson "employs her poems as instruments of persuasion and seduction, or as mock legal documents" seems valid (Guthrie 155).

He is accurate when he notes that "They maintained a weekly correspondence of which only scraps survive, all written by her to him, yet these few remnants show that Dickinson and Lord negotiated at length with each other over such issues as how much sexual license she would grant him during his visits, if and when their relationship might be formalized, and whether she might ultimately move into Lord's house at Salem" (Guthrie 156).

"My lovely Salem smiles at me I seek his Face so often—but I am past disguises (have dropped—) (have done with guises—)//I confess that I love him—I rejoice that I love him—I thank the maker of Heaven and Earth that gave him me to love—the exultation floods me—I can not find my channel—The Creek turned Sea at thoughts of thee—will you punish it—. . . " (LII 615). Dated in error 1878, this draft fragment no doubt belongs toward the end of the fragmentary correspondence, but it reveals how forthright Dickinson was. Given that both Susan Gilbert Dickinson and Lord's niece Abby were growing worried about the seriousness of the relationship, this kind of correspondence supports their observations.

When Dickinson's niece Mattie recalled the courtship, she described the Judge's bringing his niece Abby and giving her the coach for her and her friends, while he and Emily "enjoyed their own adventures in conversation at home" (in Lundin 246). They relished stories and banter; Mattie recalled that "their enjoyment of the comedy of every day was . . . broadly akin," and she remembered Aunt Emily terming certain kinds of humor and jokes "The Judge Lord brand" (in Lundin 246).

It was clear that the courtship was steadily developing during the year 1882 because the scene of Dickinson's hearing that Judge Lord's health was so fragile that Vinnie had read about his condition in the newspaper occurred early in that spring. She later writes to Lord May 14, 1882, that after Vinnie had told her, "Mr. Lord is very sick," "I grasped at a passing Chair. My sight slipped and I thought I was freezing. While my last smile was ending, I heard the Doorbell ring and a strange voice said 'I thought first of you.' Meanwhile Tom [Kelley, one of the Homestead crew] had come and I ran to his Blue Jacket and let my Heart break there—that was the warmest place. 'He will be better. Don't cry Miss Emily. I could not see you cry'" (LIII 730). Murray suggests that Dickinson's favoring Tom Kelley (leaving word that he is to be head pallbearer at her funeral) stems from this incident, which shows his evident understanding of her emotional life (Murray 192).

Emily and Vinnie send a telegram to Salem; Lord is severely ill for several days, weeks. But the correspondence begins again.

There is the comic draft of Ned's asking his aunt what church Judge Lord belongs to—and her reasonable defense, even if "murmurless" (LII 616). There is her longing for a letter "To beg for the Letter when it is written, is bankrupt enough, but to beg for it when it is'nt, and the dear Donor is sauntering, mindless of it's worth, that is *bankrupter* . . ." She closes that note with a kind of admonition, "Perhaps, please, you are sinful? Though of power to make Perdition divine, who can punish you?" (LII 616). There is, too, the often quoted letter about sexuality:

Dont you know you are happiest while I withhold and not confer— don't you know that "No" is the wildest word we consign to Language?

You do, for you know all things—[top of sheet cut off] . . . to lie so near your longing—to touch it as I passed, for I am but a restive sleeper and often should journey from your Arms through the happy night, but you will lift me back, wont you, for only there I ask to be—I say, if I felt the longing nearer—than in our dear past, perhaps I could not resist to bless it, but must, because it would be right.

The "Stile" is God's—My Sweet One—for your great sake—not mine—I will not let you cross—but it is all your's, and when it is right I will lift the Bars, and lay you in the Moss—You showed me the word.

I hope it has no different guise when my fingers make it. It is Anguish I Long conceal from you to let you leave me, hungry, but you ask the divine Crust And that would doom the Bread.

That unfrequented Flower . . . the Bible says very roguishly, that the "wayfaring Man, though a Fool—need not err therein"; need the "wayfaring" Woman? Ask your throbbing Scripture . . . (LII 617).

Images of tumescence occur regularly in her drafts, but as John Cody emphasizes about this particular letter, what is most significant is not the long quotation above but the fact that Dickinson points out to Lord, "I have a strong surmise that moments we have *not* known are tenderest to you" (in Cody 101).

Guthrie summarizes much of this drafted correspondence by describing Dickinson's "earthy sense of humor, a disputatious turn of mind, and a keen sense of pride in her identity as poet" (Guthrie 155). Perhaps more visible is Dickinson's sense of self as a woman beloved by a man trying to be worthy of her.

Obviously, not all of Dickinson's letters are sexual. To see the kinds of drafting she was doing, a shorter note—primarily about her waiting for the days to pass so that she can envision his writing—shows her careful word choices:

> Tuesday is a deeply depressing Day—it is not far enough from your dear note for the embryo of another to form, and yet what flights of Distance—and so I perish softly and spurn the Birds (spring) and spurn the Sun—with pathetic (dejected) malice—but when the Sun begins to turn the corner Thursday night—everything refreshes—the soft uplifting grows till by the time it is Sunday night, all my Life (Cheek) is Fever with nearness to your blissful words—(rippling words) . . . (LII 618).

Habegger thinks that once Emily Norcross Dickinson has died, November 14, 1882, Judge Lord's proposal materializes in fact, and that the illnesses of both the lovers eventually interfered with their love and their protestations of it (Habegger 390–1).

Reading the remnants of Dickinson's correspondence prompts a consideration of one of Cindy MacKenzie's points about the way the poet used her experience within her art. Filled with pain as her poetry often is, this critic notes that Dickinson's pain "enters the text obliquely, for the biographical elements do not constitute the subject of poetry so much as its hermeneutics. The poet's language inscribes her awareness of the inescapable condition of human experience" (MacKenzie 51).

For instance, although "I groped for him before I knew" is often connected with Dickinson's feelings for Lord, it is written on the back of a sheet of paper that Vinnie was using to compose a thank you letter, after her mother's death and in her mother's name. Dickinson might have had double narrative intentions, then, with the "him" being a religious referent (Poem #1585 Fr 1388).

> I groped for him before I knew
> With solemn nameless need. . . .

To think that the loss of Emily Norcross was not grievous is to miss a cluster of letters that Dickinson wrote to friends: for example, to Fanny and Lou, "I hoped to write you before, but Mother's dying almost stunned my spirit" (LIII 749). And the following month, to Elizabeth Holland,

> I have thought of you with confiding Love, but to speak seemed taken from me—Blow has followed blow, till the wondering terror of the Mind clutches what is left, helpless of an accent . . .
>
> Mother has now been gone five Weeks. We should have thought it a long Visit, were she coming back—Now the "Forever" thought almost shortens it, as we are nearer rejoining her than her own return—We were never intimate Mother and Children while she was our Mother—but Mines in the same Ground meet by tunneling and when she became our Child, the Affection came—When we were Children and she journeyed, she always brought us something. Now, would she bring us but herself, what an only Gift—Memory is a strange Bell—Jubilee, and Knell . . . (LIII 755).

To Judge Lord she confides, "The Month in which our Mother died, closed it's Drama Thursday, and I cannot conjecture a form of space without her timid face. Speaking to you as I feel, Dear, without that Dress of Spirit must be worn for most, Courage is quite changed." Earlier in this December 3, 1882, letter she explains, "While others go to Church, I go to mine, for are not you my Church, and have we not a Hymn that no one knows but us?" (LIII 753).

Dickinson mentions to several people that her mother had eaten some supper, and seemed more alert, "better." Then she died quietly. "She slipped from our fingers like a flake gathered by the wind, and is now part of the drift called 'the infinite . . . Mother was very beautiful when she had died. Seraphs are solemn artists. The illumination that comes but once paused upon her features, and it seemed like hiding a picture to lay her in the grave; but the grass that received my father will suffice his guest, the one he asked at the altar to visit him all his life.//I cannot tell how Eternity seems. It sweeps around me like a sea" (LIII 750).

Reading Dickinson's late life becomes a measure of cherishing what correspondence remains. Murray counts a substantial increase in the ratio of letters to poems here in the 1880s: for example, in 1883, Dickinson wrote 34 poems but 84 letters, and in 1884, the ratio remains similar: 42 poems to 80 letters (Murray 80). Habegger points out that "two thirds of Dickinson's surviving notes and letters date from her last sixteen years," a fact he attributes to her "active social and expressive impulses . . . within her well-regulated seclusion" (Habegger 541).

19

"The Poets Light but Lamps"

For all the critical attention to Dickinson's composing the fascicles (a period that ran only from sometime in 1858 through months of 1864), there has been little commentary on the long pages of copied poems (called "sets") which followed. There has been still less notice of the arrangements Dickinson used at the end of her career. A few critics have offered readings of her poetry based on the assumption that from the mid-seventies until her death, few lines separated "poem" from "letter." But more radically and more recently, the composition of each whole—however defined—has begun to come under scrutiny.

Ellen Hart and Martha Nell Smith explain the reason for their publishing *Open Me Carefully*, for example, as one attempt to capture what they see as an elusive wholeness—poems and letters, held together rather than separated. Between the 1870s and Dickinson's death May 15, 1886, "the correspondence from Emily to Susan features dramatic personal statements and remarkable manuscript art" (Hart and Smith 203).

What these critics refer to as "manuscript art," Murray explains as a tendency to create assemblage—perhaps nodding to European "artists' books, where the boundaries between image and text were blurred" (Murray 113). She points as well to Dickinson's increasing tendency during the 1870s and 1880s "to writing on wings of envelopes and fragmentary stationery, often fixed to another with a straight pin" (Murray 112).

Like Marta Werner and Aliki Barnstone, Murray sees the poet's designs as intentional rather than just a thrifty nature at work: "Sometimes the scraps and miscellaneous sheets Emily found were places to hastily make notes for the development of a poem. When the writing is squeezed into the margins around a magazine article, it's easy to picture feverish haste. On other occasions, they appear to be points of departure, an intentional mix of media with chance providing the sort of wry amusement and stimulus that artists . . . thrive on" (Murray 112). Murray would include all of Dickinson's creating art in her discussions—fascicles and sets, broadsides and relics from the natural world, as well as the later more fragmented materials. Such an elastic approach would be more useful to an artist of language than to a painter, who would privilege the visual.

This critic too sees Dickinson's poetry as stemming from the domestic arts. She points out that "Sewing book bindings was part of a continuum with needlework performed in the company of family and friends. Writing on food wrappers and old invitations was harmonious with every other frugal motion carried out on her kitchen table" (Murray 113).

Poet Susan Howe had—decades ago—called for a facsimile edition of Dickinson's poems that would replicate textures and fragments as well as language and format (Howe Birth 146). When Aliki Barnstone re-emphasizes what Howe had written, her phrase is "typographical replicas" for all dimensions of each poem (Barnstone 115). It is Barnstone's 2005 book that makes the most persuasive argument for the consideration of Dickinson's letters and poems as inseparable.

Some sense of the possibility that Howe and Barnstone suggest can be derived from comparing the seven versions of Dickinson's 1884 sextain, "Though the Great Waters sleep." All versions are written in pencil, the first known consisting of only the initial three lines. This poem is written on a fragment of stationery and coupled with two versions of a different poem, "A world made penniless by his departure."

The second version is the complete six lines, divided into tercets, but the leaf of stationery that holds the writing differs from the first:

> Though the Great Waters sleep,
> That they are still the Deep,
> We cannot doubt—
>
> No vacillating God
> Ignited this Abode
> To put it out— (Poem #1641 Fr 1438–41).

A third copy was written in "two fragments of stationery pinned together, three lines of the poem on each." A fourth is combined with different lines, memorializing Samuel Bowles and sent together to Sue for a biographer of Bowles:

> You remember his swift way of wringing and flinging away a Theme, and others picking and gazing bewildered after him, and the prance that crossed his Eye at such times was unrepeatable—

The fifth copy of the poem appears in Dickinson's letter of thanks to Catherine Sweetset, who sent her flowers in November, 1884, the second anniversary of her mother's death. In her note to her aunt, Dickinson recalls that her father Edward has been gone a decade, and her nephew Gib nearly a year:

> Father rose in June, and a little more than a year since, those fair words were fulfilled, "and a little child shall lead them"—but boundlessness forbids me.

The sixth copy was sent—after Judge Lord's death-to-Benjamin Kimball, the executor of his will. The seventh was included in early 1886 in a note of sympathy to Abigail Cooper. The poet's accompanying note reads, "Is it too late to express my sorrow for my grieved friend? Though the first moment of loss is eternity other eternities remain."

To imagine the richnesses of the way Dickinson both read and envisioned this poem through its seven versions and placements is to bring worlds of new force to it. In contrast, an important poem from several years earlier (1874, the year of Edward's death) exists in only one copy, written in pencil on "a leaf of stationery."

> Wonder—is not precisely knowing
> And not precisely knowing not—
> A beautiful but bleak condition
> He has not lived who has not felt—
>
> Suspense—is his mature Sister—
> Whether Adult Delight is Pain
> Or of itself a new misgiving—
> This is the Gnat that mangles men— (Poem #1347 Fr 1163).

Characteristic of Dickinson's pointed and always effective word play, this mélange of negatives becomes one of her riddle poems. Besides calling attention to a unique definition of "wonder," the opening lines set in motion an emphatic pace that bombards the reader. "Wonder" as "a beautiful but bleak condition" balances with the opening single word of the second stanza, and "Suspense" then folds into the combination of "Delight" and "Pain." Dickinson chooses a harsh line of direct statement to close: not dependent on any other part of the poem, both "Gnat" and "mangles" are unexpected—and irreconcilable. The poet takes the reader far from the usual connotation of "Wonder" to end in a heap of despair, far removed from the word play of the poem's opening.

One of Dickinson's most effective poems from the 1870s, "Wonder is not precisely knowing" is not embroidered by texture or arrangement: in the older pattern of the poet's aesthetic, it stands—without any need on the reader's part to visualize—monumental.

Judy Jo Small is one of the few contemporary critics who has viewed Dickinson's word play extensively. She comments on the obvious punning with "sow" "so," and "sew" in Dickinson's "Don't put up my thread and needle" as well as her use of "seed" and "intercede" in several poems—and "air" and "hair." Small points out that the poet sometimes intentionally avoids a pun, because readers are at times bothered by that kind of word play: "the more attention is drawn to words themselves and to the disorganization that exists between words as signifiers and the multifariousness of what and how they signify" the more difficult become the poet's works (Small 144, 160–6).

Throughout more than a hundred years of critique of Dickinson's poems, reviewers and literary scholars have discussed the role various speakers play in her works. From early considerations of the hypothesis that Dickinson patterned some of her speaker/persona figures after the portraits that Robert Browning gave the world of poetry to Sandra M. Gilbert's very recent commentary that Dickinson lived in "a kitchen of her own making," where she speaks in the voices of "Emilie, Brother Emily, Uncle Emily" to change her persona (Gilbert 199). Much attention has been paid to Dickinson's assumption of a male voice (a tactic that is true for her letters as well as her poems, and one sometimes intended to create comedy, especially when she writes to Ned or other of her young male neighbors). But perhaps changes in gender were less the point than was the poet's efficacy with language and sentiment: the dramatic monologue form has many uses.

Beth Doriani praises the fact that the poet's speakers in Dickinson's poems use a "variety of voices, from the sarcastic to the doubtful and from the playful to the longing." She adds, "the richness of Dickinson's poetry is due in great measure to the authenticity and immediacy of her voices" (Doriani 92).

Dickinson's various practices connected with her choices of voice provide the content for Marietta Messmer's book, *A Vice for Voices*. The author suggests that some part of Dickinson's strategy was to show her versatility with speakers and what they would have known, had they lived. Messmer also thinks the poet paid attention to what the *recipients* of her poems would have understood (138). In Dickinson's use of different speakers, too, she could subvert an expected characterization (most speakers in literary works were male, but as Dickinson had learned from her study of Elizabeth Barrett Browning's *Sonnets from the Portuguese*, a change in gender has myriad effects). Charlotte Nekola reinforces this idea, saying that Dickinson's use of "male masks" was "a rhetorical strategy," not "a personal aberration" (Nekola 153).

Messmer does not discount the fact that through her choices of speakers, Dickinson has the opportunity for subversion: even when it might appear that the poet is quoting from a famous source, she may make untoward changes in what is a literal meaning. She quotes from Diepeveen to support her observation: his commentary is "the less allusion and more quotation readers encounter, the more the questing poem . . . appropriates and works with what some would call the *writing* of another text" (Messmer 146, Diepeveen 16). Both the primary text and the source for the quotation are thereby changed. As Susan Howe had also commented, Dickinson drew where she could for her ironic tendency to subvert: "In both prose and poetry she explored the implications of breaking the law just short of breaking off communication with a reader" (Howe 11). Changing voice was not seen as defiance, however; her choices of speaker were more commonly seen as evidence of the poet's ability to create varied rhythms and themes.

Messmer also insists that Dickinson's prose—letters themselves as well as the poem-like messages in brief that accompany a poem enclosed— must be considered along with her formal poems. She calls the "letters" of whatever length "literary writings in their own right" and suggests that readers track them "in an intergeneric dialogic exchange" with the poems. This critic argues for reading Dickinson's correspondence as her "central [because 'authorized' and 'published'] form of literary expression, while challenging the superior status that her fascicle poems (unpublished during her lifetime) have enjoyed in the past" (Messmer 184).

When Paul Crumbley published his "manuscript chirography" of Dickinson's poems, all of his work was done from archival manuscripts. Originally interested in the way the poet's use of the dash (or other markings that resembled the dash) varied, and convinced that Dickinson's choices were seldom random, Crumbley provided significant information about the poems he discussed. More than intensive readings, he also began the movement toward seeing Dickinson's poems as tangible and tactile objects: "the totality of Dickinson's visual arrangements; punctuation and lineation, for example, acquire meaning within interconnected visual, syntactic, and semantic systems, not in isolation" (Crumbley Pen 171).

A related part of his book was establishing the categories of Dickinson's speakers (the bride, the Queen, the child), which we have previously mentioned. When Paula Bennett contended that Dickinson was engaging in "illegal" poetics, Crumbley agreed. Bennett's assessment for the poet's choices were somewhat more gendered than Crumbley's, as she stated that Dickinson wrote about "a world in which nothing can be known for certain and in which, therefore, the ideals of order and perfection (the foundation stones of Western phallocentrism) give way to process and incompletion. The result is a free, constantly changing form of poetry in which conclusions—whether formal or thematic—cannot be drawn and in which *variant readings are part of the very substance of the text*" (Bennett Emily Dickinson 19, her italics). Susan Howe also develops this theme, that Dickinson was very much aware of where women writers stood in the literary pantheon, and was also smart enough not to antagonize the men who were more securely placed (Bowles, Higginson). Howe refers to Dickinson's writing as her "act of lonely daring" (Howe My Emily 127). She compares Dickinson with Browning in this way, that the former poet "went further than Browning, coding and erasing—deciphering the idea of herself, dissimulation in revelation. Really alone at a real frontier, dwelling in Possibility was what she had brilliantly learned to do" (Howe My Emily 76).

As if looking ahead to this kind of critical assessment, in 1884 Dickinson writes an interesting poem or—moreorless—disclaimer in "The pedigree of Honey/Does not concern the Bee" (Poem #1650 Fr 1447–8). The stanza continues "Nor lineage of Ecstasy/Delay the Butterfly" and the poem ends praising action that leads to "A more essential thing." Dickinson herself was never known to explain her poems—or, perhaps more to the point, to explain why she preferred one to another. Throughout this study, the assumption has been that in her choosing which poems to submit to Higginson, she was playing the critic; she was in effect creating her own critique.

After she had written Higginson again, once she had read that his first-born daughter had died at only seven weeks, she again included a few new poems. This time she explained her doing so. She had been asked to contribute some of her work for a charity event: proceeds were to go to a children's hospital.

In the four poems Dickinson sent to him in late 1880, "Dare you see a Soul at the 'White Heat'" dated from 1862; she had earlier sent this identical poem to him. The other three were written very recently, and according to Franklin's notes in the variorum edition, she sent four, not three, from recent writing. Of the poems sent, Dickinson had used a common format and an almost wry message, as if thinking of possible buyers for her work. "The Savior must have been" and "Mine Enemy is growing old" were, in her letter to Higginson, titled "Christ's Birthday" and "Cupid's Sermon" though there is no indication that those titles were used elsewhere. The first opens

> The Savior must have been
> A docile Gentleman—

and the second,

> Mine Enemy is growing old—
> I have at last revenge— (Poems #1538 and #1539 Fr 1345-8).

Both of the short poems have a marked rhythm, unlike many of Dickinson's quatrain structures, and employ the poet's tendency for maxims. The second poem, for example, closes with "Anger as soon as fed is dead—/'Tis Starving makes it fat." Perhaps her most effective use of this quasi-comic tone occurs in "My Country need not change her gown," titled "My Country's Wardrobe" in her letter to Higginson. Taking her reader back to the Revolutionary War, Dickinson makes references to England so that the reader is oriented:

> My country need not change her gown,
> Her triple suit as sweet
> As when 'twas cut at Lexington,
> And first pronounced "a fit."
>
> Great Britain disapproves "the stars:"
> Disparagement discreet,--
> There's something in their attitude
> That taunts her bayonet (Poem #1540 Fr 1348-9).

Of this group, Dickinson draws from her earlier work for only one poem, which she titles to Higginson, "Hummingbirds" (Franklin points out that in one of the seven variant copies she also writes this word, as if title, at the bottom of the page. In the poem itself, this noun does not appear; instead the language used helps to represent the motion of the birds: "A Route of Evanescence/With a delusive Wheel/A Resonance of Emerald . . ." and the ending of the octave describes the amazing speed the species can attain (Poem #1489 Fr 1305–8).

Although Dickinson and Higginson did resume their correspondence, this was the last set of poems she sent him. It is as if, for most of her regular work, she has already reached the stable height of judgment that allows her to make decisions for herself. As contemporary poet Gregory Orr recently wrote, Dickinson created herself as vulnerable in every poem she wrote that began with "I." He states, "In order for a poem to come into being, the poet has had to make herself vulnerable to disorder, has had to approach her threshold, that place where disorder and order meet. This counterintuitive decision to seek disorder, to open oneself to that disorder, is the mark of the lyric poet" (Orr 12). His assessment continues, "Many of Dickinson's greatest poems are tiny dramas of survival, and Dickinson herself is a survivor, one of 'the Saved.' The writing of her poems is *how* she survived" (Orr 13).

20
The Loving Dickinson

To chart Emily Dickinson's emotional life is to include all her notes, letters, and poems, not only those written to famous literary people, or to male recipients. The love the poet shared with others was not, strictly defined, a heterosexual, physical expression (or, in the case of her decades-long correspondence with Susan Gilbert Dickinson, a homosexual expression). The key to understanding Dickinson's life—which prompted most of her emotional life—is through inclusion. Many, many of the notes and letters are written to Ned, Mattie, and the young Gib; others are written to the children's friends. And most of Dickinson's most intimate correspondence is with the two Norcross cousins, Lou and Fanny, who were enough younger than Dickinson that she thought of them, in some respects, as her children.

Because of Ned's developing both a heart condition and epilepsy, Dickinson found a special province of love for him: she shared her understanding of chronic, untreatable, illness with the young nephew. In his sister's recollection, she and Ned, and all their friends, understood that "Aunt Emily stood for *indulgence*" (Habegger 547). It was more than that in her constant attention to Ned, however, because she wrote messages that were joking, messages that were of largely personal consequence, and then—after 1877, and Ned's first attack—messages that expressed the bond she felt with her first nephew. Most of Dickinson's messages are jaunty. After he has been stung by a hornet, she sends him a one-sentence note: "You know I never liked you in those Yellow Jackets" (LII 587). Often, Dickinson plays the changing genders game: at the holidays, when she is remembering that the Northampton bridge had been blown away, she writes

> Santa Claus' Bridge blew off, obliging him to be frugal—Otherwise, he is your boundless Aunt (LII 596).

Often quoted, Dickinson's longer message:

> Dear Ned,
> You know that Pie you stole—Well, this is that Pie's Brother—Mother
> told me when I was a Boy, That I must "turn over a new Leaf"—I call
> that Foliage Admonition—Shall I commend it to you? (LII 622)

There is commentary about life on the grounds and about the grounds-
keepers, about holidays (when Aunt Emily sends him the year's first
maple sugar), about his interests. As he starts Amherst College, his
father disturbed because he takes only a partial course load—given the
unexpected health conditions he might face, Dickinson's notes are less
predictable. They usually close with a token of her love: "And ever be
sure of me, Lad/Fondly,/Aunt Emily" and "With sorrow for his illness"
(LIII 880, 893). In June, 1883, with Ned downed by a serious bout of
rheumatic fever, Dickinson writes "Stay with us one more Birthday,
Ned—[followed with a quotation from Hebrews 13:8]/'Yesterday, Today,
and Forever,' then we will let you go" (LIII 780).

There are letters as well to Mattie and a few to Gib, as well as to the
Jenkins children, Mac and Did. There is the commentary of the observing Mattie, that both Susan and Austin instilled respect for Aunt Emily
in each of their children: whereas she might have been seen as reclusive
or strange, to her niece and nephews and their friends, she was their
generous and funny aunt (Habegger 548).

There are letters to the son of Samuel Bowles, in Dickinson's greeting, "Samuel Bowles the Younger," as well as to other children of
friends she has known and mourned. There is the inclusive pattern
that the poet establishes of writing to other people who have loved an
object of her love: Mary Channing Higginson in relation to Higginson
himself, Maria Whitney in relation to Samuel Bowles, and, somewhat
later, James D. Clark in relation to Charles Wadsworth. There are the
countless letters to neighbors, usually in condolence. There is one
interchange with Dickinson's beloved Maggie Maher, when she is ill
with typhoid and staying with the Kelleys. Dickinson writes, "The
missing Maggie is much mourned . . . All are very naughty, and I am
naughtiest of all./The pussies dine on sherry now, and humming-bird
cutlets." Dickinson closes asking what her maid and friend needs
and signing herself "Her grieved Mistress." In reply, Maggie wrote,
asking about "Mother" and the household members' colds. She opens
"Sometimes I think I don't be sick at all and the next time I am sick
again . . ." (LIII 741).

Habegger points out that Dickinson sent flowers, food gifts, and notes to many others in the Amherst environs; he also notes that "Few of the locals who exchanged messages with her during her last fifteen years ever laid eyes on her" (Habegger 540). In this, as Murray has so cogently stressed, it was Dickinson's interaction with the loyal workers at both the Homestead and the Evergreens that built the rapport that insured her acceptance from the community.

In the wide range of recipients of Dickinson's letters Mabel Loomis Todd also appears, usually with a note of thanks. After the Todds arrived in Amherst in late August of 1881, they quickly became part of the town's social scene because Susan Gilbert Dickinson had made them welcome. By the fall of 1882, Mabel was brought by Austin to play the piano and sing for his aunt, who listened from her upstairs location. She never—in the five years that she still lived—met Mabel face to face; she never spoke to her. Her notes and letters tell a multi-layered story of Dickinson's reaction to the young wife's various levels of friendship with Susan, Austin, and their children—particularly the easily infatuated Ned.

By far, Dickinson sent the most messages, letters, notes—often with poems enclosed—to Susan Gilbert Dickinson. As if her communicating with her sister-in-law were a daily ritual, the poet thought readily of ways to share news, an effective phrase, a bonding image with her beloved Sue. Even in the midst of the busy days after Sue and Austin had begun their family, as they rushed from one social obligation to another, and then back home to monitor the children's bathing and bedtimes, Dickinson made her presence known. Connected with a linkage of both love and proximity—all the stronger because of the deep bond that joined Emily with Austin, and then Emily with their children, Dickinson and Susan Gilbert Dickinson were close to inseparable. Distance was immaterial. As Dickinson wrote,

> To be Susan is Imagination,
> To have been Susan, a Dream—
> What depths of Domingo in that torrid Spirit! (LIII 791)

Will my great Sister accept the minutae of Devotion, with timidity that it is no more? (LIII 791). "A fresh Morning of Life with it's impregnable chances, and the Dew, for you—" (LIII 733). To "Dear Sue," "With the exception of Shakespeare, you have told me of more knowledge than any one living—To say that sincerely is strange praise" (LIII 733). Whether Dickinson's remarks are wise compliments, as is this latter one, or a gesture of greeting, as many of them are, they solder tight the bonds that have long existed.

In the midst of Dickinson's own relief after Judge Lord began a genuine recovery from his May, 1882, illness, she saw trouble start to infiltrate the boundaries of Austin's and Susan's Evergreens. A few months later, in early September, 1882, Austin, after bringing Mabel Loomis Todd to sing for Emily, expresses his love for the young wife—and she repeats his troth to him. After Emily Norcross Dickinson's death and burial, life quiets—but more and more often Austin and Mabel are riding out together, or spending time at Mabel's studio—or, increasingly, at the Homestead. While it seems possible to ignore infidelities so long as they are part of the existing social fabric, once Austin and Mabel's relationship becomes sexual (late in 1883), such feigned ignorance is impossible: Susan carries double and triple burdens. She knows the secrets of Dickinson's health, and sees in Ned's illnesses the genetic influences of the Dickinsons. Desperately unhappy as Austin is about Ned's health (and about the fact that he is becoming educated for librarianship—which Austin sees as joining the working classes), he places some blame for Ned's health on Susan's previous attempts at abortion—denying the genetic role of his own family. There are reasons that both parents have invested a great deal of energy into developing Mattie (who is attending Miss Porter's, connected to her family largely through Ned's letters) and Gib, who as the second male child, will become the Dickinson family's promise. (Murray 190, Longsworth Amherst 180–9, Gordon 314–15).

For Austin to be increasingly distant from his family, increasingly involved with the Todds and particularly with Mabel, is a blow to the façade Susan Gilbert Dickinson has worked hard to keep in place. Always conscious of what his mother feels, Ned is also impacted negatively by his father' s strange behavior—especially because Ned's devotion to Mabel since her coming to Amherst has been relentless.

Susan had little recourse but to resent her husband's behavior, just as she increasingly resented, even if quietly, the various demands Emily made on her—not physical demands but rather emotional ones. In the torrent of emotions that changes in behavior created, and in the aftermath of the Dickinsons' losing their mother (November, 1882), as well as both Vinnie and Emily being courted by men who did not know the family's history, Susan came close to having her own equilibrium shaken. It was true that Susan as an unmarried woman had always admired Emily's humor, her verbal talents, and her love; but her resentment now, in 1882, seemed justified. If anyone was responsible for Emily Dickinson, it was *Austin*. If anyone should carry the responsibility for Ned's care, it was *Austin*. His being absent—emotionally as well as physically—enraged his wife.

Her festering dissatisfaction with their marriage, particularly with Austin's cavalier behavior toward what she saw as his responsibilities, grew into obvious hostility. The unraveling of the façade she could manage came with Gib's contracting typhoid from playing in the park: seriously ill, with seemingly no resistance to the sickness, the beloved baby of the Dickinson family died during the night of October 4, 1883. Maggie Maher had brought Emily to visit him, carrying a lantern for them both, though it had been months since she had last walked across the lawn to the Evergreens. As she sat by his bedside, the smells of disinfectant in his room coupled with her sorrow at his passing activated her own illnesses and she collapsed at three a.m. (Longsworth Amherst 189). In the words of Hart and Smith, the child's death was the beginning of a despairing end for both Susan and Aunt Emily, the real beginning of the latter's unbroken seclusion (Hart and Smith 203).

Dickinson was in bed for a week. Gib's funeral was October 9, 1883. Susan Gilbert Dickinson was in heavy mourning for a year. Of the many messages that Dickinson wrote to Susan after the loss of the beloved little boy, most seem abstract, filled with "immortality" and "his sweet velocity," but as usual Dickinson is at her best crafting narratives about his life. In an early letter, she wrote

> Gilbert rejoiced in Secrets—
> His Life was panting with them—With what menace of Light he
>   cried, "Don't tell, Aunt Emily!" (LIII 799)

On the first anniversary of Gib's death, Dickinson writes to Susan, "Twice, when I had Red Flowers out, Gilbert knocked, raised his sweet Hat, and asked if he might touch them--//Yes, and take them too, I said, but Chivalry forbade him—Besides, he gathered Hearts, not Flowers—" (LIII 842).

As is sometimes her custom, she takes one sentence from an early letter of condolence to Susan, and shapes a poem around it: "Without a speculation, our little Ajax spans the whole,"

> Pass to thy Rendezvous of Light,
> Pangless except for us—
> Who slowly ford the Mystery
> Which thou hast leaped across! (Poem #1624 Fr 1423–4)

Difficult as it was to be united through such deep sorrow, Dickinson's messages to her beloved Susan remained consistently positive, phrases of praise, never admonition.

Within the walls of the Evergreens, however, the Dickinsons were at war. A few weeks after Gib's funeral, Austin and Mabel began the sexual phase of their affair, and with that involvement, their sometimes frantic search for seclusion led them to trysts in the Homestead dining and living rooms (doors closed), to spaces on the Amherst College campus, and finally, to openly sexual meetings in the Todds' newly-rented house. With the seeming support of David Todd, who later spoke in admiration of Austin, the sexuality that Austin described as something he had never known took over the previously upright Dickinson's life.

It is no wonder that Emily Dickinson tried to close out Austin's behavior. Even before he was bringing Mabel Todd into the Homested, she was turning her emotional life back to Judge Lord—though her love already seemed less intense than it had been before his spring, 1882, illness. Her letters show that she is still participating in his marriage quest: definitions of "home" are frequent as are suggestions of physical intimacy, and her acquiescence to changing her name, "Emily Jumbo! Sweetest name, but I know a sweeter—Emily Jumbo Lord. Have I your approval?" (LIII 747).

Supported by her silence about the relationship between Austin and Mabel (and her continued intimacy with the increasingly-angry Susan) and characteristically quiet about her possible plans for life with Judge Lord, Dickinson's letters to all her regular correspondents read much as they had in the early 1880s. Elizabeth Holland, Higginson, and the Norcross cousins would have been oblivious to the poet's personal narratives—except for the deaths of, first, her mother and then, more unexpectedly, her young nephew. The discretion that bound people who wrote tied Dickinson's confessional impulses into tight knots. That practice is one reason critics and biographers have found even the drafts of Dickinson's letters to Judge Lord so surprising.

Late in 1883, Dickinson's retrospective poem "The Summer that we did not prize/Her treasures were so easy" was written on the back of her letter draft which began "I feel like wasting my Cheek on your Hand tonight." The poem moves on,

> Instructs us by departure now
> And recognition lazy—
> Bestirs itself—puts on it's Coat
> And scans with fatal promptness

> For Trains that moment out of sight
> Unconscious of his smartness (Poem #1622 Fr 1422–3).

In "The Heart has many Doors," written at about the same time, Dickinson may be referencing the death of Gib but she may also be linking this opening metaphor to her relationship with Judge Lord.

> The Heart has many Doors—
> I can but knock—
> For any sweet "Come in"
> Impelled to hard—
> Not saddened by repulse,
> Repast to me
> That somewhere, there exists,
> Supremacy— (Poem #1623 Fr 1423).

The tonal symmetry between Dickinson's late draft entries to Lord and some of her language in this group of poems suggests that her heightened sense of happiness permeated much of her writing. As she wrote to the Judge, probably about this same time, "The Withdrawal of the Fuel of Rapture does not withdraw the Rapture itself" (LIII 786). Or, more personally, "I feel like wasting my Cheek on your Hand tonight—Will you accept (approve) the squander—Lay up treasures immediately—that's the best Anodyne for moth and Rust and the thief whom the Bible knew enough of Banking to suspect would break in and steal . . . Night is my favorite Day—I love silence so" (LIII 786).

Some of Dickinson's best late poems are written after Judge Lord's death, which occurred on March 13, 1884; because of both distance and her personal reclusiveness, she would not attend his funeral. Instead, she writes,

> Morning, that comes but once,
> Considers coming twice—
> Two Dawns upon a Single morn
> Make Life a sudden price— (Poem #1645 Fr 1444–5).

There is the lovely "Not knowing when the Dawn will come" with its fantasy feathers and bellows; "So give me back to Death/The Death I never feared," and the aptly metaphoric "A World made penniless by his departure" (Poems #1647, #1653, and #1642 Fr 1445–6, 1449–50, and 1441). To the Norcross cousins, soon after Lord's death, Dickinson writes in both prose and poetry, "Thank you, dears, for the sympathy. I hardly dare to know that I have lost another friend, but anguish finds it out.

> Each that we lose takes part of us;
> A crescent still abides,
> Which like the moon, some turbid night,
> Is summoned by the tides (Poem #1639 Fr 1432–3).

Whereas many of these Dickinson poems about death, written during 1884 and 1885, have been related to her grief after losing Gib, it seems reasonable to assume that any poem after these two paired losses—her nephew and her lover—stem from the same welling of sorrow and dismay. For instance,

> My life closed twice before it's close;
> It yet remains to see
> If Immortality unveil
> A third event to me,
>
> So huge, so hopeless to conceive
> As those that twice befell.
> Parting is all we know of heaven,
> And all we need of hell (Poem #1773 Fr 1518).

There is also her summary, later, three months after Lord's dying, when she has lost consciousness for most of a day, to friends about her own illness. She reported that her doctor told her she had experienced a "revenge of the nerves." She continues, about Gib's death, "The little boy we laid away never fluctuates, and his dim society is companion still. But it is growing damp and I must go in. Memory's fog is rising."

> The going from a world we know
> To one a wonder still
> Is like the child's adversity
> Whose vista is a hill . . .

The poem closes with a couplet that clearly speaks to her loss of Judge Lord, "But will the secret compensate/For climbing it alone?" (Poem #1662 Fr 1454–5).

Eventually diagnosed as Bright's disease, a malfunction of the kidneys, Dickinson's illness truly invalided her. Starting with her faint on June 14, 1884, as she was baking a cake with Maggie, her health was poor and her activities were carefully restricted. Not that her correspondence lessened; as she wrote to Mabel Loomis's parents, "A Letter is a joy of Earth—/It is denied the Gods" (Poem #1672 Fr 1465–6). Particularly noticeable were the letters from Helen Hunt Jackson, still intent on leading Dickinson to publication. The intermittent illnesses that plagued both Jackson and Higginson worried the poet, but she was writing less and less poetry herself. Even during the year following her difficult syncope experience, she wrote 69 letters as well as 13 poems. She also looked anxiously over Ned, because as the affair between his father and Mabel Todd continued, and his mother's anger threatened to destroy the family, he spent 1885 "ill and suffering"—subject to seizures amid the hostility he felt from Austin (Mattie, too, was experiencing her father's anger, because both the Dickinson children sided with their mother) (Longsworth Amherst 200).

Dickinson experiences more severe bouts of illness during the next two years, and finally her writing diminishes, her quick mind slows, and even when Austin comes to sit by her bedside, she has little to say. During the last months of her life, early in 1886, Dickinson talks with Vinnie and Maggie about the kind of funeral she would like to have—such direct participation in the ritual surprised them, but they both knew that their promise to her was earnest. Early in May, 1868, Dickinson wrote a two-word message to the Norcross cousins, a wry good-bye that drew from recent fashionable culture to create a smile along with what Dickinson knew would be immense sorrow. "Called back," her message read to the beloved women she identified as "Little Cousins" (LIII 906). The phrase was the title of a popular novel (made into a melodrama for stage) by Hugh Conway, a text no real student of literature would have claimed.

On May 13, Dickinson went into the coma in which she died at evening, Sunday, May 15, 1886. Vinnie had called both Austin and Dr. Bigelow to be in attendance. Throughout the two previous years, Dickinson—for symptoms of blacking out, vomiting, and severe headaches—had been treated with combinations of digitalis, glycerine, extract ustilago and an anti-spasmodic compound used by epilepsy expert Sir Edward Sieveking, arsenic—as well as nux vomica, which contained strychnine (Gordon 216). Regardless of what her death certificate said, her illnesses were not exactly those of the kidneys.

Emily Dickinson's funeral was held on Wednesday morning, May 19. She had asked that men who worked for the Dickinsons' would be her casket bearers—all were Irishmen, though Austin had also invited some of his local friends to be honorary pallbearers. Tom Kelley would be chief pallbearer, and whether or not she expressed it, Dickinson wanted the procession—from the Homestead to the gravesite—to have some of the qualities of an Irish wake (Murray 377–8).

Furniture maker and undertaker Edwin Marsh built a $5.00 pine box for the 5 foot 6 inch-long white casket. Everything was white. "The casket was furnished with five-sixths of a yard of Russian white flannel and white textile handles at a cost of $85. Adding the flannel wrap with ribbons ($9.25) and the making of the bier upon which the casket was carried to the cemetery ($2.50) and other miscellaneous items, caused expenses to reach $121.75." (Murray 183). It was Marsh's thirty-first funeral that year, and turned out to be one of his most expensive. Susan Gilbert Dickinson handled all the arrangements, and hired Eunice Powell to make the flannel robe for Dickinson . . . and Susan wrote the very lengthy obituary (Murray 184).

The brief service was held in the Homestead's library, with Reverend George S. Dickerman reading from Corinthians. Higginson read Emily Brontë's solemn yet joyful "No Coward Soul Is Mine." Then the processional moved from the rear door of the central hall of the Homestead, the casket covered with violets and ground pine. The scene of apple blossoms was strong (Habegger 617). Attending were Susan and Austin, Ned, Mattie, Vinnie, Maggie, Mabel Loomis Todd and David Todd, and community representatives (Murray 187). (Murray says Susan attended the service; Habegger says she was no where in sight, though she had done most of the work.)

From Susan's obituary came the earliest exacting, and understanding, criticism of both Dickinson and her work. As several excerpts show, Susan did comprehend all the nuances, and the at time effortless veracity, of her sister-in-law's art. "As she passed on in life, her sensitive nature shrank from much personal contact with the world, and more and more turned to her own large wealth of individual resources for companionship, sitting thenceforth, as some one said of her, 'in the light of her own fire.'" She continued that "the sacred quiet of her own home proved the fit atmosphere for her worth and work. All that must be inviolate. One can only speak of 'duties beautifully done'; of her gentle tillage of the rare flowers filling her conservatory, into which, as into the heavenly Paradise, entered nothing that could defile, and which was ever abloom in frost or sunshine, so well she knew her subtle chemistries; of her tenderness to all in the home circle . . ." (Hart and Smith 266).

Susan's prose continued, "Her talk and her writings were like no one's else . . . A Damascus blade gleaming and glancing in the sun was her wit.

Her swift poetic rapture was like the long glistening note of a bird one hears in the June woods at high noon, but can never see . . . So intimate and passionate was her love of nature, she seemed herself a part of the high March sky, the summer day and bird-call. Keen and eclectic in her literary tastes . . ."

Susan concludes, "To her life was rich, and all aglow with God and immortality. With no creed, no formalized faith, hardly knowing the names of dogmas, she walked this life with the gentleness and reverence of old saints, with the firm step of martyrs who sing while they suffer" (Hart and Smith 267–8).

Susan Gilbert Dickinson chose a different poem as closing, but here Emily Dickinson's "To make a prairie" seems most illustrative of not only her poetic qualities but her life values.

> To make a prairie, it takes a clover and one bee,
> One clover, and a bee,
> And revery.
> The revery alone will do,
> If bees are few (Poem #1779 Fr 1521).

Afterword

The publication of Emily Dickinson's poems took nearly half a century, and the wonder is that it was finally accomplished at the end of the twentieth century by Ralph Franklin. His 1998 variorum edition has drawn from many different publications, both published and archival, starting with the first book of Dickinson's poems edited by Higginson and Mabel Loomis Todd. Bound in white, edged in gold, with Mabel's drawing of Indian pipes as design, the book was titled *Poems*, and appeared November 12, 1890, from Roberts Brothers in Boston. A year later, the second series appears. In eleven printings in 1891, the book would sell almost eleven thousand copies (Wineapple 287–8). There would be a third edition, edited by Mabel Todd alone, on September 1, 1896.

Getting to the stage of publishing even some of Dickinson's poems was a scenario of unpleasantness. The personal warfare extended, moving past the alliance between Austin and Mabel, to the exclusion of Susan Gilbert Dickinson and her children, Ned and Mattie. At first, Susan wanted control of the poems—at least partly because so many of them were written to her. Those works, however, were Vinnie's property: she had found the bound fascicles in Dickinson's chest after Maggie Maher had brought them back from her room as she cleared out Emily's clothing. Amazed at the quantity of writing, Vinnie destroyed an even larger quantity of letters, as she had promised Emily she would. But she realized some kind of value in these hundreds of poems, so carefully preserved by her sister.

Vinnie may have realized worth, but Austin did not. And it was Maggie Maher who preserved the only daguerreotype extant of Emily Dickinson taken just before she turned sixteen. But after allowing Susan to have possession of the poems, and seeing that what she did was read to friends from them, Vinnie decided—surreptitiously—to allow the

185

eager Mabel Loomis Todd to do the editorial work (not to mention the copying of Dickinson's sometimes illegible handwriting. Mabel bought a World typewriting machine and laboriously printed out Dickinson's poems). Maggie worked in the Todds' household for two years, paid by Vinnie, while this copying was being done. (Murray 253).

Less than a month after Emily Dickinson's death, Austin prepared a deed for Vinnie to sign, giving the Todds a small parcel of land (on which they would build a large red house, called The Dell, funded partly by Austin). An earlier deed that transferred land had stalled because Emily would not sign it, although Vinnie did. According to the terms of this 1886 deed, the Todds paid $1200 for the land, but since they had no funds, no such payment was ever made (Gordon 228).

Austin's will, dated November 3, 1887, left everything to Susan except the two paintings that went to Mabel and the Homestead and its meadow which were to be Vinnie's. His understanding with his sister was that she would leave those properties, at the time of her death, to Mabel Todd. She did not do so—partly because of a lawsuit that was adjudicated in March of 1898.

The battles between Austin and Mabel (who primarily wanted to marry him) continued until his death, playing out in their unsuccessful attempts to have a child together ("The Experiment") and in Mabel's various trips—sometimes to Boston for singing and painting lessons, sometimes with David on his astronomical photography journeys—which existed as punishment for Austin's resistance to her demands (Gordon 244).

Austin was ill during much of 1894 and 1895; during this time, Mabel was prevented from seeing him. He died August 16, 1895, and Mabel and David Todd were not allowed to come to the funeral on August 19—but Ned left a French door cracked so that Mabel could see her beloved in the coffin.

Mabel Todd had also typed and readied a two-volume collection of Emily's letters, which were published in 1894. When Susan Dickinson heard that plans for more publications were in process, she was appalled—mostly at the complicity of her sister-in-law Vinnie who had evidently stayed in league with Mabel throughout both the affair and its highly public ramifications, as well as its financial fall-out, and Vinnie's allowing Mabel to become the published voice of Emily Dickinson. As a means of appeasing Susan, Vinnie filed suit against Mabel for fraud. Maggie Maher was deposed May 28, 1897, before Judge Everett Bumpus in Northampton (Murray 201). During the two days of the trial, March 1 and 2, 1898, Maggie remained at Vinnie's side, and though Sue was not there, Ned and Mattie were. (Several weeks after the trial, Ned had the first of his heart attacks; because of his engagement to a woman his parents considered lower class—just as he had supposedly changed class status, by taking a job in the Amherst College Library—Susan asked him not to see Alix Hill for three months. Alix had been Mabel's assistant on the work she had done for the first series of Dickinson's poems, so there may have been political anger afoot as well. The three months did not pass; instead, Ned died May 3, 1898) (Gordon 315).

The verdict of the trail was Vinnie's, and she lived until August 31, 1899, "attended to the last by Maggie" (Gordon 319). Vinnie left the Homestead to her niece Mattie. Susan Gilbert Dickinson died May 12, 1913, leaving the Evergreens as well to Mattie. Angry that she had lost the lawsuit, Mabel Loomis Todd put a quantity of Dickinson's poems, letters, and other papers into a camphor-lined trunk, and there the materials stayed for 30 years. Mabel died October 14, 1932.

The narrative continued, however, through the next generation. Because Austin had lost his daughter Mattie (Martha) through his chicanery both romantic and financial, she chose Aunt Vinnie's side. She became an adversarial competitor for control of Emily Dickinson's materials—as *Martha Dickinson Bianchi*. Representing Mabel Loomis Todd was her only child, *Millicent Todd Bingham*.

Mattie—an accomplished musician, and Millicent, with the PhD in geography from Radcliffe, gave up their professional lives to study, investigate, preserve, and publish the writings of Emily Dickinson. Their countless books came to fruition in 1955, when Thomas H. Johnson edited *The Complete Poems of Emily Dickinson*.

Bibliography

Barker, Wendy. *Lunacy of Light: Emily Dickinson and the Experience of Metaphor.* Carbondale: Southern Illinois University Press, 1987.

Barnstone, Aliki. *Changing Rapture: Emily Dickinson's Poetic Development.* Hanover, NH: University Press of New England, 2006.

Benfey, Christopher. "'Best Grief is "Tongueless"': Jerome Liebling's Spirit Photographs," *The Dickinsons of Amherst.* Lebanon, NH: University Press of New England, 2001, 169–209.

———. *A Summer of Hummingbirds.* New York: Penguin, 2008.

Bennett, Paula. *Emily Dickinson, Woman Poet.* Iowa City: University of Iowa Press, 1990.

———. *Poets in the Public Sphere: The Emancipatory Project of American Women's Poetry, 1800–1900.* Princeton, NJ: Princeton University Press, 2003.

Bianchi, Martha Dickinson. *Emily Dickinson Face to Face: Unpublished Letters with Notes and Reminiscences.* Boston: Houghton Mifflin, 1932.

———. *The Life and Letters of Emily Dickinson.* Boston: Houghton Mifflin, 1930.

Bingham, Millicent Todd. *Emily Dickinson's Home: Letters of Edward Dickinson and His Family.* New York: Harper, 1955.

Blasing, Mutlu Konuk. "Poetry, 1850–1976." *Oxford Companion to Women's Writing in the United States,* eds. Cathy N. Davidson and Linda Wagner-Martin. New York: Oxford University Press, 1995, 670–2.

Browning, Elizabeth Barrett. *Aurora Leigh.* 1856. New York: Norton, 1996.

Budick, E. Miller. *Emily Dickinson and the Life of Language: A Study in Symbolic Poetics.* Baton Rouge: Louisiana State University Press, 1985.

Burr, Zofia A. *Of Women, Poetry, and Power: Strategies of Address in Dickinson, Miles, Brooks, Lorde, and Angelou.* Urbana: University of Illinois Press, 2002.

Cameron, Sharon. *Choosing Not Choosing. Dickinson's Fascicles.* Chicago: University of Chicago Press, 1992.

Capps, Jack L. *Emily Dickinson's Reading: 1836–1886.* Cambridge: Harvard University Press, 1966.

Carruth, Hayden. "Emily Dickinson: Unexpectedness," *Suicides and Jazzers.* Ann Arbor: University of Michigan Press, 1992, 150–9.

Chase, Richard Volney. *Emily Dickinson.* Westport, CT: Greenwood Press, 1951, 1971.

Cody, John. *After Great Pain: The Inner Life of Emily Dickinson.* Cambridge: Harvard University Press, 1971.

Cooley, Carolyn Lindley. *The Music of Emily Dickinson's Poems and Letters: A Study of Imagery and Form.* Jefferson, NC: McFarland, 2003.

Crumbley, Paul. *Inflections of the Pen: Dash and Voice in Emily Dickinson.* Lexington: University of Kentucky Press, 1997.

———. *Winds of Will: Emily Dickinson and the Sovereignty of Democratic Thought.* Tuscaloosa: University of Alabama Press, 2010.

Dandurand, Karen. "New Dickinson Civil War Publications," *American Literature* 56 (1984), 17–27.

Deppman, Jed. *Trying to Think with Emily Dickinson*. Amherst: University of Massachusetts Press, 2008.

Dickinson, Emily. *The Complete Poems of Emily Dickinson*, ed. Thomas H. Johnson. Boston: Little, Brown, 1975.

———. *The Letters of Emily Dickinson*, eds. Thomas H. Johnson and Theodora Ward. Cambridge: Harvard University Press, 1986.

———. *The Manuscript Books of Emily Dickinson*, ed. Ralph W. Franklin. 2 vols. Cambridge: Harvard University Press, 1980.

———. *The Poems of Emily Dickinson*, Variorum Edition, ed. R. W. Franklin, 3 vols. Cambridge: Harvard University Press, 1998.

Dickinson, Susan. "Annals of The Evergreens," Writings by Susan Dickinson, in eds. Martha Nell Smith et al. *Dickinson Electronic Archives*, http://archive. emilydickinson.org/susan/tannals.html.

Diehl, Joanne Feit. *Dickinson and the Romantic Imagination*. Princeton, NJ: Princeton University Press, 1981.

Diepeveen, Leonard. *Changing Voices: The Modern Quoting Poem*. Ann Arbor: University of Michigan Press, 1993.

Dobson, Joanne. *Dickinson and the Strategies of Reticence, The Woman Writer in Nineteenth-Century America*. Bloomington: Indiana University Press, 1989.

Doriani, Beth Maclay. *Emily Dickinson: Daughter of Prophecy*. Amherst: University of Massachusetts Press, 1996.

Duncan, Douglas. *Emily Dickinson*. London: Oliver and Boyd, 1965.

DuPlessis, Rachel Blau, "Poetry," "Contemporary Women's Poetry" in *Oxford Companion to Women's Writing in the United States*, eds. Cathy N. Davidson and Linda Wagner-Martin. New York: Oxford University Press, 1995, 672–6.

Eberwein, Jane Donahue. *Dickinson, Strategies of Limitation*. Amherst: University of Massachusetts Press, 1985.

Ehrenreich, Barbara and Deirdre English. *Witches, Midwives and Nurses, A History of Women Healers*. New York: Feminist Press, 2010.

Erkkila, Betsy. The *Wicked Sisters: Women Poets, Literary History, and Discord*. New York: Oxford University Press, 1992.

Faderman, Lillian. "Emily Dickinson's Letters to Sue Gilbert," *Massachusetts Review* 28 (Summer 1977), 197–225.

Farr, Judith. *The Gardens of Emily Dickinson*. Cambridge: Harvard University Press, 2004.

Fast, Robin Riley and Christine Mack Gordon, eds. *Approaches to Teaching Dickinson's Poetry*. New York: Modern Language Association, 1989.

Franklin, Ralph W. *The Editing of Emily Dickinson: A Reconsideration*. Madison: University of Wisconsin Press, 1967.

Freedman, Linda. *Emily Dickinson and the Religious Imagination*. Cambridge: Cambridge University Press, 2011.

Gelpi, Albert. *Emily Dickinson, The Mind of a Poet*. New York: Norton, 1965.

Garbowsky, Maryanne M. *The House without the Door: A Study of Emily Dickinson and the Illness of Agoraphobia*. New Jersey: Associated University Presses, 1989.

Gilbert, Sandra M. *Rereading Women*. New York: Norton, 2011.

Glaspell, Susan. *Alison's House*. In *The Complete Plays*, eds. Linda Ben-zvi and J. Ellen Gainor. Jefferson, NC: McFarland, 2010, 310–53.

Goodman, Susan. *Republic of Words, The Atlantic Monthly and Its Writers, 1857–1925*. Hanover, NH: University Press of New England, 2011.

Gordon, Lyndall. *Lives Like Loaded Guns, Emily Dickinson and Her Family's Feuds.* London: Virago, 2010.

Gray, Richard. *A Brief History of American Literature.* Oxford: Wiley-Blackwell, 2011.

Griffith, Clark. *The Long Shadow: Emily Dickinson's Tragic Poetry.* Princeton, NJ: Princeton University Press, 1964.

Guthrie, James. *Emily Dickinson's Vision: Illness and Identity in Her Poetry.* Gainesville: University of Florida Press, 1998.

Habegger, Alfred. *"My Wars Are Laid Away in Books": The Life of Emily Dickinson.* New York: Modern Library, 2002.

Harris, Morag. *Emily Dickinson in Time: Experience and Its Analysis in Progressive Verbal Form.* London: Karnas, 1999.

Hart, Ellen Louise. "The Encoding of Homoerotic Desire: Emily Dickinson's Letters and Poems to Susan Dickinson, 1830–1886," *Tulsa Studies in Women's Literature* 9 (Fall 1990), 251–72.

—— and Martha Nell Smith, eds. *Open Me Carefully: Emily Dickinson's Intimate Letters to Susan Huntington Dickinson.* Ashfield, MA: Paris Press, 1998.

Heginbotham, Eleanor Elson. *Reading the Fascicles of Emily Dickinson: Dwelling in Possibilities.* Columbus: Ohio State University Press, 2003.

Higgins, David. *Portrait of Emily Dickinson: The Poet and Her Prose.* New Brunswick: Rutgers University Press, 1967.

Higginson, Thomas Wentworth. "Emily Dickinson's Letters," *Atlantic Monthly* 68 (October 1891), 444–56.

——. "Letter to Mrs. Higginson on Emily Dickinson," *Heath Anthology of American Literature,* Vol. 1, fourth edition, eds. Paul Lauter et al. Boston: Houghton Mifflin, 2002, 1957–9.

Hirschhorn, Norbert. "A Bandaged Secret: Emily Dickinson and Incest," *Journal of Psychohistory* 18.3 (1991), 251–81.

——. "Was It Tuberculosis? Another Glimpse of Emily Dickinson's Health," *New England Quarterly* 72 (March 1999), 102–18.

—— and Polly Longsworth. "'Medicine Posthumous': A New Look at Emily Dickinson's Medical Conditions," *New England Quarterly* 69 (June 1996), 299–316.

Howe, Susan. *The Birth-Mark: Unsettling the Wilderness in American Literary History.* Hanover, NJ: University Press of New England, 1993.

——. *My Emily Dickinson.* Berkeley, CA: North Atlantic, 1985.

Jenkins, MacGregor. *Emily Dickinson, Friend and Neighbor.* Boston: Little, Brown, 1930.

Johnson, Greg. *Emily Dickinson: Perception and the Poet's Quest.* Tuscaloosa: University of Alabama Press, 1985.

Juhasz, Suzanne. *Naked and Fiery Forms: Modern American Poetry by Women, A New Tradition.* New York: Harper and Row, 1976.

——, Cristanne Miller, and Martha Nell Smith. *Comic Power in Emily Dickinson.* Austin: University of Texas Press, 1993.

Katcher, Philip. *The American Civil War, Day by Day.* Gloucestershire: Spellmount, 2007.

Kelley, Mary. *Private Woman, Public Stage: Literary Domesticity in Nineteenth-Century America.* New York: Oxford University Press, 1984.

Kher, Inder Nath. *The Landscape of Absence: Emily Dickinson's Poetry.* New Haven: Yale University Press, 1974.

Kirk, Connie Ann. *Emily Dickinson, A Biography*. Westport, CT: Greenwood Press, 2004.

Kirkby, Joan. *Emily Dickinson*. London: Macmillan, 1991.

Lease, Benjamin. *Emily Dickinson's Readings of Men and Books: Sacred Soundings*. New York: St. Martin's Press, 1990.

Leder, Sharon with Andrea Abbott. *The Language of Exclusion, The Poetry of Emily Dickinson and Christina Rossetti*. Westport, CT: Greenwood Press, 1987.

Lee, Hermione. "Introduction." *On Being Ill by Virginia Woolf and Notes from Sick Rooms by Julia Stephen*. Ashfield, MA: Paris Press, 2012, xiii–xxxvi.

Leyda, Jay. *The Years and Hours of Emily Dickinson*. 2 vols. New Haven: Yale University Press, 1960.

Liebling, Jerome, Christopher Benfey, Polly Longsworth and Barton Levy St. Armand. *The Dickinsons of Amherst*. Lebanon, NH: University Press of New England, 2001.

Loeffelholz, Mary. *Dickinson and the Boundaries of Feminist Thought*. Urbana: University of Illinois Press, 1991.

Longsworth, Polly. *Austin and Mabel: The Amherst Affair and Love Letters of Austin Dickinson and Mabel Loomis Todd*. New York: Farrar, Straus and Giroux, 1983.

———. "The 'Latitude of Home': Life in the Homestead and the Evergreens," *The Dickinsons of Amherst*. Lebanon, NH: University Press of New England, 2001, 15–106.

Loving, Jerome. *Emily Dickinson: The Poet on the Second Story*. Cambridge: Cambridge University Press, 1986.

Lundin, Roger. *Emily Dickinson and the Art of Belief*. Grand Rapids, MI: Eerdmans, 1998, 2004.

MacKenzie, Cindy. "'It ceased to hurt me,' Emily Dickinson's Language of Consolation," *Wider than the Sky, Essays and Meditations on the Healing Power of Emily Dickinson*, eds. Cindy MacKenzie and Barbara Dana. Kent, Ohio: Kent State University Press, 2007, 47–59.

Maffly-Kipp, Laurie. "Religion, 1700 to the Present," *Oxford Companion to Women's Writing in the United States*, eds. Cathy N. Davidson and Linda Wagner-Martin. New York: Oxford University Press, 1995, 755–7.

Mamunes, George *"So has a Daisy vanished."* Jefferson, NC; McFarland, 2008.

Martin, Wendy. *An American Triptych: Anne Bradstreet, Emily Dickinson, Adrienne Rich*. Chapel Hill: University of North Carolina Press, 1984.

McIntosh, James. *Nimble Believing: Dickinson and the Unknown*. Ann Arbor: University of Michigan Press, 2000.

McIntosh, Peggy and Ellen Louise Hart, "Emily Dickinson," *Heath Anthology of American Literature*, Vol. I, fourth edition, eds. Paul Lauter et al. Boston: Houghton Mifflin, 2002, 2969–74.

Messmer, Marietta. *"A vice for voices": Reading Emily Dickinson's Correspondence*. Amherst: University of Massachusetts Press, 2001.

Miller, Cristanne. *Emily Dickinson: A Poet's Grammar*. Cambridge: Harvard University Press, 1987.

Mitchell, Domhnall. *Emily Dickinson: Monarch of Perception*. Amherst: University of Massachusetts Press, 2000.

Montefiore, Jan. *Feminism and Poetry: Language, Experience, Identity in Women's Writing*. London: Pandora, 1987.

Morgan, Victoria N. *Emily Dickinson and Hymn Culture, Tradition and Experience*. Surrey: Ashgate, 2010.

Mossberg, Barbara. *Emily Dickinson: When a Writer Is a Daughter.* Bloomington: Indiana University Press, 1982.

Mudge, Jean McClure. *Emily Dickinson and the Image of Home.* Amherst: University of Massachusetts Press, 1975.

Murray, Aife. *Maid as Muse: How Servants Changed Emily Dickinson's Life and Language.* Durham: University of New Hampshire Press, 2009.

Nekola, Charlotte. "'By Birth a Bachelor': Dickinson and the Idea of Womanhood in the American Nineteenth Century," in *Approaches to Teaching Emily Dickinson's Poetry*, Robin Riley Fast, Christine Mack Gordon (eds.) New York: Modern Language Association of America, 1989, 148–54.

New, Elisa. *The Regenerate Lyric: Theology and Innovation in American Poetry.* Cambridge: Cambridge University Press, 1993.

Oates, Joyce Carol. "'Soul at the White Heat': The Romance of Emily Dickinson's Poetry," *(Woman) Writer: Occasions and Opportunities.* New York: Dutton, 1988, 163–89.

Oberhaus, Dorothy Huff. *Emily Dickinson's Fascicles, Method & Meaning.* University Park: Pennsylvania State University Press, 1995.

Olney, James. *The Languages of Poetry: Walt Whitman, Emily Dickinson, Gerard Manley Hopkins.* Athens: University of Georgia Press, 1993.

Orr, Gregory. "From the Province of the Saved, Emily Dickinson and Healing," *Wider Than the Sky, Essays and Meditations on the Healing Power of Emily Dickinson,* eds. Cindy MacKenzie and Barbara Dana. Kent, OH: Kent State University Press, 2007, 11–26.

Peel, Robin. *Emily Dickinson and the Hill of Science.* Teaneck, NJ: Fairleigh Dickinson University Press, 2010.

Perriman, Wendy K. *A Wounded Deer, The Effects of Incest on the Life and Poetry of Emily Dickinson.* Newcastle: Cambridge Scholars Press, 2006.

Petrino, Elizabeth A. *Emily Dickinson and Her Contemporaries.* Hanover, NH: University Press of New England, 1998.

Pohl, Josephine Pollitt. "Emily Dickinson—Loaf Giver," Appendix A of Murray, Aife. *Maid as Muse* (2009), 228–35.

Pollak, Vivian R. *Dickinson: The Anxiety of Gender.* Ithaca, New York: Cornell University Press, 1984.

———, ed. *A Historical Guide to Emily Dickinson.* New York: Oxford University Press, 2004.

Pollitt, Josephine. *Emily Dickinson: The Human Background of Her Poetry.* New York: Harper & Brothers, 1930.

Porter, David T. *The Art of Emily Dickinson's Early Poetry.* Cambridge: Harvard University Press, 1966.

Quinn, Sister M. Bernetta, O.S.F. "Religious Poetry." *Oxford Companion to Women's Writing in the United States,* eds. Cathy N. Davidson and Linda Wagner-Martin. New York: Oxford University Press, 1995, 681–2.

Reynolds, David S. *Beneath the American Renaissance: The Subversive Imagination in the Age of Emerson and Melville.* Cambridge: Harvard University Press, 1988.

Rich, Adrienne. "Vesuvius at Home: The Power of Emily Dickinson," *Parnassus* 5.1 (1976), 49–74; in *On Lies, Secrets, and Silence, Selected Prose 1966–1978.* New York: Knopf, 1979.

Sewall, Richard B. *The Life of Emily Dickinson.* 1974. New York: Farrar, Straus and Giroux, 1997 (Third Edition).

Showalter, Elaine. *A Jury of Her Peers: American Women Writers from Anne Bradstreet to Annie Proulx.* New York: Knopf, 2009.

Shurr, William H. *The Marriage of Emily Dickinson: A Study of the Fascicles.* Lexington: University Press of Kentucky, 1983.

———, ed., with Anna Dunlap and Emily Grey Shurr. *New Poems of Emily Dickinson.* Chapel Hill: University of North Carolina Press, 1993.

Small, Judy Jo. *Positive as Sound: Emily Dickinson's Rhyme.* Athens: University of Georgia Press, 1990.

Smith, Martha Nell. *Rowing in Eden: Rereading Emily Dickinson.* Austin: University of Texas Press, 1992.

——— and Ellen Louise Hart, eds. *Open Me Carefully, Emily Dickinson's Intimate Letters to Susan Huntington Dickinson.* Ashfield, MA: Paris Press, 1998.

Smith-Rosenberg, Carroll. *Disorderly Conduct: Visions of Gender in Victorian America.* New York: Knopf, 1985.

———. "The Female World of Love and Ritual: Relations between Women in Nineteenth Century America," *Signs* 1, 1 (Autumn 1975), 1–29.

St. Armand, Barton Levi. *Emily Dickinson and Her Culture: The Soul's Society.* Cambridge: Cambridge University Press, 1984.

Stewart, Susan. "Children, Women, Queens," *A New Literary History of America;* eds., Greil Marcus and Werner Sollors. Cambridge: Harvard University Press, 2009, 322–8.

Stokesbury, James L. *A Short History of the Civil War.* New York: Morrow, 1995.

Stonum, Gary Lee. *The Dickinson Sublime.* Madison: University of Wisconsin Press, 1990.

Taggard, Genevieve. *The Life and Mind of Emily Dickinson.* New York: Cooper Square, 1930.

Tate, Allen. "Emily Dickinson," *Essays of Four Decades.* Chicago: Swallow Press, 1959, 281–98.

Vendler, Helen. *Poets Thinking: Pope, Whitman, Dickinson, Yeats.* Cambridge: Harvard University Press, 2004.

Walsh, John Evangelist. *Emily Dickinson in Love: the Case for Otis Lord.* New Brunswick: Rutgers University Press, 2012.

Ward, Theodora Van Wagenen. *The Capsule of the Mind: Chapters in the Life of Emily Dickinson.* Cambridge: Harvard University Press, 1961.

———, ed. *Emily Dickinson's Letters to Dr. and Mrs. Josiah Gilbert Holland.* Cambridge: Harvard University Press, 1951.

Watts, Emily Stipes. *The Poetry of American Women from 1632 to 1945.* Austin: University of Texas Press, 1977.

Weisbuch, Robert. *Emily Dickinson's Poetry.* Chicago: University of Chicago Press, 1975.

Werner, Marta L. *Emily Dickinson's Open Folios: Scenes of Reading, Surfaces of Writing.* Ann Arbor: University of Michigan Press, 1995.

Whicher, George Frisbee. *This Was a Poet: A Critical Biography of Emily Dickinson.* New York: Charles Scribner's Sons, 1939.

Wilbur, Richard. "Sumptious Destitution," *Responses: Prose Pieces, 1953–1976,* Expanded Edition. (No city.) Storyline Press, 2000, 11–26.

Wineapple, Brenda. *White Heat, The Friendship of Emily Dickinson and Thomas Wentworth Higginson.* New York: Knopf, 2008.

Winters, Yvor. "Emily Dickinson," *Maule's Curse.* Norfolk, CT: New Directions Press, 1938, 149–65.

Wolff, Cynthia Griffin. *Emily Dickinson.* New York: Knopf, 1986.
Wolosky, Shira. *Emily Dickinson: A Voice of War.* New Haven: Yale University Press, 1984.

Web sites

Dickinson Electronic Archives: http://www.emilydickinson.org/
Emily Dickinson International Society: http://www.emilydickinsoninternationalsociety.org/
The Emily Dickinson Museum—The Homestead and The Evergreens: http://www.emilydickinsonmuseum.org

Index

African American population 1, 45, 53, 88
Agassiz, Louis 89
Amherst-Belchertown Railway 1, 32
Amherst, Massachusetts 1, 3, 9, 17, 18, 27, 30, 32, 39, 52–3, 62, 67, 72, 75, 84, 90, 93–4, 96, 104–5, 110, 113, 125, 127, 130, 139–40, 142, 144, 151, 176
Amherst Academy 1, 3, 5–8, 10, 12, 92
Amherst College 1, 5–6, 12, 39–41, 53, 92–3, 114, 136, 140, 159, 175, 179
Amherst Observatory 6
Arthur, T. S. 9
Seed-Time and Harvest 9
assassination 64, 89–90, 104
Atlantic Monthly 3, 55–6, 61, 88–90, 116, 125–6

Bancroft, George 90
Beauregard, Pierre 62
Bianchi, Martha Dickinson 187
see also Dickinson, Martha
Bingham, Millicent Todd 187
Booth, John Wilkes 64
Bowles, Mary 37–41, 46, 48–9, 52, 86, 139, 143–4
Bowles, Samuel 24, 37–41, 48–9, 52, 57–8, 73, 114, 125, 144, 150–1, 156, 168, 171, 175
Bowles, Samuel, The Younger 175
Bright's Disease 181–82
Brontë, Charlotte 8–9, 27, 33, 40
Jane Eyre 9
Brontë, Emily 8, 27, 33, 40, 183
"No Coward Soul Is Mine" 183
Brown, John 46, 61
Browning, Elizabeth Barrett 8, 11, 33, 54, 170
Aurora Leigh 11, 33
Sonnets from the Portuguese 11, 170

Browning, Robert 11, 116, 132, 169, 171
Dramatis Personae 116

Carlo (Emily's dog) 10, 18, 29, 61, 64–5, 67, 86, 90, 110, 114, 116–17
Carruth, Hayden 14, 51
Cary, Alice 89
Civil War 45–53, 54–66, 74, 88–90, 104
class 12, 114–15, 136, 177
Confederacy 53, 62–63, 89
consumption *see also* tuberculosis
Conway, Hugh 182
Craik, Dinah Maria 11
Head of a Family 11
Olive 11
Creeley, Robert 103

Darwin, Charles 56
Origin of the Species 56
Davis, Jefferson 46, 90 *see also* Civil War
Davis, Rebecca Harding 55, 88–9
Life in the Iron Mills 55, 88–9
Dickens, Charles 11–12
Bleak House 11
Dickinson, Edward 1, 3–5, 7, 10, 16, 19–20, 28, 31–2, 40–2, 53–4, 58, 67, 72, 84, 90, 94, 113–16, 122, 125, 128, 135–8, 142–5, 147–50, 161, 168
Dickinson, Emily Elizabeth
conservatory 31–32, 116
education 1, 5–6
fascicles 6, 24, 33–4, 77–82, 112, 153, 166
gardening 5, 17–18, 31–2, 67
gendered roles 3, 51–2, 84–5
health concerns 1–2, 8, 28–33, 54, 58–9, 61, 64–6, 83–5, 89–90, 181–82 *see also* tuberculosis, epilepsy

CPSIA information can be obtained at www.ICGtesting.com
Printed in the USA
LVOW12*1306220515

439527LV00002B/205/P